T0369375

PEANUT BUTTER FRIDAYS

Robert S. Pehrsson

abbott press®
A DIVISION OF WRITER'S DIGEST

Abbott Press books may be ordered through booksellers or by contacting:

Abbott Press
1663 Liberty Drive
Bloomington, IN 47403
www.abbottpress.com
Phone: 1-866-697-5310

ISBN: 978-1-4582-0915-3 (sc)
ISBN: 978-1-4582-0914-6 (e)

Library of Congress Control Number: 2013907845

Printed in the United States of America.

Abbott Press rev. date: 06/25/2013

Contents

Read this first!

Demolition signs announce the impending death of the old apartment house. Tomorrow a pile of bricks, plaster and concrete will rest in its place. I walk across the street directly toward the entrance and without looking around I lift the yellow ribbon that cautions me not to do that. On the first floor the boarded store windows preserve panes of glass for one more day. The door, the entrance to the apartments in back and above, hangs off a single hinge and caught by a passing breeze twists slightly. An official white paper with large black print informs me that this building is condemned and unsafe to enter. I enter.

A few short steps take me to the foot of the stairs. I hug the wall as I ascend the steep and narrow staircase leading to that apartment of long, long ago. The stairs creak and sag. The heavy carved banisters gone, ripped out, but the steps still support my climb. The doorways to each apartment stand open and bare, doors missing. The apartment I seek on the second floor seems to welcome me back as would a dying patient in a cold hospital bed.

I stop in the center of the empty living room. Oh, the memories of more than 60 years ago flash before my eyes. I hesitate for just a second. The wallpaper looks the same as when I stood here, right here in this very spot, so many years ago. Anticipation chills my spine. The autumn breeze passes through every window's shattered glass. I shiver. The setting sun glances off a building across the street. Shadows slowly ascend its walls.

A door slams shut. I brace myself. Is there actually a door remaining in this building? Is that a foot step creaking in the hallway? Am I alone? My heart races. I have this strong urge to run down the stairs and I truly wish to do so. But I don't. It's the wind I convince myself. Besides, my mission must be accomplished, indeed a very important one. I peek out into the hallway. All clear, sufficient evidence to convince me I am alone. Still wary, I tiptoe into the bedroom.

Would I find those letters? I know where Bobby Anderson hid them. I have always known and I have reason to believe he never removed them. The closet door is in splinters, some of which rests on the floor and some scraps of wood have been kicked to the rear of the closet. I pull large chunks out onto the bedroom floor and push splintered wood aside. Now on my knees, I crawl my way to the back wall. The floor board rests in its rightful and undisturbed place. I withdraw a Swiss Army knife from my pocket and dig its blade between two boards. Time, many seasons and the Brooklyn humidity, have swollen the floor boards tight together. I withdraw the blade and unfold the screwdriver tool and jab it into the seam at the end of the board. It loosens and I pull it up and out. After removing two splinters from my right hand, I lie flat on the floor and reach into the small hole, no easy task for someone my age. It is now too dark to see. I should have brought a flashlight but I did not think to do so. I feel around, my hand touching nothing but wood, and my heart nearly sinks. As I carefully withdraw my hand toward the front of the opening I feel something move. I almost feel my blood pressure shoot up several points. I do not budge. I try to persuade myself that whatever moved was not a rat. That it was caused by a breeze coming through the never insulated wall and sweeping through the opening in the closet floor. I reach down, open my hand wide and clutch something. I withdraw my hand and stare at the brown bag stuffed with wrinkled papers and two notebooks. These I place on the floor beside me. My hand returns to that breezy space. I feel another bag and then another. I crawl out of the closet with my bounty of five bags of wrinkled papers and four notebooks. The last glow of sunlight allows me to see the handwritten letters I had hoped to find. I smile. I almost dance. I feel the joy of finding a buried treasure.

As I exit the ill fated building no one gives me a tumble, not even a hardhat or two who are paid handsomely to look up and down the street. And this is a very good thing because I have plenty on my mind and plenty in my arms as I head for my car. I place the treasure on the passenger seat and drive one block north on Manhattan Avenue and left on Grand Street which brings me to the Williamsburg Bridge. I descend onto old Delancey which once again is becoming, as the song says, very fancy. I park in front of my present home on Mulberry Street.

For the next few weeks I spread wrinkled letters on the parlor floor and place them, as best I can, in chronological order. Bobby had been decent enough to provide hints about the sequence and at times had even written the dates.

Let me inform you about the reason for my recent daring activity which I already shared with you. I was sort of, like the Blues Brothers, on a mission for God. Bobby and I grew up in the Williamsburg section of Brooklyn.

Almost everyone in the neighborhood was Catholic. Bobby attended the local public school, PS 18, but later changed to the Catholic school diagonally across the street. He began writing letters because his teacher assigned each boy to write a friendly letter to someone named John. As I remember the girls in the class were told to write a letter to Jane. At first Bobby hated the idea but it grew on him and John, although imaginary, became the recipient of nearly four years of letters. Bobby wrote a letter mostly everyday and sometime twice a day. They were short letters and today he would likely be tweeting. The letters started when he was in fourth grade at PS 18 which still stands at 101 Maujer St. His first letter is dated September 10, 1950. As I read each letter I recall life as it was in the 1950s. Much was different then. However, I have noticed that schools have not changed very much at all. Many teachers today continue practices that Bobby described in the 1950s. From Bobby's perspective some teaching practices such as he describes can do harm. I agree.

Other than educational practices, the world as Bobby describes it, exists no more. It is almost another universe. It's not that times were better then but they were most certainly different. Something, like the very axis of the universe, has shifted and that which was central to almost every one of Bobby's letters deliberately changed in the 1960s and since has been caught up in a tornado of change. I speak of the Catholic Church which Bobby would hardly recognize.

After weeks, probably months, of organizing the letters into a chronological sequence, I was done, at least with that part of the project. Then I read them, every one, every word. It wasn't easy because Bobby's spelling was what some would euphemistically call nonstandard. He spelled words as he pronounced them and thus *water boiling* became "wadda berling" and *ideas and words* became "idears and woirds". I wanted to preserve his Brooklyn dialect so I left many of Bobby's own spellings in the letters. As Bobby matured so did his writing. The spellings and grammar became more standard and his letters easier to read.

I sat at my computer and began to transcribe each letter. The letters were far from isolated comments. Each letter contributes to events and episodes as they unfolded. I did some editing, changed much of the spelling because in some cases the spelling was so nonstandard that the reader would be challenged beyond frustration. This was the case especially for those beginning epistles. However, I wanted to preserve his development in the letters. I considered how Samuel Clemons (Mark Twain) had maintained the dialect in much of his writing. I actually think of Bobby Anderson as an inner city Tom Sawyer and you'll meet his friend, Earnest, who appears to be a city version of Huckleberry Finn. There were episodes in the letters and I was able to organize these into chapters. The first few chapters contain spellings that would be best described as reflecting the pronunciation at that time and place, 1950s Brooklyn, New York. As I read the letters I considered which spellings to edit and which to preserve, I realized these misspellings were actually rule based. Based on the regularities of these words I employed Bobby's dialect and developed what I call "Bobby's Rules of Brooklynese" which follows this introduction.

Maybe it's just me, but these letters seemed well worth my efforts to preserve them. I wanted to go back to that time of yesteryear; a time so different from today, a time more innocent and less complex. Since I found great pleasure in peering back to those days, perhaps others will appreciate the nostalgia as well. What follows is Bobby's story, actually many stories, about a youngster, innocent in most ways but nevertheless dealing effectively with first love, school adventures, nuns and growing up as a Catholic in Brooklyn in the 1950s.

Bobby's Rules of Brooklynese

what will help you unnerstand better
Peanut Butter Fridays

Rules for pronunciating English woids de rite way like we do in Brooklun!

1. Whenever you gots an "r" written in the woid, try an leave it out.
    Examples: dinner = /dinna/, dollar = /dolla/, New York = /Noo Yock/

2. Whenever you don't gots an "r" in a woid, try to put one in.
    Examples: idea = idear, Brenda = Brender, lost = /lorst/, wash = /warsh/

3. Woids what gots "ir" or "or" in dem, get pronunciated like /oi/.
    Examples: girl = goil, word = /woid/

4. Woids what gots "oi" in dem, get pronunciated like /ir/ or /er/ . . .
   Examples: oil = /irl/, Greenpoint = /Greenpernt/, ointment = /erntment/

5. Woids what begin and end wid "th," the "th" gets pronunciated like a /d/.
   Examples; these = /dese/, and them = /dem/

6. Woids what gots a "th" in the middle get pronunciated like the "th" is a /dd/.
   Examples: another = /anudder/

7. And the same ting in rule 6 goes for a "t" or two in the middle of a woid what is then pronunciated like /dd/ and when you apply rule number 1, you get woids what end in—dda.
   Example: butter = /budda/, brother = /brudda/, water = /wadda/

8. Woids like "new" are pronounced /oo/ as in too.
   Example: New York = /Noo/ /Yock/, stupid = /stoopid/

9. Sometimes letters are reversed.
   Examples: ask = /aks/ (sounds like axe)

10. It's a good ding to pronunciate the "ing' like /in/ or /na/
    Examples: going = /go-in/, and sometimes /go-na/ or /gonna/

11. What the teacher's call "double negatives" don't cancel each udder out. It makes it stronger.
    Example: I don't gots no milk. I ain't gonna do dat no more!

12. There are lots of udder woids what you godda loin but this is gonna be a real good start and it'll all woik out jist fine once you get the idear.

Chapter 1

A Monster in my Closet

Fourth Grade

I hate writing letters! I hate it! I hate it! Ding it, dang it darn!
I hate writing letters. But I gotta do it.

Dear John,
    Today is Septumber 10, 1950. How are you? I am fine.
I am riting this ding dang letter for school and I hate it.
The teacher sayz we gotta rite a friendly letter to somebody
what's named John. I hate it. I hate riting. I hate this friendly
letter. Rite now I ain't feelin all that friendly. But I gotta do
it. Ding it, dang it, darn!

Dear John,
    Today is Septumber 11, 1950. How are you? I am fine.
No. I ain't reelly fine mostly cause I gotta rite this here
stoopid letter for the stoopid teacher in this stoopid school.
Now I gotta start all over. This stoopid letter shore ain't
gonna do the stoopid trick. Ding it, dang it, darn!

Dear John,

Today is Septumber 12, 1950. I am Bobby Anderson and I am in the fourth grade and I am ten years old and I go to P.S. 18 what's on Maujer St in Willamsboig, Brooklun. I am riting this here letter cause the stoopid teacher sayz I gotta rite this here stoopid letter. That's why. But I don't gots no time to rite no stoopid letters to no stoopid imajinary person what ain't even reel and all. I don't even like riting letters to peoples what are reel. My time is jist too valyoubull. I got more portent stuff to do. Now I gotta start all over. Ding it, dang it, darn. I gotta do it.

Dear John,

I am pretty good. How are you? I go to P.S. 18 what is a very nice school. I have a very nice teacher when she ain't screaming her stoopid head off which is mostly all the time. I jist can't get serius about riting this here letter cause I hate riting STOOPID letters and I don't even know nobody what's named John. This is reelly stoopid. I gotta start over. This here letter ain't gonna do the trick.

Dear John,

I am fine. How are you? I go to P.S. 18 what is a funny looking school. It gots four floors up and it gots only four classrooms on eech floor. About a coupla hundred years ago it was a big school but most of it got burned down or sumthin like that happened. Now we gots a big little school.

Dear John,

That last letter ain't all bad. I was gonna give it to the teacher but when I read it over, I figger the teacher's gonna think its stoopid. It jist don't sound right. It don't sound like the way the teacher talks. It don't sound like the kinda stuff what a teacher's gonna like. I gotta try riting a nudder letter. I hate riting. Ding it, dang it, darn. I gotta do it.

Dear John,

Today is Monday, Septumber 18. I am fine. How are you? I hope you are fine. The sun is shiny today. Is the sun shiny where you is at? I hope the sun is shiny where you is at. This gotta be the most stoopidist stuff what I ever rote. I gotta do it all over. Ding it, dang it, darn. I gotta do it.

Dear John,

The teacher aks me for my homewoik but I tell her I don't got it cause I forgot it. The teacher wrinkles her stoopid face and tells me to stand in the stoopid corner for a half a stoopid hour so I remember not to forget. But maybe I'm gonna forget to remember or maybe I'm gonna remember to forget.

Dear John,

I told the truth about the letter. It's at home. And that's the truth. It's at home but it ain't alone. I got lots of friendly letters what I started and some even got finisht. All them letters are all over my bedroom floor. I'm gonna stuff them in a bag and hide them reel good where nobody is ever gonna see them. They are so stoopid.

Dear John,

I gotta remember to rite anudder stoopid friendly letter. I gotta do it! Ding it, dang it, darn!

Dear John,

I am fine. How are you? I got this here note from the teacher in my pocket. It's to my mom. The teacher sayz it's a secret note and I can't look at it or nuthin. So she puts it in this envelope and licks it and presses it reel tight. I ain't shore but I figger it ain't gonna be good news. My mom ain't home from woik yet and I got about a hour alone in this partment, alone with this here note. I think I'll get some wardda berling. Be right back.

Dear John,

I'm back. The note sayz my mom gotta go see the teacher cause I don't got that stoopid friendly letter wrote, and I day dream in school, and don't read and rite good enuff, and I got 3 F's on my spelling tests in the last 3 weeks and I ain't doing so good in arithmetic. The teacher wants my mom to go see her at school. I steamed it open.

Dear John,

Today is Monday Septumber 25, 1950. How are you? I am fine. I go to P.S. 18 what's in Brooklun. We got this new kid what jist moved into the neighborhood and he's in my class.

Dear John,

That new kid's name is Earnest something. He got a reel funny last name what nobody can pronunciate because its longer than this page and what ends with a skee sound. Everybody even the teacher jist calls him Earnest. He's jist Earnest.

Dear John,

Today the teacher gives Earnest lots of tests to do. Then she checks what he done and she gets reel mad. She yells at him, "Earnest, didn't you learn anything in your last school?" She sayz he don't know how to read and he don't even spell rite.

Dear John,

The teacher sits us kids together on account of how good we learn and how fast we get the woik done and all. Earnest sits next to me and Nicholas.

Dear John,

Me and Earnest and Nicholas get to do the same woikbook and stuff cause we don't do good woik. Nicholas woiks reel hard but he don't never get it rite. I do the woik when my day dreams get boring. Earnest always looks like he's woiking at something but it ain't never school woik.

Dear John,

The teacher tells me and Earnest and Nicholas to copy a long list of about 25 woids from the blackboard what's on the right side of the classroom wall. We gotta write every woid 20 times. She says we gotta praktice spelling cause praktice makes poifect."

Dear John,

Yesterday the teacher's riting on the board and everybody's copying what she rites. Then all a sudden I hear a reel loud noise, a disgusting noise, you know, a fart. Some kids turn arown but the teacher don't. She keeps riting like she ain't heard nothing. But there ain't no way she coulda mist that one. All the kids are looking at me. "Not me," I whisper and shake my head. Then it gets reel quiet again. Then a louder one! The teacher don't budge. I think I know where it comes from. I look over at Earnest but he's jist buttoning up his shirt like nothing happened.

Dear John,

Today I'm copying the notes from the board but I keep one eye on Earnest. He's opening his shirt button. His right hand goes inside his shirt and his left arm goes up and down reel fast and that's how he makes the noise! I think me and Earnest are gonna be friends.

Dear John,

Remember that note what the teacher gives me for my mom? I still got it. I was gonna give it to my mom when she gets home from woik but then I find out it ain't good news and all. So me and Earnest was talking and I tell him about the note what I got from the teacher. Before I get to tell him the hole story, Earnest sayz I should steam it open to find out what it says. I tell him I all ready done that. Earnest ain't all that stoopid. Me and him thinks alike. Me and Earnest are gonna be reel good friends.

Dear John,

I been trying to make the noises what Earnest makes but I don't got it down yet. Earnest says I gotta cup my hand more. Earnest says I'll get reel good at it if I jist keep prakticing. Like the teacher says, "Praktice makes poifect."

Dear John,

I always keep things like notes from the teacher in my pocket and I don't never leave nuthin like that around my bedroom cause my mom cleans up sometimes. And if she don't find it, maybe my sister Maggie will find it. Either way it ain't good. If my mom finds it, I'm in big trubble. If Maggie finds it, she'd black mail me to keep a note like that from getting to my mom. Maggie's blackmail is back rubbing. That letter could cost me big time in back rubbing.

Dear John,

I lorst the teacher's note. This is what happens. I'm walking to school this morning and Earnest catches up with me and says he's been doing some thinking about my problem with the note what I told him about. He says it'd be a reel good idear to put the note in my pocket what gots the biggest hole. I aks him how he knows I got holes in my pockets. He says every kid what's worth a darn got a hole in at least one of his pockets. At first I got the note in the pocket what's got the small hole but then I figger Earnest's right. The notes better off in the udder pocket what got the biggest hole. So I make shore it's all the way down near the bottom right near the hole. By the time me and Earnest get to school, the note's gone. It jist got lorst all by itself. I don't even hafta give it no extra little push. I don't even hardly know when it falls out. Earnest says he don't see nuthing. Earnest says, "You never wanna see nuthing you don't never wanna see. That's a good principle for living longer." So now I don't gotta give the note to my mom. There ain't nothing to give her. It's gone. It got lorst!

Dear John,

I still don't got that friendly letter done for the teacher. None of them udder letters can go to the teacher cause I say stuff what she ain't gonna like. I gotta try again. Ding it, dang it, darn!

Dear John,

How are you! I am fine. I go to school at P.S. 18 what's in Brooklyn. My teacher is a very nice and kind person. But there is one kid in my class what I can't stand and her name is Christine Carney. She thinks she's the greatest gift to the hole woild. She always gets the best grades in the hole class. Maybe she's smart but I bet she can't make no great noises like Earnest.

Dear John,

I hate riting letters. Ding it. Dang.

Dear John,

The teacher wants that letter reel bad. I hadda stand in the stoopid corner for a nudder stoopid hour this morning cause I don't got it done yet. I hate riting letters.

Dear John,

Christine Carney's the smartest kid in the class and the teacher said she rites the best letters and even showed us her letter with a big A+ on it.

Dear John,

At lunchtime I aks Christine Carney how much she charges for riting letters and she shows me her hands and aks me, "Are my hands clean?" And I says, "Yeah, there ain't no dirt or nuthin on them." And she says "My hands will always stay clean."

Dear John,

The teacher told me it was very bad for me to aks Christine Carney how much she charges to rite a letter for me and I hadda stand in the stoopid corner for two hours. Christine Carney kept looking at me and smiling and showing me her hands. Ding it, dang it!

Dear John,

I hate riting letters. But what I really hate even more is Christine Carney.

Dear John

No problem with writing letters now. Me and Earnest found this here old book in the liberry. It's called How to Write Letters and it's all about how to write reel good letters and it got lots of letters in the book what you can jist copy. Now I can get the letter done reel fast. I'm gonna get a good grade. I won't just copy cause that's like wrong and all. I'll take some stuff from different letters and I'll add some of my own idears and woirds. It's a reel good book what somebody done wrote way back in 1895.

Dear John,

Me and Earnest finally figgered how to write a reel good letter for school. First thing is you just gotta get a letter what somebody else already done wrote and then you copy some of the stuff like the sentences and move some of the woirds arown. Then you add some stuff in your own woirds. I even used a diktionary to make the woirds sound more grown up

9

and all. This friendly letter looks reel good. Earnest helped me pick out the good parts from the book and helped me add some other stuff. Here's what I wrote in my letter. It's a reel good friendly letter.

Brooklyn, New York
November 4, 1950

Dear John,

How are you? I am delightful. I have just received your response, in which you intimidate, in no gentle terms, upon my conduct and acts accusing me of faithlessness to you in accepting the attentions of frivolous women and all. However, light you make of promises, yet I am foolish enough to consider them as something more than trifles; and likewise induced to believe that the woman who voluntarily breaks a promise will not pay much regard to no oath no more; and if so, in what light must I consider your conduct? After all, you must own my delightful project ain't all that bad. I hope this letter finds you respectable and otherwise O.K. Will you not, dear John, for the sake of our happiness banish all thoughts however light you make of promises and all. We did so enjoy your tea yesterday at your old lady's house.

With veneration,
Bobby Anderson

Dear John,

Earnest says my friendly letter sounds reel good to him. It sounds like the way teachers talk mostly but it gots some parts where you can tell it's the way I say it.

Dear John,

I bet the teacher's gonna love my friendly letter. I ain't gonna hafta stand in no stoopid corner no more.

Dear John,

Remember I was telling you about the disgusting noises what Earnest makes? Now Earnest got lots of practice cause he's been helping me and he's reel good. He makes even louder noises now. One thing what the teacher said was right. Praktice makes poifect. When the teacher ain't lookin, he lets one go. But then sometimes he don't use his arm. Those are reelly disgusting. I sit next to Earnest and the window is on the udder side of him. The wind blows everything my way. I keep telling Earnest it's lots better when he makes them noises with his arm.

Dear John,

Big trouble! That friendly letter what I wrote for the teacher don't exactly win me no prize. The teacher says I copied it. But she ain't got no proof. Besides, I don't copy all of it. I just copied most of it. I took parts from different letters and I even added some of my own woirds to make it sound reel. But now I gotta write the letter over again without no copying. I hate writing letters. Ding it, dang it, darn. I gotta do it.

Dear John

Earnest says the teacher ain't fair for accusing me of copying the letter. She ain't got no proof and I'm innercent until guilty. Earnest says that's the lawr of the land.

Dear John,

Teachers don't forget much. The teacher aks me how come my mom don't come to school yesterday afternoon. I says, "I don't know." Then she aks me if I gived that note to my mom. I told the truth. It got lorst. I told her about the hole in my pocket and how it ain't my fault. Then she writes anudder letter and licks the envelope and gives it to me. She says, "Don't lose it."

Dear John,

The teacher's riting on the blackboard and swings arown just in time to hear that noise and she catches Earnest with his hand inside his shirt and up his arm pit. Next thing the teacher picks up the eraser and throws it at Earnest but her aim ain't so good. The eraser's flying through the air and hits me right in the face. I start coughing from the chalk dust. She's down at my seat reel fast and picks up the eraser and throws it again at Earnest. The eraser hits Earnest right in the head so hard that it bounces off and hits the window. The window already gots this tiny little crack in it and the eraser hits right there in that crack and makes a hole when it goes through. But then all the glass starts cracking from the top to the bottom and chunks of glass start falling and then all the glass falls out. Then there's a scream down in the school yard. The teacher looks out what used to be the window. She puts her hand to her mouth and backs right into Earnest's desk. She kinda falls back and sits on the desk. Right on Earnest's fountain pen what squashes and shoots black ink across the room and hits Christine Carney in the face. Then the teacher runs to the door and opens it. She backs into the room. The principal walks in. She got glass and chalk dust all over her hair and a little blood dripping over her left eye and some blood is tricking down her nose.

Dear John,

Earnest says people gotta be reel careful when they walk near a school what's in Brooklun.

Dear John,

Today we got a sub. Earnest got suspendered.

Dear John,

Christine Carney's nose is still a little bit dark cause of the indellabell ink what don't come off all that easy.

Dear John,

The teacher is back. Earnest is back. Everything's back to normal.

Dear John,

This time I don't lose the note. Somebody stoled it. Earnest says if I leave it hanging outta my pocket jist a little maybe it could get stoled. Earnest's getting to be reel helpfull.

Dear John,

Everything's back to normal. The teacher ain't sick no more, Earnest ain't suspendered no more and the principal ain't bleeding no more. The teacher really hates Earnest but that ain't no different. She hates him from the start. She jist hates him a lot more now.

Dear John,

The teacher aks me if I give the note to my mom. I tell the truth. It got stoled. She aks why would anyone wanna steal a note. Then I tell her that people steal all kinds of stuff around here. Like jist the udder day somebody stole the front door to the partment house what I live in. And Mr. Durango got his car stole tree times in one week. Mrs. Zizack got her false teeth stole last night. And I had some more stuff to tell her but she yells "STOP!" Then she writes a nudder note and tells me to make shore my mom gets it.

Dear John,

This time I hadda give my mom the note. I can't figger out no udder way. This is getting to be a big monsterous problem. My mom's reel upset but she figgers the problem is that I jist ain't all that smart. She don't say it but I figger she thinks I'm kinda stoopid.

Dear John,

My mom's got a plan that's gonna make me smarter. She figgers a novena's gonna do the trick. A novena is like a deal Catholics make with God. You gotta go to church nine Monday nights in a row and say all the prayers and sing all the hyms and then God gotta give you any miracle what you wants. That's why it's called a Miraculous Medal Novena. God's gonna give me more brains if my mom makes the novena nine Mondays in a row. If my mom makes the novena, God gotta keep His end of the deal.

Dear John,

I told Earnest about the deal my mom's making with God by her making the novena. Earnest says a novena's a real good thing. His mom made a novena last year cause his dad was looking at udder women. Then Earnest's dad smashed his car into a telefone pole and got two black eyes and broke his nose. Women don't look at him no more. He don't look at no women no more when he's driving.

Dear John,

A deal's a deal! God don't never back out of a deal. The novena's gonna do the trick for me alright.

Dear John,

Jist in case the novena don't work my mom and the teacher are gonna come up with a backup plan. Tomorrow my mom and the teacher are gonna talk about a plan to get me to be smarter. The novena plan sounds reel good to me mainly cause my mom and God gotta do it all. But when my mom and the teacher get together, they're gonna come up with something reel terrible. I probably gotta do something like work harder and stop day dreaming. This ain't good.

Dear John,

Last night I heard a noise in my bedroom closet and I peeked out from under the covers jist a little and then I hears it again. Don't look, covers up. Peek again and then I seen a monster with green eyes and blue hair coming out of the closet. AH, HELP! Then my mom comes into my bedroom and the monster's back in the closet. My mom says it was a dream but I reelly seen it. Mom goes to the closet. "Don't open it, Mom." She opens it. Nuthin. That monster musta come up from the cellar by a secret passage. Now he's back in the cellar again. I jist know it. I don't sleep after that, not even a wink. Jist keep one eye on that closet and the rest of me under the blanket. The monster don't come out again all night.

Dear John,

My mom and the teacher got together and made the new back up plan. My mom calls the plan skykology, no that ain't spelled write. It got a p in the beginning, a p _ it's spykology, no, it got a ch what sounds like a k, it's spychology or something like that, yeh, that looks right, spychology. Well anyways, they figger I ain't got the best brains but my mom told me that ain't none of my fault. When God was handing out brains, I got short-changed. But my mom says the teacher and her want me to use better what little I got. Psykology. Spychology. It's gonna do the trick.

Dear John,

This is the plan. When I do good stuff like pay attenshun and don't day dream and do all my homewoik and get good grades, then I get a piece of candy. That ain't a bad plan!

Dear John,

I got ten gumdrops today from the teacher cause I was paying attenshun. This spychology ain't a bad plan.

Dear John,

The candy's O.K. and all but spychology's cutting into my day dreaming time. Besides I got only 8 gumdrops today and I was paying better attenshun than yesterday when I got 10 gumdrops.

Dear John,

I got a problem. I like day dreaming more better than gumdrops.

Dear John,

The teacher makes a little change in the plan. I get 4 pieces of candy if I get a A on my spelling, 3 for a B, 2 for a C, 1 for a D, and nuthin else for nuthin lower. I'll give it a try.

Dear John,

Now Earnest is getting spychologized too.

Dear John,

Ding it, dang it, darn. It ain't fair. I reelly worked hard on my spelling woirds but it got me no gumdrops. I looked at the words real hard and spelled them but I forgot how to write them for the test. Earnest got 2 pieces of candy. He got 12 woirds right and I got 11 right. But I reelly got more stuff spelled right. I only got one letter wrong on all the 9 woirds what I mist and Earnest reelly messed up his 8 woirds bad. I mean I got closer than him to the woirds but you don't get no gumdrops for near misses in spelling. In spelling it's all or nuthin.

Dear John,

I got a D on my spelling test today so I get 1 piece of candy. But it don't exactly woik out that way. See the teacher opens a pack of chuckles and looks at them. Then she opens her desk drawer and pulls out a penknife. Then she opens six packages of chuckles on her desk and cuts them in half. Then she comes over to my desk and puts a candy down. I got half a chuckle.

Dear John,

The teacher catches me day dreaming about a million times today so I get not even one chuckle. Ding it. Dang!

Dear John,

All us kids what are Catholic got class at St. Mary's what is really called Immakulate Konseptshun but I'm gonna call it St. Mary's cause I don't spell that udda name so good and besides its tooooooo long. Well anyways on Wednesday afternoon us kids what are Catholics, and that's most of us in the whole school, gotta go to St Mary's. It's called religion instrukshun. The teachers at PS 18 look real happy on Wednesday afternoons.

Dear John,

The nuns at St. Mary's wear these long black robes and they got these big beads hanging down. They're called Rosary Beads. Earnest useta go to Catholic school for a week where he useta live and he says he thinks of Pistol Packin Momma. The nuns pack yard sticks under them black robes. Tomorrow's Wednesday.

Dear John,

I aks Earnest how come he only got to go to Catholic School for one week. He says, "Me and nuns don't exactly get along all that good. So the nun tells my mom a public school is better for me."

Dear John,

I was at religion instrukshun today and I was day dreaming and this nun comes over and hits me on the arm with the yard stick. That hurt. She had it hid reel good under the black robe. Earnest was right. Yardstick packin nuns.

Dear John,

Joey Dominica goes to St. Mary's and he says I ain't a Catholic. He says reel Catholics go to Catholic schools. He says I'm a public.

Dear John,

Earnest says his mom reelly wants him to go to Catholic school again because he needs a dish of plin. But the nuns told Earnest's mom they don't got no room. Earnest is on the waiting list.

Dear John,

If this spychology stuff don't woik, they're gonna come up with something a lot worser and reel ugly. I jist know it.

Dear John,

That monster's back. It comes out of my closet again last night and he's a lot worser and reel ugly. He's green and red and got a big black robe on with chains hanging down. He comes right near my bed and he's gonna hit me with a big bat. I yell and duck under the blankets. My mom comes into my room and puts on the light but the monster's gone. Back in that closet, down in the cellar.

Dear John,

I'm reel tired today in school and keep thinking about that monster in my closet and I got only 2 half chuckles.

Dear John,

I checked my closet. I can't find the secret trap door but it's gotta be there. I hope that monster don't come back tonight.

Dear John,

He's back. He got a black hood on his head and them chains hanging down and white dust all arown his head and he's holding a big bat to bam me. "AH! HELP! The Monster!" My mom and dad come running in. I aks them if I can sleep in their bed. My mom's almost gonna say yes but my dad says, "No!" I don't sleep the rest of the night and I keep the covers up over my head.

Dear John,

Earnest says, "Everybody knows about the rules what monsters gotta keep. When a monster is under your bed, you gotta stay in the middle of the bed without hanging your hands or feet over the side. A monster can get you if you hang any part of you over the sides." I told Earnest I know about the other rule, "Monsters can't get you if you got a blanket covering you all up. But a monster can get you when you come up for air." Earnest says, "You are right about that."

Dear John,

I gotta give my mom a nudder note. I know it ain't good news. I been too sleepy to pay attenshun in school what with holding my breath all night and all. I ain't been day dreaming cause I went to sleep and got to real dreaming. I ain't been getting many chuckles.

Dear John,

Well, it's Friday and I got all weekend to think about the note. Besides we're gonna have a party at are partment tonight and there ain't no sense in sperling the fun for my mom. I'll jist keep it in my shirt pocket.

Dear John,

I gotta help get ready for the party tonight. I gotta dust all the furniture except for the reel high stuff like the top of the player piano. My mom and dad got short friends.

Dear John,

My mom jist aks me to go down to the cellar to get some glasses what are packed away in are bin. "But, Mom, that's where the monster lives!" But she don't got no time to go with me. I gotta go. The monster is gonna get me and I ain't never gonna write you again. Goodbye, John.

Dear John,

He almost got me. I go down the stairs reel slow. Maybe he don't know I'm coming. Reel quiet. Maybe he's sleeping. Monsters gotta sleep too, espechully ones what come outa closets at night and hide under beds. Dark. Light switch on. Nuthing. Somebody stoled the bulb again. Glasses. I gotta get them. Something moves. It's the monster. Fast. Upstairs. Run.

Mom aks, "Where's the glasses." "I don't got them cause there ain't no light bulb in the cellar and the monsters waiting for me in the dark." "There are no monsters in the cellar," says mom. "How'd you know that? You ain't never seen that monster in my closet and he got a secret trap door to the cellar." Mom says, "Here take the flashlight." I says,

"O. K. but now he's probably woke up cause I make so much noise before. Goodbye mom, you'll by sorry."

Step, step, step, creak, stairs are creaky, very creaky. Stop, listen, step, step, listen, step, creak, last step, CREAK!!! Shine flashlight all around. Listen, quiet. I whisper, "Where ya hiding monster?" Nuthing. Step, step. Dark in back of me, shine flashlight. Nuthin. Box of glasses. Unlock and open the bin. Pick up the glasses, put them down, lock bin. Shine flashlight all around. Nuthin. Flashlight on box, pick up box. Flashlight rolling, rolling, off the box. CRASH! Dark, dark, very dark. Noise. The monster's coming. Run, run, bump, wall, wrong way. Turn around. Stairs. Step, step, step, run, run. SLAM cellar door. "Mom, the monster almost got me, but I got most of the glasses. Only two of em got busted and one dead flashlight smashed on the cellar floor."

Dear John,

Earnest found out we're having a party. Earnest says he ain't doing nuthin speshal and he got time to come to the party tonight. So I invite him.

Dear John,

All my ants and uncles was at the party and some friends on the block. My dad plays the piano and when he gets tired he put on the rollers and it looks like a ghost is playing the piano. They had Rheingold beer and lots of potater chips and stuff. Everybody laffed a lot when my Dad aks, "What'll you have?" and Uncle Al says, "Rheingold Blue Ribbon." Mr. Remson laffed so much he fell off the chair. He looks up and says, "It's Pabst Blue Ribbon."

Earnest said, "People think stoopid stuff is funny after they had a few beers."

Me and Earnest helped take the empty glasses into the kitchen to get them washed. But before we washed any we got the last drops out and into a bottle in the closet. We had Mission orange soda in the living room but in the kitchen we had are own beer in the closet. We had lots of last drops. Then me and Earnest laffed a lot about lots of stoopid stuff. Then we went to sleep under the kitchen table.

Dear John,

This morning my mom gives me a aspirin and says no more beer for me. She cleans up the mess what Earnest made under the table when he throwed up and she finds all the empty bottles with the last drops all gone. I hadda take a bath today cause I smell reel bad. My dad says, "The darn kid stinks like a brewery."

It was pretty late or maybe early in the morning when the party broke up and we was found sleeping under the table. Earnest's mom and dad was looking for him all night. His dad helped Earnest stagger home.

Dear John,

I ain't hungry for no breakfast. My head hurts. Earnest is right about lafting a lot after a few beers but he don't say nuthin about the next morning when there ain't nobody lafting.

Dear John,

My shirt stinks cause of the beer and what Earnest done and all. My mom's got the shirt and holding her nose and now she's checking the pocket. I says reel fast, "Mom, I can wash the shirt. Jist don't you worry about that smelly shirt. I love washing stinky shirts." But my mom puts her fingers into the shirt pocket and finds the paper and aks, "What's this?" "What?" I says. She shows me the note. "Oh, that? Yeah, oh yeah. I almost forgot, lucky thing you found that. It's a note from Earnest. It's a secret message, nobody else can . . ." Too late. She's already reading and looks up and very seriusly says, "This note is from your teacher." "Oh that one, oh yeh that one. I almost forgot to give you that one. That's a different one."

Dear John,

Earnest figgered out what the problem was. He throwed up cause he shouldn't never mix drinks like we done. He sayz, "I can usually hold my beer better than that. The problem is that I should of knowed not to drink two different kinds of beers. That Rheingold's better than Pabst Blue Ribbon beer and never makes me sick before." Earnest sayz Rheingold's the best. Earnest knows a lot about important stuff.

Dear John,

My mom's reel mad at me. She wrote a note back to the teacher. My mom can't see her cause she gotta woik and can't take no more time off. But my mom says she's gonna try spychology on my homewoik. If I do my homewoik reel good, she's gonna give me a Milky Way or a Tree Musketeers. That's good but how about a Rheingold Blue Ribbon? Only fooling, Mom.

Dear John,

The nun told us that they're gonna make a movie about Our Lady of Fatima. These three little kids what lived a long time ago in a country named Fatima had a vishon of the Blessed Virgin Mary and she told them lots of stuff what will save the world and all. God sent her to tell the world that we better be good and pray or else! These kids got to see the mother of God in person. Wow! That's pretty good.

Dear John,

I was tawking with Earnest about them three kids and seeing the mother of God in person and Earnest says if they was really smart they shooda aks for her autograph.

Dear John,

Earnest aks me if I voted. I told him I can't vote cause you gotta be reel old to vote. Earnest says he voted in the Miss Rheingold contest. Maybe Earnest likes Rheingold cause every year they got a reel pretty Miss Rheingold.

Dear John,

The teacher don't forget. I still gotta rite that friendly letter. Ding it, dang it, darn. I gotta do it.

Dear John,

How are you? I am fine. It is raining out. Is it raining out where you is? I like to play. Do you like to play? I go to school. Do you go to school? I am in 4th grade. What grade are you in? Do you have a nice teacher? I have a very nice teacher. My teacher is the best teacher in the woild. Do you have the best teacher in the woild? I hope to hear from you.

With deepest sincerity,
Bobby Anderson

Dear John,

I handed my teacher my friendly letter to John. First thing, she takes her red pencil and crosses out _ is _ and writes _ are. Then she says she'll correct the rest of the mistakes later.

Dear John,

She read it. She smiles at me and says, "That's the right way to write a friendly letter. It's almost perfect, only three spelling mistakes." I told Earnest that the teacher likes my letter. Earnest sayz, "You done a good thing to make the teacher happy." Sometimes I ain't shore if Earnest is serius or not.

Dear John,

I reely done a good job on my homewoik and I got a Tree Musketeers. But I figger maybe it ain't worth all that trouble. I spent a hole hour doing the woik and about five seconds eating the Tree Musketeers.

Dear John,

Remember I told you about the party last week? Well I almost forgot to tell you about Uncle Norman. Uncle Norman was at the party last week. He's a reely big man, like kinda fat and reely old. Before me and Earnest falls asleep under the table, Uncle Norman tells us to come up to the roof with him. He's a little drunk but we go up to the roof and Uncle Norman points to the Brooklyn Bridge. You can see the top of the Brooklyn Bridge all lit up and all. Uncle Norman told us that a long time ago he was one of the men what builded the Brooklyn Bridge. Uncle Normam says, "One time I was up on the bridge and a big wind comes along and blows me right off the bridge. I fell a long way down to the street below." I aks him if he got hurt. But Uncle Norman looks down and says, "No, not much." Then Uncle Norman don't say one more word. He jist turns around and goes down stairs. When me and Earnest got back to the party, Uncle Norman was gone.

Dear John,

The candy ain't worth it. Too much woik to pay attenshun and its jist a little crummy piece of a chuckle. I don't even get a whole chuckle. Earnest says it ain't woikin for him neither. He says he's gonna figger out a plan so that they up the ante. He figgers cold cash will do the trick.

Dear John,

I told my mom about what Uncle Norman told us about falling off the Brooklyn Bridge. My mom says she knows about that. My mom said, "Yes, Uncle Norman fell and there were two men below and he fell on them and that's why he didn't get hurt bad." Then my mom tells me that when Uncle Norman falls the two men were killed instantly. Uncle Norman did get hurt but not in the regular way. After all these years he still has to go to a speshal hospital cause sometimes the two guys what are dead talk to him and he talks to them about how sorry he is and all.

Dear John,

I told Earnest maybe the dead guys are ghosts. I don't see no reason for Uncle Norman to go to a speshal hospital jist because he sees the ghosts of two guys what got dead when he falls on them. I see that monster and I don't gotta go to no speshal hospital. Earnest agrees with me and he says people see strange stuff all the time and they ain't crazy. Saints see Mary and angels and dead people all the time and nobody thinks they're crazy. They're jist having vishons like the three kids at Fatima and what they seen was a real good thing.

Dear John,

Me and Earnest ain't got no chuckles in tree days and now we both got anudder note. Earnest figgers the teacher's cooking up a new plan with spychology.

Dear John,

Earnest aks me if I ever hear about hallusinations. I never heard about them. So Earnest tells me his dad always tells his mom she's having hallusinations because she sees him looking at udder women when he ain't. Earnest's dad says she's jist seeing things that ain't there.

Dear John,

Earnest told me he's been thinking about ghosts and vishons and all. He aks me, "What's the difference between vishons and hellusinations?" I don't know the anser to that but I figger it's worth thinking about.

Dear John,

Me and Earnest been doing lots of thinking about vishons and hellusinationss. What's the difference?

Dear John,

I don't know if ghosts are reel or jist hellusinationss. That monster what comes outta my closet looks reelly reel.

Dear John,

So yesterday we was at religion instrukshun cause it was Wednesday. The nun's talking about the three little kids that had six vishons and saw Our Lady of Fatima. Earnest puts up his hand and aks the nun what's the difference between a vishon and a hellusinations. First the nun looks real mad but then she says that the Pope is the only one who knows because he has infullibility and he can't be wrong. The Pope says what the kids seen was a vishon. Then the nun stops and thinks and then she says there is another difference. Hellusinations don't mean anything but vishons always commyounicate an important message.

Dear John,

I axadentally put my shirt in the hamper and then I took all the shirts to the Chinese Laundry. My mom told me to. It ain't my fault. So the last note what I got from the teacher went to the cleaners. Too bad.

Dear John,

Earnest says it comes down to one thing or the udder. People who see ghosts either got visions or hallusinations. He says hallusinations are when you see something what ain't there and vishuns is seeing what's there but what nobody else can see.

Dear John,

Earnest says he seen a movie on television called Topper and it was about these two people what get killed and come back as ghosts. Earnest says that ghosts are always hanging around on earth cause they got some kind of unfinished business and they gotta comyounicate with people what are still alive. That's the way it always is in the movies. So those ghosts are trying to comyounicate with Uncle Norman. Earnest don't think Uncle Norman's having hellusinationss. Earnest says Uncle Norman is having a vision.

Dear John,

My mom got the note. The Chinese guy saved it for her. I ain't going to that cleaners no more. Ding it, dang it, darn!

Dear John,

I told my mom we gotta tell Uncle Norman that he ain't having hellusinationss. He's having a vision. The two ghosts are trying to comyounicate something to him. But my mom says they aren't really ghosts. She says they're hellusinationss. She knows about that too.

Dear John,

My mom and the teacher had anudder meeting. New plan. When I do good, I get gumdrops or chuckles but when I do bad, I get a punshment. Spychology got two sides, good and bad. I like only one side.

Dear John,

I told Earnest that my mom says Uncle Norman is having hellusinationss. Earnest aks me how can anybody tell when it's a vision and when it's a hellusinations? I told him we gotta aks the Pope.

Dear John,

My mom's kinda sad cause the novena ain't woikin yet. But she's only done it for 6 weeks. The deal woiks only when she got all nine weeks done.

Dear John,

The teacher watches me reel close now all the time. Well, I was day dreaming during health. A reel exciting day dream about my fighting off that monster what comes outta my closet and I'm gonna do sumthin what scares him away for good but then I seen the teacher coming. Well, it's either candy or punshment. So I sit up reel fast and look reel smart. Think fast. The last woirds she said was something about brushing teeth. So I up my hand and says, "I think it's reel important to brush our teeth tree times a day and we should bring are toothbrush to school to brush after lunch." She's reel surprised and says, "Very good." Then she gives me a chuckle, one crummy little half piece but it beats a punshiment.

Dear John,

Peter Ackerman is the smartest boy in this hole school. He should really like Christine Carney cause she's the smartest girl in P.S. 18. Earnest agrees, "Peter Ackerman and Christine Carney got so much in common what with their matching thick glasses and buck teeth. They should get married." And then he stops and thinks and says their kids would be real ugly but real smart.

Dear John,

Earnest got lots of gumdrops and chuckles. More than he can eat. I was watching him and I figgered him out. He sets it up so the teacher catches him being bad and then changes reel fast to being good. That's when he gets candy. Today whenever he wants more candy he makes like he ain't paying no attenshun and then the teacher aks him a question and he shows he was listening and she gives him candy for paying reel good attenshun. Earnest got spychology figgered out reel good.

Dear John,

I told Earnest that I got him figgered out and he jist smiles and says, "You ain't so dumb as you look, Bobby Anderson."

Dear John,

What Earnest done woiks reel good for me too. I make it look like I'm daydreaming. I get the teacher's attenshun that way. Then I open my eyes real wide and shake my head like I agree what with she's saying. I get candy by acting good after acting bad. It woiks better than jist being good. Earnest told me, "You always gotta plan these things out."

Dear John,

I told Earnest I figger the monster's trying to comyounicate and I figger he wants sumthing. Earnest says, "You got that right!" Earnest is gonna think about it and help me figger out what the monster wants.

Dear John,

Earnest says he's been thinking about my monster. He had kinda the same problem what with monsters and ghosts but they was always in his kitchen at night and they was always floating around the ice box. But they don't come up to his kitchen no more cause he figgered what they want and he gives it to them so they don't gotta come looking for it.

Dear John,

Earnest told me he got a plan about keeping my monster down in the cellar. I gotta go talk to him about it.

Dear John,

Earnest's saves up his mom and dad's left over beer and he puts a cup of beer down in the basement. The beer keeps Earnest's monsters reel happy. Earnest aks me if I keep candy and stuff in my bedroom. I tell him I always keep some candy and cookies in a drawer in the table what's next to my bed. Earnest says that's how come the monster's in my bedroom. The monster wants my candy. Earnest says I gotta make a deal with the monster so he gets candy but he don't gotta come up to my bedroom to get it.

Dear John,

I bet Earnest is right! The monster wants the candy I keep in my bedroom. So this morning before school I go down in the cellar. The light bulb woiks. I got a bag of candy and a little plate. "You here monster?" Nuthing. "I got a deal for you. You don't come up and outa my closet cause I'm leaving you candy, ten pieces every day. O.K.?" Nuthing. But he's listening. So I leave the candy on the floor near my bin jist like Earnest and me desided. "There. There's the candy, in a little plate. You can get it when I leave but don't come outa my closet no more." I go upstairs reel slow. I don't see the monster, but he's there. He ain't no hallyousination. I know he's there.

33

Dear John,

I checked when I got home from school. The candy's still there. I'm worried. Maybe the monster don't like chuckles. Maybe Earnest's plan ain't gonna woik.

Dear John,

I told Earnest I left the candy for the monster. I don't tell Peter Ackerman or Patrick Garino or nobody else cause they don't believe I got a monster in my closet. But Earnest believes me and he says I done the right thing.

Dear John,

Earnest went into business. Earnest told me he figgered out a way to turn his candy into cold cash. He's selling candy to udder kids at lunch. He gives them a better deal than the lunch counter what sells 2 candies for a penny. Earnest sells 3 for a penny.

Dear John,

Earnest aks me if the candy's gone. I don't know. Better check. Earnest says he put some beer in his cellar cause that's where his monsters and ghosts live. Earnest says it woiks reel good and they don't come up to his kitchen no more. He says, "I bet your candy's gone."

Dear John,

The candy's gone! The plate's empty. The monster got the candy. I'm gonna put 10 pieces there everyday. I made a deal with the monster. I'll keep my end of the deal. I hope he keeps his.

Dear John,

I don't need no more than ten pieces of candy every day. I just make shore I get ten pieces from the teacher except on Fridays when I gotta woik reel hard at being bad and then good. That way I can keep that monster down in the basement for the hole weekend.

Dear John,

I keep doing more better in school. I think it's cause I get to sleep reel good and I don't gotta worry about that monster no more. He's real happy staying in the cellar with all that candy.

Dear John,

I told Earnest about my needing to woik only hard enuff to get ten pieces of candy. Earnest says that I probably should get as much candy as I can and keep puttting as much as I can on the plate. Earnest says it is a well known fact that monsters are greedy and the more candy I put on the plate the better they like it.

Dear John,

I gotta pay reel good attenshun to the teacher so I can trick her into thinking I'm paying reel good attenshun.

Dear John,

I got a nudder note from the teacher in my pocket. I already checked it out with steam. It's good news. It says I done better. I aint gonna lose this note and nobody's gonna steal it.

Dear John,

Today's my mom's birthday and we're gonna have a party tonight but my mom and dad both told me Earnest ain't invited.

Dear John,

I gave my mom the teacher's note for her birthday present. She liked it and told me it was a reelly good present.

Dear John,

The candy's gone everyday. I told Earnest, "If that monster comes outa my closet again, I got a plan. I ain't gonna leave no more candy. But Earnest's got a better idear. He says, "Leaving the candy's a reel smart thing to do. But if that monster ever comes out again, you gotta leave him even more candy." Earnest says, "I got lots of candy. If you need candy for the monster, I can sell you some at a discount."

Dear John,

Earnest is getting to be a real good friend. He got helpful suckgestions.

Dear John,

I was a little worried about having hellusinations and being crazy and all but now I know that monster was a vision cause hellusinationss don't eat candy and drink beer.

Dear John,

My mom's reel happy cause the teacher says I do reel good in school now. I even got that ding dang friendly letter done reel good. It's all cause my mom finished the nine weeks. The novena done the trick.

Chapter 2

The Correct Way

Fourth Grade

Dear John,

My mom says "Clean your closet." I told my mom, "Mom, I got lots to do and it ain't all that messy." My mom says, "Clean it." I aks my mom, "How come I gotta clean it?" She says, "Cause I say so." Then she opens her eyes real big and makes a big circle with her mouth. I don't say nuthing else when I see that look cause there just ain't nothing to say. Anyways I'm reel glad I done it. You was under my toys and shirts and pants and shoes and underclothes and boxes and games and books and some dead socks. Probably the worstest was the dead socks. Pretty stinky, John. I'll write a lot more now that I found you again. You probly missed me and all.

Dear John,

See, I told you I was gonna write you again. I gotta bring you up to date on what's going on around here. First thing is I jist got promoted from 4A to 4B and the next thing is we got a new teacher. See in some schools the kids get the same teacher for a hole year but here they got it figgered better. If a teacher gets stuck with a hole bunch of kids like Earnest, at least she don't gotta spend a hole year with them. That helps teachers from going nutty and it helps us kids when we got a real mean and nasty teacher. We keep hoping things will get better sooner.

Dear John,

I gotta tell you about this here teacher what I got in 4B. Her name is Mrs. Cornwall. She don't never ever smile. She wrinkles her nose up and her mouth down. She got only two dresses. One is all grey and her udder's all brown. She talks loud and squeaky and she always yells at us. She says that reading and writing and correct English are reel important cause they are bay sicks. But what's reelly reelly important is that we do everything the right way.

Mrs. Cornwall says, "There is only one way to do anything. Boys and girls, what is that way?"

Then we all gotta say, "The correct way."

Dear John,

Remember I was telling you about having a mean teacher? We got one.

Dear John,

Earnest keeps making funny faces in class at nobody. So I aks him, "Earnest, why do you make funny faces at nobody?" Earnest says he's trying to wrinkle his nose up and his mouth down. He says, "It's reel hard to do that but I'm gonna keep practicing til I gets it right. Praktice makes poifect and I gotta do it the correct way."

Dear John,

I aks Earnest how come he wants to look like Mrs. Cornwall. Before he can anser me, I tell him, "You're already ugly enuff." Earnest shakes his fist at me but he's smiling so it's O.K.

Dear John,

Sumtimes Earnest is like a dog what growls and wags his tail. You're never shor what end to believe.

Dear John,

Yesterday Mrs. Cornwall called on kids to read up and down the rows in the geography book. I figgered I could get ready to read my pargraph and figger out some of the tuffer woids because she called on the foist kid in the row for the foist pargraph and then the second kid for the second pargraph and I sit in the fifth seat. But I got the same problem every time. See the fifth pargraph always begins at the bottom of the page and the rest is at the top of the next page. You gotta turn the page to see it. But I can't do that. Mrs. Cornwall says we gotta keep one finger on the place where the kid's reading. She watches reel close so we don't lose the place.

So when it's my turn to start reading, I done O.K. on the foist five woids on the bottom of the page but then I turn the page. I get to the third woid on that page and bam! Dead in my tracks. So I'm trying reel hard to sound it out.

Then Mrs. Cornwall tells me, "Sound it out."

Well, that gets me mad cause that's the very thing what I'm trying to do anyways. And then Christine Carney raises her hand and says the right woid and then she looks at me like ain't she the greatest gift to the woirld. Then Christine

Carney tells me about every udder woid to the end of the pargraph. I get finished reading and Mrs. Cornwall says, "Class, tell Bobby Anderson the way to read."

Mrs. Cornwall aks, "What way?"

Everybody looks at me and they all say, "The correct way."

Dear John,

Me and Earnest are getting to be betterer and betterer friends everyday. Earnest says friends gotta have lots in common and we got something real big in common. We both hate school and we really hate Mrs. Cornwall.

Dear John,

Mrs. Cornwall does a surprise attack on Earnest. She sees he ain't keeping his finger on the woids so she tells Peter Ackerman to stop reading right in the middle of a sentence. Then she skips the next three kids and tells Earnest to read the rest of that sentence. Well, Earnest don't know the next woid. Even if he kept his finger on the rite woirds, he probably ain't gonna know the next woid cause Earnest can't read all that good. Mrs. Cornwall tells Earnest to stand in the stoopid corner. That don't bother Earnest none cause he practiced wrinkling his nose up and his mouth down.

Dear John,

I aks Earnest, "Do you think it's fair for a teachers to make us read without letting us check out the woids foirst?" Earnest says, "Teachers like it that way because they're better at correcting than teaching."

Dear John,

Earnest's dad got a ticket for speeding on the Grand Central Parkway. Earnest says the cop was hiding on his motorcycle behind a bridge jist waiting to catch somebody. Earnest says Mrs. Cornwall shoulda been a motorcycle cop. She's sneaky.

Dear John,

My dad told my mom that a lot of the houses around here are gonna get nocked down so they can put up big partment houses for poor people. Lots of the rich people are selling their houses and moving to Nassaw County. That's way far out on Long Island. The people what ain't so rich are moving to Queens.

Dear John,

I told Earnest about the rich people what are moving to Queens and Earnest says he's been to Queens and it's a real nice place. That's the country and they got farms with horses and cows.

I think Earnest is thinking about Nassaw. I been to Queens. It's a lot like Brooklyn only jist a little nicer.

Dear John,

Mrs. Cornwall told us that starting tomorrow we're gonna have a student teacher. She's from St. John's College and she's learning how to teach and is gonna be a reel teacher some day but she's gonna be practicing on us foist. Her name's Miss Donnelly.

Dear John,

Miss Donnelly showed up today and Mrs. Cornwall innerduced her and then she told Miss Donnelly to sit in the back of the room. Miss Donnelly mostly watches Mrs. Cornwall teach and erases the blackboard and stuff. Sometimes she types on stencils and makes copies on the mimeograph. I think she likes going on errands best of all.

Dear John,

Miss Donnelly's got a reel nice big smile and long and curly blond hair. She's kinda tall and kinda thin. Today she got on a reel bright colored dress with red and green and purple flowers all over it.

Earnest says Miss Donnelly looks reel professional. Then he says he can tell right away jist by looking at her that she's gonna be a really good teacher.

I figger that means Earnest thinks Miss Donnelly is pretty. When it comes to teachers Earnest knows what's important.

Dear John,

Ding it, dang it, darn! You won't believe it! Anudder friendly letter. I hadda do that in 4A and now I gotta do it again in 4B. I hate them friendly letters. Mrs. Cornwall says that the most important thing about writing a friendly letter is to make sure you say something inneresting and creative. You also gotta write something what makes them wanna write back. Like aksing a question makes them wanna write back. Ding it, dang it, darn. I gotta do it.

Dear John,

Earnest aks Mrs. Cornwall, "How come we gotta write a friendly letter when we done that in 4A?"

Mrs. Cornwall says, "Because I said so." Then Earnest got a punchiment for aksing too many questions. Earnest gotta stay after school to write his friendly letter. Mrs. Cornwall don't trust him to write a friendly letter at home.

Earnest whispered to me, "I ain't in a friendly mood."

Dear John,

I got nuthing to write about. I ain't got nuthing inneresting ever to say. Nuthing inneresting ever happens around here. I hate writing letters.

Dear John,

I found that letter what I wrote in 4A and I wrote it again with no mistakes. I gave it to Mrs. Cornwall and she looked at it. She can't find no mistakes and she looks real sad about that. She wrinkles her nose up and her mouth down and puts my friendly letter on her desk. She says, "I'll correct it later." That means she'll find sumthing wrong with it even if she gotta woik real hard.

Dear John,

Earnest says that staying after school ain't all that bad cause Mrs. Cornwall goes home right away after school and Miss Donnelly hadda stay to watch him so he don't copy. Miss Donnelly told Earnest that it can be fun writing a letter to an imaginary friend and, if nothing exciting happens, he can invent lots of exciting things. Then Miss Donnelly and Earnest wrote a letter together. I think I'll aks Miss Donnelly if I can stay after school and maybe she can help me.

Dear John,

A lot of people are moving away. My dad says it's because the city's gonna put up the partments for the poor people and the richer people don't wanna live here no more. He says the people what are moving away got predujuices.

Dear John,

Mrs. Cornwall hates my friendly letter. She says, "It is too short and the handwriting is horrible." Then Mrs. Cornwall wrinkles her nose up and her mouth down and says, "Write it again but this time write it the correct way." I told you she was gonna find sumthing wrong with it no matter what I do. But at least she hadda woik hard to come up with sumthing.

Dear John,

How come one teacher loved my friendly letter and the udder teacher hates it? It's the same letter but even better! It's got corrections.

Dear John,

I aks Miss Donnelly to help me with the friendly letter and she done it. It's the foist time I liked staying after school. We had fun planning out the idears for the friendly letter. Foist Miss Donnelly blind folds me and I hadda walk over to the map and put my finger on some spot. I put my finger on a place what nobody never heard of. I'm pretending you live in this little place out west somewheres with maybe a couple of udder people. Miss Donnelly says that it's a great place to have a imaginary friend because you'll wanna know more about everything if you live in a place like that. Miss Donnelly never even heard of the place and probably nobody else does neither. It's called Pocatello and it's way far from everything in a state what's called Idaho.

Dear John,

Miss Donnelly helped me with the idears for the letter and we made it reel inneresting and then set it up so you wanna write back. Then I hadda write it out myself. Miss Donnelly says planning out the idears is the most important thing. Writing it out is the easy part. Here's the letter what I wrote myself.

Dear John,

I was in the Museum of Natural History jist last week. You probably don't got no museum where you live in Pocatello, Idaho. So I'll tell you about this place what's in New York City. The Museum of Natural History is a reelly big place and it's got great dinosores bones, stuffed animals, and great mummies and lots of udder stuff. The dinosores are pretty good but mostly I like them mummies the best. So I spend lots of time looking at this one mummy's coffin. The body is carved into the top and the reel one, the axtual mummy is inside the coffin. It's been dead for a coupla million years. But I talk to it anyways and aks questions like, how come you got dead? And what's it like to be dead so long? What was it like to be a Ejiptian queen and all?

Well one day I'm in the museum and I was kinda like day dreaming in the dinosaur room. Then I hear the guys in uniforms telling everybody the museum's closing but I figger I got plenty of time. But I was wrong. I hear the doors all closing up for the night and there ain't nobody else around. After I hear all the doors shut, SLAM, SLAM, SLAM, the lights all go out. I yell, "Hey, let me outta here." But nobody comes.

Then I think I hear a noise, like the creaking of something opening, very rusty creaky hinges, creak, creak, and then Boom, it sounds like a door shuts. The noise comes from the mummy room. So I walk reel quiet and careful because there ain't no big lights, jist little ones near the floor. So I go into the mummy room and look around. Then I seen it. The mummy's coffin is wide open and it's empty. Then I hear a noise like a swishing of a dress coming right at me from a dark corner.

Well, John, you can guess pretty good that I was scared alright but if you wanna know what happened next, you gotta write back and ask me about it. I hope to hear from you soon.

Scenery,
Bobby Anderson

Dear John,

I figger that's a reel great letter because Mrs. Cornwall says you gotta make the letter inneresting and give John a reason to write back. I done that. And this time it's a lot longer and I wrote it in my very best handwriting.

Dear John,

Mrs. Cornwall looks at my letter and wips out her red pen and crosses out dinosores and Ejiptian and says, "Too many mistakes." Then she holds up my paper with all the red marks on it and she yells, "Boys and girls, tell Bobby Anderson how to write a letter. What way?"

All the kids yell back, "The Correct Way."

Dear John,

Miss Donnelly's gone for a week back to St. John's College for classes. She says she'll miss us. Earnest says he'll miss her a lot cause she's such a good student teacher what with her pretty dresses and all. Earnest knows what's important about being a good teacher.

Dear John,

Before Miss Donnelly left I aks her to read my letter and she says that my letter was fine. It jist needs editing. I don't know what that means. So I aks Earnest and he says, "You gotta send it to editors in the Daily News or the Daily Mirror. That's where all the editors are. Then they put the letters in the paper on the editors page. That's how you get edited." Earnest knows a lot but I ain't so sure about this.

Dear John,

Peter Ackerman is like the smartest boy in the class but today he got one arithmetic problem wrong when he was up at the blackboard. Mrs. Cornwall keeps us practising, "Class, tell Peter Ackerman how he should do his arithmetic problems. What way?" Then we all yell together, "The correct way."

Peter Ackerman turned all red in the face and I think I saw a tear drip onto his desk.

Dear John,

Everybody gets their turn except Christine Carney cause right from the start she always does everything the correct way.

Dear John,

Earnest thinks Mrs. Cornwall ain't such a good teacher. I told him that she ain't no different from most of the udder teachers what I had. Earnest exsplained to me that Mrs. Cornwall wants everything done the correct way but she don't never show us the correct way foist. Then when we do stuff, Mrs. Cornwall is like the motorcycle cop hiding behind the bridge on the Grand Central Parkway. She gets us for all the mistakes. Earnest says, "It ain't right. Good teachers ain't motorcycle cops."

Dear John,

Earnest aks me, "How come we gotta write a letter when the teacher ain't never told us how to write a letter?" I told him I don't know. Earnest says, "Teachers are better at correcting than teaching."

Dear John,

Mrs. Cornwall says, "Boys and girls you must hand in a paper with absolutely no mistakes. It must be totally correct." Then Mrs. Cornwall aks, "What way?" And we all say, "The correct way."

Dear John,

If we don't make no mistakes, Mrs. Cornwall's got nuthing to do. She never teaches how to do anything. She jist tells us to do stuff and then she corrects what we done wrong. Everybody does sumthing wrong, except for Christine Carney.

Dear John,

Mrs. Cornwall gives me back my friendly letter and it got red marks all over it. I gotta write it over with no spelling or udder mistakes.

Dear John,

I hate writing. But I gotta write that letter over again and I gotta do it the correct way. Ding it. Dang it. Darn!

Dear John,

I corrected all the stuff what was marked in red and then I wrote the hole thing again. Then I give it to Mrs. Cornwall. I think she's gonna like it now cause she jist puts it on her desk without looking for the mistakes.

Dear John,

Mrs. Cornwall still hates my letter. She says, "This is not a real letter! This is a story and a pack of lies indeed!" She wants a real letter to an imaginary friend without no imagination.

Dear John,

I don't tell Mrs. Cornwall about Miss Donnelly helping me write the letter and all because I don't want Miss Donnelly getting into no trouble.

Dear John,

I asked Earnest, "How can it be a real letter if it's to sumbody what ain't real?"

Earnest thinks and says, "We should be writing letters to people what are real. We could be writing letters to real kids what live far away or famous people. Writing letters to people what ain't real don't make no sense. You are right, Bobby! They ain't real letters."

Dear John,

Mrs. Cornwall never read my friendly letter the first time. She jist looked for all the spelling and udder mistakes!

Dear John,

Everybody in the class gotta do their letter over again except, of course, Christine Carney. Mrs. Cornwall tells Christine Carney to stand in front of the room and show everybody her friendly letter what got a big A on it. I looked real hard at her letter. It was real short but Christine Carney skipped lines and wrote real big. Then Mrs. Cornwall says, "Christine Carney is the only one in this class who always does everything the correct way." Christine Carney's jist standing there with the biggest smile on her face, like she's saying, "Ain't I swell?"

Dear John,

Earnest says, "If Christine Carney does everything the correct way, how come everybody in the class hates her? She ain't making no friends the correct way."

Dear John,

Mrs. Cornwall says, "The correct way to write is to make no mistakes." But then she says, "Remember, boys and girls it must also be creative just like Christine Carney's."

Dear John,

Earnest says that Mrs. Cornwall got it all upside down about making no mistakes and being creative too. Earnest says, "You can't do both at the same time. Correct and creative ain't good mixers."

I told Earnest it's like mixing Rheingold and Pabst Blue Ribbon.

Earnest says, "Eggsactly!

Dear John,

Mrs. Cornwall yells all the time, "No mistakes!" She says if we make a mistake we'll learn to do it the wrong way and then it's harder to learn the correct way. Mrs. Cornwall keeps saying over and over and over, "What way?" "The correct way." Then she says, "And remember your letters must also be creative!"

Dear John,

Mrs. Cornwall exsplained something about writing a friendly letter. She says the most important thing is that we write it with no mistakes. Correct spelling is the most important thing because it's bay sick. And we gotta woik at making it inneresting and creative and we must use our imaginations.

But Earnest says Mrs. Cornwall got it upside down. He says foist you gotta make it inneresting and creative and then you do the correcting of the spelling and uther stuff. He says that's editing. I guess he looked that one up cause that ain't what he told me before.

Dear John,

I aks Earnest if he knows what bay sick is. He says it's got something to do with Jamaica Bay near Rockaway Beach. The crabs and clams and fish are all sick cause of the bad stuff what people throw in the bay. It's a sick bay so it's bay sick.

Dear John,

I think sometimes Earnest makes up stuff like deafnitions and then he goes and checks it out in a dikshonary.

Dear John,

Earnest knows a lot but sumtimes it's a good idear to check on what he says. So I aks Mrs. Cornwall what bay sick means. She wrinkles her nose up and her mouth down and tells me the correct way is to look it up in the dikshonary.

Dear John,

Bay sick ain't in the dictionary.

Dear John,

We got these reading groups what are named after flowers. Christine Carney's in the rosebuds. I'm in the carnations. Earnest and Nicholas are in the dandylions.

Dear John,

I hadda stand up and read out loud today. I was reading in *Roads to Everywhere* the story called the Milkmaid and Her Pal. I come to where it says that the milkmaid's pal spilled the milk and I keep reading but Christine Carney raises her hand and Mrs. Cornwall points to her and Christine Carney says, "Bobby Anderson says 'pal' and the woird is 'pail'." That gets me reel mad because Christine Carney's in the rosebuds and nobody in the carnations cares if it was her pal or her pail what spilled the milk. Who cares who spilled the milk anyways?

Dear John,

Earnest wasn't eggsactly there. He was daydreaming when Christine Carney corrected me so I told Earnest what happened and he says, "No use crying over it." Then he winkles his nose up and his mouth down. He's getting good at that.

Dear John,

We gotta take turns reading the geography book out loud and most of us do nuthing but make mistakes and get corrected and nobody listens to what we read because the good readers are waiting to correct the kid reading and the bad readers are trying to figger out what they're gonna hafta read. And the rest of the kids are day dreaming. Nobody learns nuthing about geography.

Dear John,

At least I know where Pocatello Idaho is.

Dear John,

Earnest says it ain't fair that we get in trouble when we lose our place in reading because Christine Carney don't ever get in trouble when she's in the wrong place. I aks him what ya mean? He says she's outta place when she buts in the carnashons when she's suppose to be in the rosebuds.

Dear John,

I told Christine Carney to stay outta of my carnashons. She jist smiles and says, "Roses on vines always look down on carnations."

Dear John,

I wrote the new letter over about ten times and I don't think I spelled any woids wrong. I was reel careful. The letter ain't long but I don't think that's gonna matter cause I skipped lines and rote real big. Here is my letter.

Dear John,

How are you? I am fine. It is raining out. Is it raining out where you are? I like to play. Do you like to play? I go to school. Do you go to school? I am in 4th grade. What grade are you in? Do you have a nice teacher? I have a very nice teacher. My teacher is the best teacher in the world. Do you have the best teacher in the world? I hope to hear from you.

With deepest sincerity,
Bobby Anderson

Dear John,

It woiked! Mrs. Cornwall loved my letter. She looked it over reel careful and she says, "Not one mistake! You did it the correct way."

I gotta tell you a little secret. It's the same letter what I wrote in 4A and I gave Mrs. Cornwall the first time. She forgot she read it before. I had my sister Maggie write it over with sort of my hand-writing and I rubbed her back for half an hour. It did the trick!

Deaar John,

I told Earnest that Mrs. Cornwall mostly holds up the stuff what got mistakes. If it got no mistakes the udder kids don't get to say, "The correct way."

Earnest says, "I told you. No mistakes sperls all her fun. She lives for mistakes"

Dear John,

I figgered out how to write letters. The most important thing is not to make no mistakes. You jist gotta be reel careful and not write much because the more you write, the more mistakes you make. That's my correct way.

Dear John,

Miss Donnelly's back and starting tomorrow she's gonna teach the carnations. Earnest is jealous because he's a dandylion.

Dear John,

When we was reading today Miss Donnelly told the carnations that sometimes it's O.K. to make a mistake but when you do, you gotta try and correct it yourself. Miss Donnelly said, "The most important thing about mistakes is what you learn from them. Some people are afraid to make mistakes. But if you don't make mistakes, you don't learn as much."

Dear John,

Earnest says, "If you get smart from mistakes, me and you gotta be the smartest kids in Brooklyn.

Dear John,

Starting today Miss Donnelly says no one can correct somebody else when we read. She says that if you make a mistake or don't know a woird, then everyone should wait and see if you can get it right all by yourself without any help. She says it takes time to figger things out.

Dear John,

We was reading the story of the Stonecutter in the *Roads to Everywhere* and it was my turn to read and I come to this woird what I don't know. So I stop and wait for Christine Carney to help but she don't because Miss Donnelly's got her finger up to her lips, that way telling everybody to jist wait. So I looked down at the book again and I seen that it says, ". . . he sat." I look again and read, "In the . . . the king sat." Then it says something about white horses in the next sentence and so I look back at the woird and the woird begins with car . . . but it gotta have horses. So I figger the woird gotta be carriage and it was! I done figgered it out all by myself without any help!

Dear John,

For now on when I come to a woird what I don't know right off, I'm gonna look at all the other woirds around it and figger out what woird belongs there and makes sense and all. That way before I sound it out I know already what it's supposed to mean. That makes it easier to sound it out.

Dear John,

Miss Donnelly told us about Thomas Alva Edison and all the mistakes he made when he was trying to invent a battery. She wrote on the blackboard what he said and I copied it. Edison said, "I have not failed. I've just found 10,000 ways that won't work." He learned lots from making mistakes and then he invented other stuff what didn't come out as batteries. He got smart and rich and famous from making lots of mistakes.

Dear John,

Nancy Trotta was reading at the end of the Stonecutter story and she comes to the woird "wizard" and she says, "magician." Miss Donnelly don't correct her until Nancy Trotta's done reading and then Miss Donnelly writes the two woirds on the board and says, "They mean almost the same thing and that means Nancy Trotta was thinking when she was reading. That's very good, Nancy Trotta, but we need to see how these two woirds are different."

So this is what I figger Miss Donnelly was saying. Sometimes it's O.K. to say the wrong woird if it means the same thing and you're reading for fluantsy. Grown-ups do that all the time. But you also gotta know how to get the woirds exactly right because when I grow up, I don't wanna read the wrong woirds like on my income tax papers and udder stuff like that.

Dear John,

Now we done something new in reading. Miss Donnelly tells us what pargraph each kid is gonna read. We gotta read it foist reel quiet and practice it before we gotta read it out loud to the other kids. Then, when we read, all the other kids gotta turn their books upside down and jist listen.

Dear John,

Us kids in the carnations sound a lot better reading and the story is more inneresting when you're listening.

Dear John,

Earnest says Miss Donnelly don't need to do all that much correcting because she's good at teaching. But Mrs.

Cornwall's gotta do lots of correcting because when it comes to teaching, she stinks.

Dear John,

When Earnest reads, he don't read the exact same woirds what are on the page but he still makes it sound reel good. When nobody's watching he can get away with it real good. Besides most of the time Earnest's story is lots more inneresting than the one what's in the book.

Dear John,

Earnest was right about Miss Donnelly. All the kids in the class, except maybe Christine Carney, say Miss Donnelly's a good teacher.

Dear John,

Earnest aks Miss Donnelly to teach the dandylions. Miss Donnelly says that she gotta get more practice teaching and work up to that group.

Dear John,

Earnest thinks it's jist great that Miss Donnelly's gotta work up to his group. I figger she gotta work down to that group but I don't say nuthin about that to Earnest.

Dear John,

Earnest aks Mrs. Cornwall, "How come Miss Donnelly don't teach the dandylions?" Mrs. Cornwall says, "Miss Donnelly is not ready for that much of a challenge." Earnest aks, "How come?" Mrs. Cornwall says, "Because I said so."

Dear John,

Now Miss Donnelly's gonna teach the whole class writing. She says starting tomorrow we gotta write and she's gonna give us a good grade only if we write something inneresting. We don't gotta worry about the spelling because it's a foist draft. She wants it to be fun and inneresting for her to read.

Dear John,

Miss Donnelly's been teaching the carnations and Mrs. Cornwall's been teaching other groups. But now Miss Donnelly's gonna teach us everything jist like a reel teacher and Mrs. Cornwall's ain't gonna to stay in the classroom. She tells us to be good because she'll come in sometimes to check on us and to see how good a teacher Miss Donnelly is.

Dear John,

Earnest is telling everybody that if they're bad in class when Miss Donnelly's teaching, he's gonna get real mad at them. Nobody wants Earnest to be mad at them because it might be unhealthy for them. I think everybody's gonna be real good for Miss Donnelly and even better than they are for Mrs. Cornwall.

Dear John,

Earnest told Nicholas and some udder kids, "Anybody what ain't good, better stay out of dark alleys."

Dear John,

Miss Donnelly showed us how to write a real good story. First we got lots of good idears and Miss Donnelly wrote them on the blackboard. Then we took one idear and we all helped write even better idears about it. Miss Donnelly called it brainstorming. Nobody can correct anybody's idears and no making funny faces at stoopid idears. Miss Donnelly wrote all the idears on the blackboard. She even wrote Christine Carney's boring idears. Then we all wrote a story together. Writing stories can get to be fun.

Dear John,

I told Earnest the truth. Christine Carney's idears was stoopid and boring but his idears for the story were the most fun and exciting. Earnest smiles and pushes me away. I think Earnest was embarrassed. But it was Earnest's idear that started the class story. It was about pirates and treashures and, of course, damsels in dis dress.

Dear John,

I wrote a inneresting story for Miss Donnelly. Here it is. It's about you.

The Lorst Verse

Once upon a time John wakes up and his mom says, "Good morning."

Well John opens his mouth and says, "g . . . g . . . g." Then pain in the throat! No verse. He tries again, "g . . . g . . . g." Nuthin comes out. John got no verse.

His mom says, "Uh oh, you lorst your verse." She says, "That's O.K." And goes to the telefone.

John is real upset like worried and noivous because he lorst his verse. He gets up and foist looks under his bed, then in his droors, then in his toy chest. He looks in his closet under the toys and shirts and pants and shoes and underclothes and books and some dead socks. He throws everything on the floor.

His mom comes in and is mad at the mess but she says, "Quick get drest because we got an apperntment with the doctor."

John gets dressed and into the car and two minutes at the doctor's place. The doctor says, "Open your mouth."

John opens and something good tasting goes in. Then something bad tasting. Sulfur medsin. Back in the car.

Johnn says, "That medsin taste real bad."

Then his mom looks serprized.

John says, "My verse! I got my verse back. The doctor found it."

His mom looks and says, "What do you mean?"

He says, "You know, I lorst it. Where was it?"

She laffs and says, "I see. You lorst your verse and you were looking for it. Is that why you turned your room upside down?"

When John got home he was reel glad to see his room wasn't upside down. It was jist the way it always is, messy.

Dear John,

In the school yard Earnest don't wanna talk to me no more. He spends all his time talking to Miss Donnelly. He says it's because she's a reel good teacher.

Dear John,

Miss Donnelly gives us back the stories what we wrote and says she only graded it for creative thinking and she gave the best grades to the most innerersting stories. Then she gives me back the story and it got A+ and she says that it's a wunnerful first draft. She says if I wanna, I can write it again and she will give it another grade for gas stations.

Dear John,

I don't unnerstand why she's gonna grade my story for gas stations. So I aks Earnest what he thinks about that. He don't know. She told him she's gonna grade his for plumbers or something.

Dear John,

Earnest and me aks Miss Donnelly how come she's gonna grade for gas station and plumbers. She says, "No, I didn't say that. I said that I would grade your paper for mechanics." Me and Earnest both says, "Oh, thanks."

That don't help. Mechanics still don't make no sense. But me and Earnest don't want Miss Donnelly thinking we're stoopid or something so we don't aks about it again.

Dear John,

Earnest's staying after school to help Miss Donnelly wash the boards and clean erasers. This is very strange stuff for Earnest.

Dear John,

Miss Donnelly was teaching the carnations group and Mrs. Cornwall walks into the classroom and sits down in the back of the room. She's watching and writing down what's going on. Andy Scarpino's reading and he comes to a woird and stops because he don't know it. He starts reading to himself the woirds around the woird he don't know and trying reel hard to figger out what belongs there. Nobody helps him. Then Mrs. Cornwall looks up and looks around. Christine Carney's staying out of the carnations and nobody's saying nuthing. Mrs. Cornwall wrinkles her nose up and her mouth down. Then Mrs. Cornwall says the right woird real loud. Then Andy Scarpino messes up another woird. Mrs. Cornwall waits for somebody to correct him and then she corrects him again. Then Mrs. Cornwall tells Miss Donnelly to change places and she finishes up the lesson by correcting everybody for everything.

Dear John,

Mrs. Cornwall's back teaching the carnations and Miss Donnelly is watching. Mrs. Cornwall yells, "What way?"

"The correct way."

Dear John,

I was reading today and I was trying to read fast and I come to the woird "home" and I say "house." I know right away it's wrong but I jist keep going and hope nobody catches it. No such luck! Mrs. Cornwall gets up and writes it on the board and says, "Home! The correct woird is home and you said house." Then she turns to the reading group, "There is only one way. What is that way?"

"The correct way."

Dear John,

Some professor from St. John's College came to P.S. 18 today. First he sits and watches Miss Donnelly teach the carnations. Miss Donnelly teaches real good and everybody woiked real hard figuring out the woirds and not correcting nobody else. We wanted to do the right thing so she looks good.

Then the professor and Mrs. Cornwall got together. They had a big meeting. First Miss Donnelly watches us. She keeps walking back and forth, back and forth, and I never seen her bite her nails before. Then Mrs. Cornwall comes in and tells Miss Donnelly to go the liberry because the professor wants to talk to her. Then all three of them get together and we was real good and quiet. But when they all come back into the classroom, none of them was smiling.

Dear John,

I hope Miss Donnelly don't get fired. It's my fault she's in trouble. When I said *house*, I shoulda said *home.*

Dear John,

Miss Donnelly started back teaching us again but she says, "Mrs. Cornwall is right. The correct way is the only way." Now Miss Donnelly says we gotta correct each other when someone makes a mistake.

Dear John,

Christine Carney looked real happy at lunch and says, "This is definitely the correct way." Then Christine Carney says, "The correct way is the only way." Christine Carney's real happy to be butting into our carnations again.

Dear John,

Earnest says he don't like it this way. He likes it better when nobody corrects nobody. He says that Miss Donnelly's been brainwashed but I can see he still thinks she's a real good teacher. She wore a red dress today.

Dear John,

I hadda stay after school today because I don't do my homewoik. Mrs. Cornwall makes us sit in the hallway and do the woik so everybody can see us getting a punchiment.

Mrs. Cornwall and Miss Donnelly are inside the room talking and I move my chair closer to the door and listen jist a little. Mrs. Cornwall's telling Miss Donnelly that she needs to learn how to teach the correct way. She says the professor never told her to teach the wrong way and Miss Donnelly got one more chance or she gotta stop student teaching and go back and learn to teach the correct way.

But Miss Donnelly don't wanna leave. She's hoping to graduate in June and get a teaching job in September. She needs to finish and get a job because she needs money. She got nobody to take care of her.

Then Mrs. Cornwall says, "It's very simple. You must always correct every child for every mistake every time. That's the correct way to teach. By correcting them, children learn."

Dear John,

Miss Donnelly says we gotta correct other kids when they make mistakes. She says that we gotta tell kids the right woirds when they read and make mistakes.

Dear John,

Today Andy Scarpino was reading and he ain't got no time to check out the woirds because Miss Donnelly calls on him first. He starts reading and messes up five woirds in the first sentence. That's pretty bad on account the sentence got six woirds. He got the woird "a" correct. When he gets to the second sentence he keeps messing up and his face gets a little red and everybody's helping him and correcting him and then his face gets reel red and he starts shaking and then he can't see none of the woirds because his page is getting wet from the tears what's coming out of his eyes and running down his face. Miss Donnelly tells Andy Scarpino it's O.K. and he can stop reading.

Then I see Miss Donnelly. She got a handky and pretends she's jist blowing her nose. But Miss Donnelly got tears running down her face too.

Dear John,

Miss Donnelly changed the rules again. She don't let nobody correct me when I'm reading today and I done pretty good even if I changed some of the woirds to ones I already know. When I get done reading, Miss Donnelly puts the right woirds on the board and exsplains them. Next time I won't miss them because I really woiked at remembering them. I don't want Miss Donnelly getting fired when Mrs. Cornwall hears me say the wrong woirds.

Dear John,

Earnest says Miss Donnelly is real brave because she ain't giving up all that easy. He says Miss Donnelly is real strong even if she ain't a man. Strong men don't ever cry but sometimes strong ladies cry. But then Earnest says it don't matter because Miss Donnelly ain't giving up and that's the main thing.

Dear John,

Mrs. Cornwall was absent today because she got a daughter that needs help because she's gonna have a baby. So Miss Donnelly was the teacher for the whole day.

Miss Donnelly told us, "The most important thing is to correct your own mistakes and learn for yourself what is correct. You should not have to depend on others for help. When you make a mistake, you have to correct it. You must become independent learners. When you grow up no one else will help you."

Miss Donnelly said that correcting kids for every mistake can make some kids feel bad and hurt them. For now on she's gonna tell us what pargraph we're gonna read the next day and we can check out all the woirds for a whole day. This way nobody should make lots of mistakes.

Then she says the way we're gonna do it and all is a secret and we don't gotta tell nobody else.

Dear John,

Earnest told all the carnations they better practice their reading so Mrs. Cornwall don't get Miss Donnelly fired. And he told them to keep their mouths zipped.

Dear John,

Earnest says we got a problem. Christine Carney told Mrs. Cornwall everything what Miss Donnelly says. Christine Carney should stay outta the carnations.

Dear John,

The professor was here again today and they had another big meeting. Only this time the principal was in on it.

Dear John,

Miss Donnelly ain't gonna be a student teacher no more.

Mrs. Cornwall told the class that Miss Donnelly will student teach again next year when she learns to teach the correct way and when she learns to follow orders. She says that right in front of Miss Donnelly who gets real red with tears in her eyes. Miss Donnely hadda turn around so we don't see her crying. Jist her shoulders shaking.

Dear John,

Today Miss Donnelly said goodbye. We're real sad to see her go. Miss Donnelly's walking with her stuff out the door near the stairway and Earnest runs down the hall and gives her a hug. He's all red in the face when he comes back to the classroom. Mrs. Cornwall looks at Earnest and wrinkles her nose up and her mouth down. Earnest looks at Mrs. Cornwall and wrinkles his nose up and his mouth down. Earnest hadda go to the principal's office for the rest of the day.

Dear John,

The kids in the class are real sorry Miss Donnelly got fired from the student teacher job. She's the best teacher we ever had.

Dear John,

I told Earnest I was real sad because I got Miss Donnely fired when I said *house* when the woird was *home*. But Earnest sayz it wasn't me what got her fired. It was Christine Carney.

Dear John,

Earnest aks Mrs. Cornwall, "How come Miss Donnelly ain't gonna be a student teacher no more?" Mrs. Cornwall says, "Anymore." Earnest says, "Right. How come she ain't gonna teach us anymore." Mrs. Cornwall says, "Isn't going to." Earnest says, "Right. How come she isn't going to teach us no more?" Mrs. Cornwall says, "Sit down and ask no more questions until you learn the correct way to speak English."

"Class, what way do we speak?"

"The Correct Way!"

Dear John,

I always really hate writing letters. Now I really hate reading too. I said *house* when I shoulda said *home*. I shoulda read it the correct way.

Dear John,

I keep telling Earnest I shoulda read *home* when I said *house* but it's still my fault that Miss Donnelly got fired.

Earnest says, "It ain't your fault. Mrs. Cornwall and Miss Donnelly got different idears about what's the correct way."

Dear John,

There we was standing in front of the mirror and Earnest wrinkles his nose up and his mouth down real good now. He makes a face jist like Mrs. Cornwall's. I say, "You got it. That's the way!" We both smile and shake our heads.

Then Earnest aks, "What way?"

I say, "The Correct Way!

Chapter 3

Straight and Narrow

Fifth grade

Dear John,

I'm switching schools! Tomorrow's the first day of school and I'm gonna go to St. Mary's. That's the Catholic school what's across the street from P.S. 18. They got lots of room at St. Mary's now cause of all the rich kids are moving away. My mom never even told me I was on the list. I'm gonna be in fifth grade.

Dear John,

I told Earnest I ain't gonna be in P.S. 18 no more cause I'm gonna go to St. Mary's. Earnest says his mom wants him to go to St. Mary's but the nuns keep putting him on the bottom of the list and that's O.K. with him cause he don't never get along all that good with the nuns anyways.

Dear John,

Earnest says St. Mary's should be real different for me. When he went to the Catholic school, he never hadda write no friendly letters.

But I told Earnest, "You only went to Catholic School for about one week. Right?"

Earnest says, "Right. But they don't got no time writing friendly letters cause when I was there, they mostly prayed."

I told Earnest, "After you switched to the public school, they probly don't pray all that much cause that's what they was praying for."

Dear John,

Today's the first day of school and I'm standing in the school yard with lots of other kids. Then a really big fat nun comes out of St. Mary's School with a big school bell. That's the principal and she rings this big school bell, clang clang, and everybody gotta stand right where they is and not make one little move. Then the nun rings the bell again, clang clang, and everybody gotta walk to a line. A kid's standing with a big sign and it says 5A. That's my class and there's a nun standing in front of the line of kids. I figger I better make a good impreshon. So I go up to the nun and I say, "Good morning, nun. I'm Bobby Anderson. Is this my class?"

She looks at me and says, "It is and I know very well who you are. I know all about you. You shall call me Sister, and never call me Nun." Then she tilts back her head and looks down her nose and says, "Go to the rear of the boy's line."

Dear John,

When we get upstairs we all gotta wait outside in the hall. Everybody jist stands there and nobody don't say a word. Then the nun tells us to come into the classroom one at a time and tells us what seat to sit in. Everybody else already got a desk when I get in there cause I'm the last one on line. The nun pernts to a desk and says, "You sit here in this seat right in front of me. You public school children always need more discipline."

My desk's right in front of the nun. But then in the back of the room, somebody's smiling and waving at me. Oh, no! It's Christine Carney!

Dear John,

I guess the nun knows Christine Carney don't need no more discipline. She's overloaded with the stuff.

Dear John,

The first day at St. Mary's went pretty good mostly because it took most of the day to get to our desks and getting our books and saying the Pledge of Allejance and about a hundred other prayers. Then we hadda copy fifty rules what the nun writes on the blackboard. Every rule starts with don't. Rule 1 is "Don't stray from the straight and narrow road." The number 50 rule is, "Don't use double negatives." I don't got no idear what that means.

Dear John,

The nun says, "A new boy is down in the office and he will be in this class."

We was all wondering who it is and then the big fat nun what's the principal walks in and right behind her, it's

Earnest. Earnest switched to St. Mary's. He's in my class! He was a day late. That ain't all that bad for Earnest.

Dear John,

I aks Earnest how come he got to go to St. Mary's. He said they got to the bottom of the list.

Dear John,

The nun checks our notebooks to make sure we wrote the fifty rules and wrote them right and all. I wrote all the rules but she gets real mad at me cause I made the number 50 rule sound better. I wrote, "Don't use no double negatives." How come she gets mad at that? It sounds better and like stronger than the way she wrote it.

Dear John,

I aks Earnest, "How come you don't tell me all summer about switching to St. Mary's? Earnest said, "I don't even know about it 'til this morning. See, I go to P.S. 18 yesterday but the teacher and me don't hit it off good right from the start. She sends me to the principal's office three times."

Then the principal calls up Earnest's mom and tells her she heard that Earnest is on the waiting list for St. Mary's and the waiting list jist got real short. The principal told Earnest's mom that St. Mary's is a real good school and Earnest should go there.

Dear John,

It's nice to hear those familiar noises coming from the back of the room. Earnest jist keeps getting better with practice.

Dear John,

We had one empty desk way in the back of the classroom. That's where the nun put Earnest but then when those noises start coming from the back, the nun tells Peter Ackerman to change seats with Earnest. Now Earnest sits next to me. This is gonna be fun.

Dear John,

It ain't no fun cause the nun always looks at me and Earnest. She don't look at nobody else in the class.

Dear John,

Earnest gotta copy the fifty rules from somebody cause he got to school a day late and the nun erased all the rules from the blackboard. The nun sees him copying from my book and she takes it away and gives him Christine Carney's notebook. Christine Carney always gets all the rules right.

Dear John,

I aks Earnest, "What a double negative?.

Earnest says, "That's when you say no two times. Like when a baby's doing something bad and the mom says, 'No, no,' That's a double negative.'"

Dear John,

Christine Carney told me she heard Earnest telling me about the double negatives and she says, "Earnest, as usual, is wrong. A double negative is not lojical because one negative cancels out the other negative. For example, if you say, 'I can't go nowhere,' it means you can go anywhere."

I said, "I got it now and I ain't gonna do no more double negatives."

Christine Carney jist shakes her head and walks away.

Dear John,

I told Earnest what Christine Carney said and Earnest says, "So when a mom says, 'No, no,' she really means 'yes.'"

I said, "I guess that's what it means.

Earnest walks away talking like to himself, "That's stoopid cause a mom don't mean yes."

Dear John,

Me and Earnest think rule 50 is a stoopid rule. Everybody knows when you say you ain't gonna do nothing, it sounds better and a lot more stronger than when you jist say you ain't gonna do something.

Dear John,

Earnest aks Christine Carney, "If a double negative means yes, do two yeses mean a no?"

Christine Carney just shakes her head and walks away.

Dear John,

Earnest told me his dad wrecked his truck last night but he ain't hurt bad. See, he was driving home on Ocean Parkway and lots of big bugs hit his windshield. Well the bugs splat, squashed all over it. He's looking at all the bugs on the windshield and he ain't watching the road and where he's going. The road turned but the truck kept going straight. Then the truck goes off the road and winds up in a baseball field upside down. Earnest's dad is O.K. but the truck's squashed and looks a lot like them squashed bugs on the windshield.

Dear John,

I told Earnest his dad strayed from the straight and narrow road.

Earnest told me that was pretty funny but he ain't about to tell his dad what I said. His dad ain't in the mood right now for religion jokes.

Dear John,

I hadda write a story about my summer vacation and it can't have no double negatives. I aks my sister Maggie to read it and help me with the double negatives. She crossed out one word what said something like "no" in almost every sentence. I read it and it don't sound right but I wrote it real short and real careful and it's all correct and I got B+. I ain't gonna copy it here because it's the most boring stuff what I ever wrote and it don't sound like the way nobody I know talks. I hate writing.

Dear John,

I was over Earnest's apartment today and Earnest's dad's gonna get another truck cause he needs it for work. He fixes roads for Kings County which is jist a fancy name for Brooklyn. Earnest's dad don't got much money to get a real good truck so he got a old one what runs O.K. But both the windshields got big cracks in them.

Earnest told his dad to keep his eyes on the road and not on all the cracks. Then his dad chases Earnest around and picks up a dead cockroach from the floor and puts it down Earnest's shirt. We was laffing when Earnest tries to get the dead bug out cause it wasn't dead and it got into Earnest's pants. Earnest's dad ain't in such a bad mood no more.

Dear John,

Earnest keeps talking about rule number one, the straight and narrow, and he is definitely not for it. He says, "Think about it. The whole thing ain't natural. No real road is ever straight and narrow. If you keep going straight along a narrow road when there is a bend in the road, you'll land upside down and maybe dead. Straight and narrow ain't the way to go."

Dear John,

In P.S. 18 there was three reading groups but in St. Mary's we got two reading groups. The nun always starts with the eagles. Christine Carney's in that group and they get done real fast. Next comes the group what Earnest and me are in, the blue jays. Most of the time we gotta read in the reader. Its called *Roads to Everywhere*. It's the same one as last year in PS 18. I kinda liked that book last year but now it ain't all that inneresting, like boring on account I know all the stories. But that makes it all easy to read so I don't mind none. Anyways it's a 4th grade book and all the blue jays gotta read it again and the eagles got the 6th grade book. It's embarrassing and very youmilleyating, John. And we gotta do other stuff like really stoopid stuff in the woikbook. The nun calls them fun to do pages. Maybe she thinks so but I don't.

Dear John,

Reading is just like it was at P.S. 18. It goes like this. When another kid's reading, you gotta keep your finger on the woird so the nun sees you're keeping your place. That way when the kid reading makes a mistake, quick hand in the air, wave at the nun till she looks at you, then you gotta

77

shout out the right woird and then give the reading kid a dirty look. That's the way everybody learns how to read better. It ain't all that different from the correct ways what we done at PS 18.

Dear John,

The nun says, "It is very important to read each and every word correctly and you do that by reading every letter correctly."

I aks the nun if she knows Mrs. Cornwall and she says, "No."

I said, "She teaches at P.S. 18 right across the street. You should meet her. You'd like each other."

Dear John,

I told Earnest, "The nun and Mrs. Cornwall are a lot the same but the nun don't know Mrs. Cornwall. We should innerduce them."

Earnest says, "The two of them would be a double negatve!"

We laff at that so much we both fall on the floor.

Dear John,

Earnest says, "Teachers are all the same."

I say, "Not Miss Donnelly. She's different."

Earnest says, "And that's why she ain't a teacher no more."

Dear John,

The nun says we're gonna learn to write a poem. But first we gotta learn to appresheate a wonderful and great poem. It's about trees and God. The nun tells us that it's hard to believe that the poet wasn't a Catholic but it's still one of the most beautiful poems that was ever written. We gotta memorize it. It's called Trees.

Dear John,
    I got this part memorized.

> I think that I will never see
> a poem lovely as a tree.

Dear John,
    Today the story in the reader is called "Diego Wins." It's about a kid what lives in Cuba. Well, that's a problem cause I musta been sick last year when they read that story cause I don't remember a darn thing about it. So I look at the pictures to try to figger out what the story's about but it don't look nuthing like Brooklyn so that don't help.
    I'm sitting in the first seat in the second row. The six kids in the first row gotta read first. I figger I'm gonna read pargraph seven. So Johnny Paizano's reading pretty good what with the other kids helping him read better. So I keep my finger kind of around where he's reading and I start looking for the pargraph what I'm gonna read. It ain't there. Two pargraphs on the first page, four pargraphs on the other page and pargraph seven's on the other side of the page. Big problem.
    I can't never read out loud good until I check out all the woirds foist. Most of the time I can sneak ahead and check out what I'm getting into. But most of what I'm gonna hafta read is on the back of the page.
    Johnny Paizano finishes his pargraph. He got only about five dirty looks from all the helpers. Then Marie

Magatarino's reading. Pretty bad. She gets lots of help and lots of dirty looks. Next Jimmy DeAndro. He reads real fast and never misses a woird and don't unnerstand a darn thing. Barry Dranski's up next swinging. He musta checked out the woirds in the foist sentence O.K. but then he strikes out. They gotta help him with almost every woird. It's getting closer and closer. I'm trying to keep my finger on the right woird and I lift the page jist a little so I can see the woirds through the paper but it don't help much.

So I lift the page to jist get a little peak and wam the nun shouts, "Young man, what do you think you are doing?"

I say, "Uh, a fly's crawling under the page and I'm shooing him."

She says, "A fly in October? Absurd!" "How dare you lie to me. The audacity of you!" Nuns like big woirds and they really like woirds what nobody else ever says.

Then she tells me to read where Barry Dranski stopped reading. That's to see if I was keeping my place. But I remember the last woird he reads and I find it and finish reading the pargraph what was only like about five words. Then Franky Alvareddi starts reading the next pargraph and the nun jist gives me a dirty look.

One problem was that I messed up Herbie Marino real bad. He told me he was checking out the next pargraph and he gotta read the one what I was sposed to read. Then all the other kids gotta check out new pargraphs. They don't like that none. I gotta come up with a plan so I don't get cort like that no more.

Dear John,

       I think that I will never be
       so lovely as a tree.

I'm working on the rest of the poem now that I got that part memorized real good.

Dear John,

I was telling Earnest I'm gonna bring a mirror to school so I can see what's on the next page and Christine Carney hears me. She says, "Dont ever try to read with a mirror. You're eyes will see backwards." She says she read in a scientific jurnal that some children reverse letters and words because their eyes see backwards. She says, "I should think you should consider this to be a major concern for boys like you who can't read well. Perhaps you see letters and words backwards and if this be the case, perhaps you should see a doctor before you both grow up to be complete illiterates."

Earnest says, "Christine Carney, there ain't no problem about kids like that growing up"

Christine Carney aks, "Pray tell, why will there be no problem?"

Earnest says, "Because if they see things backwards, they ain't gonna live long enuff to grow up."

Christine aks, "And why would they come to such an unfortunate end?"

Earnest said, "Because they're gonna walk in front of cars what they think are driving the other way."

Dear John,

I keep practicing that poem so I get it memorized real good. Here it is again.

> I think that I will be a tree
> or a poem as lovely to see.

Dear John,

Earnest says he's got a plan so we don't get cort not being prepared and all like last time. He says we gotta do what Miss Donnelly done because when we practiced first everybody got to sound like a real good reader. So we gotta get readers for home so we can check out all the woirds for the next day.

"Good idear but only one problem. We ain't allowed to bring no readers home."

Earnest says, "I'm woiking on it."

Dear John,

Tomorrow I gotta have the rest of the poem memorized. I only got the first two lines down but I know them real good.

> I think I see a lovely bee
> in the tree across the sea.

Dear John,

The nun really hates it when you look ahead to check out the woirds foist. I don't know why she gets upset. Miss Donnelly let us check out everything foist and that way everybody reads better and listening to everybody else wasn't so boring. I figger if you check out the woirds first, you're gonna read better.

Dear John,

Earnest says, "I'm working on a plan to get us some of our own *Roads to Everywhere* but there are a few bugs in the plan I gotta woik out.

Dear John,

The nun calls on me to say the poem what I got memorized but I don't got it memorized exactly the right way. I figgered it was close enuff but the nun don't exactly agree.

I gotta write the poem ten times. But at least she don't say nothing about memorizing it.

Dear John,

Me and Earnest both hadda write the poem ten times. Earnest got it done real fast and he showed me how he done it. He don't write the whole poem ten times. He writes each line ten times by using a special writing helper. It's a piece of wood what got ten holes in it and you put a pencil in each hole. Then Earnest holds the writing helper at one end and writes. It comes out the same ten times. Earnest's dad made it for him cause he says there ain't no use in writing something ten times.

Dear John,

I got my poem done ten times real fast. It was kinda fun cause Earnest lent me his writing helper.

Dear John,

Today me and Earnest are walking home and Earnest reaches in his jacket and gives me *Roads to Everywhere*. I aks him, "How come you got *Roads to Everywhere*?" He says, "I woiked the bugs out of my plan."

Dear John,

Last night I practiced reading the next story in the *Roads to Everywhere*. I figgered out most of the woirds so I don't get cort if the nun calls on me to read tomorrow. This morning I go over to Earnest's apartment and I hadda wait for him to get his shoes on. I seen Earnest got his own reader so I practiced reading that next story in *Roads to Everywhere.*

Earnest's dad's home and he looks at the reader and says, "*Roads to Everywhere.* That's a darn good idear. I'd like to take one and jist keep going. But all I'll ever get to do is fix them."

Dear John,

Earnest says, "The nun keeps looking at the wrong stuff. She's kinda like my dad when he was driving and crashed. My dad was looking at the bugs when he shoulda been looking at the road."

Dear John,

Sometimes Earnest don't make much sense and now I know where he gets that from.

Dear John,

We gotta make up our own poem and it gotta rhyme and it gotta have something called I am big pent ameter. It's gotta be about a tree or birds or sumthin in nature.

Dear John,

The nun told us today, "There are two roads. One leads to heaven. But the devil wants us to take the other road which is filled with temptations and the fires of hell. Only one road will take us to heaven. That road is the will of God and we must always keep our eyes on that road."

Then Earnest whispers to me and says, "There are lots of roads."

The nun hears Earnest whispering and says, "There are no secrets in this classroom. Tell the class what you said."

Then Earnest gets up and says, "I'll show you what I said." Then Earnest walks to the back of the room and pernts to the readers. He says, "See, there are about 25 Roads to Everywhere."

Dear John,

Earnest hadda stay after school today. So I waited outside school and we walked home together. Earnest said, "Walking home from school the same way gets boring. Let's go home a different way every day. There gotta be more than two ways to walk home."

Usually it takes about five minutes to walk home. Today it took almost an hour.

Dear John,

I hadda read out loud today and I don't make even one little teeny mistake. The nun's real sirprized and she says, "Very good reading." Then she looks even more sirprized at herself for letting that slip out.

Dear John,

The nun says, "Poetry is beautiful because it has rules about rhyme and meter. Beauty is in following rules and people who don't follow the rules write ugly things. Some poems don't rhyme and they are not real poems. They are just ugly writing."

Dear John,

We hadda write a poem about nature. Here's the poem what I wrote:

The Tree and the Bee

I think that I shall never be
as big as a tree
or as small as a bee.

A tree is really big and tall
and a bug is real tiny and small
I'll jist be me or nothing at all.

Dear John,

I let Earnest read my poem and he thinks it's real good. He says it's about taking roads but I told him it ain't. It's about trees and bugs. My poem don't say nothing about no roads.

Dear John,

Earnest made up a short poem about nature. I think it's pretty good.

Bugs on the Windshield

Where are the bugs at?
All over that windshield.
Splat. Splat. Splat!

Where's the truck at?
All over that infield.
Splat. Splat. Splat!

Dear John,

I got my poem back and it got a star on top and it got A+. The nun musta slipped up again.

Dear John,

Earnest got his poem back. He got a D. The nun wrote "Never end a sentence with at!"

Earnest showed me what the nun wrote and he aks me, "What's the last word in her sentence?"

I got it.

Dear John,

Ten kids are in the bluejays and everybody's reading real good. Almost nobody makes mistakes. Except Earnest. He gets the story real good but he don't say the same exact words what are in the reader. He needs to practice more. I know he got his own the *Roads to Everywhere*.

Dear John,

Earnest said there ain't so many *Roads to Everywhere* as there use to be. Now there are only 15 in the back of the classroom.

Dear John,

The nun got her own *Roads to Everywhere* but when she opens it today, lots of dead bugs fall all over the floor. Some what don't fall on the floor are squashed in the Roads to Everywhere.

Dear John,

The nun can't prove nothing but she knows Earnest put the dead bugs in her *Roads to Everywhere*. The nun and Earnest ain't exactly hitting it off all that good.

Dear John,

The nun told us today, "Beginning next week we will have a student teacher and you must be very good because last time she failed student teaching in a public school. The college is letting her teach in a Catholic school because the children are much better and smarter and it will be easier for her to pass this time."

Dear John,

I aks the nun what's the student teacher's name.

The nun said, "I don't know her name yet but she at St. John's College."

Earnest is hoping it's Miss Donnelly.

Dear John,

The nun called on Earnest to read today and it sounded real good if you wasn't looking at the woirds in the reader. Everybody keeps telling him the right woirds but he don't stop reading to listen. He jist keeps going fast in the *Roads to Everywhere*.

Dear John,

I aks Earnest, "How come you got so many woirds wrong what with your having your own *Roads to Everywhere* and all."

Earnest said, "I remember the story. I jist don't remember the exact woirds. So I read the story in my own words."

Dear John,

Earnest ain't a blue jay no more cause the nun says he don't read the words right. The nun made another group for about three kids. Earnest and Nicholas and a nudder kid what got a name I forget are pidgeons.

Dear John,

Earnest aks the nun again what's the name of the student teacher. The nun smiles and says like this, "The student teacher's name is" and then she stops and looks at Earnest and then she says, "something you will learn when she gets here." But Earnest don't give up so easy. He aks her in a real nice way and even said please. But the nun jist looks at him and gives him a kind of evil smile and walks away. I never ever before heard Earnest say that please word.

Dear John,

The student teacher is Miss Donnelly. The nun broke down and told us Miss Donnelly's gonna be here next Monday. The please from Earnest done the trick.

Dear John,

Earnest don't jist walk home today. He's jumping and laffing and hooting and yelling. He jumped over every fire hydrant. If he don't calm down, it's gonna be one wild weekend in Brooklyn.

Dear John,

Last night there was a lot of loud noises like guns shooting outside my apartment house. So real careful I look out the window and there's a kid looking up at me. I turn off the lights so I can see better out the window. It's Earnest setting off a hole bunch of firecrackers. I opened the window and called down to him, "What are you doing?" He shouts up, "I'm cellarbrating." I told you it was gonna be a one wild weekend.

Dear John,

It's Sunday and I seen Earnest at Mass. He was really good in church. He says he let out all the badness in him yesterday and now he's getting into being real good. He don't wanna do nothing bad when Miss Donnelly comes to school tomorrow.

Dear John,

Miss Donnelly was waiting for us when we got up to the classroom today. She looks different. She got her hair real short and she got on a dress what's all brown.

Earnest figgered she was gonna be sirprized to see us but she don't pay no attenshun when he waves at her.

The nun told Miss Donnelly to sit in the back of the classroom and watch her teach.

Earnest kept turning arownd to look at Miss Donnelly but the nun keeps telling Earnest, "Face front."

Miss Donnelly ain't paying no attenshun to Earnest.

Dear John,

Earnest's trying real hard to be good even in school now because he wants to show Miss Donnelly how good he's doing. Miss Donnelly's gonna sit in the back of the room and watch how the nun teaches for about two weeks. Then she's gonna get to teach us.

Dear John,

Today Miss Donnelly got on a dress what's all grey. She don't smile, not even once.

Dear John,

The pidgeons don't got no readers. They get only woikbooks and mimeograffed papers. The nun says they gotta learn all the skills first before they can read. The nun told the pidgeons that first they must learn the sounds and then they will learn to say the words correctly.

The nun and Mrs. Cornwall got lots in common. If they ever meet they're gonna be real good friends.

Dear John,

The nun told the blue birds to get the *Roads to Everywhere* from the back shelf because it was reading time. But there was a big problem. There was only two *Roads to Everywhere*. All the other *Roads to Everywhere* was gone.

Dear John,

It took me and Earnest twenty minutes to walk home today. We keep finding new ways but they take more time. But we get more time to talk.

Dear John,

Earnest told me he was a real big help to the nun cause he made it right for her. There are only two *Roads to Everywhere*.

Dear John,

We gotta write another poem. Earnest aks Miss Donnelly if she can help him write it after school like she done before. Miss Donnelly tells Earnest she can't and that he must go back to his seat and be quiet. She don't smile not even one little bit.

Dear John,

Today Miss Donnelly got up from her desk in the back of the room and walked over to the window. She just looked out for a few minutes and then she went back to her desk.

Dear John,

Me and Earnest are gonna help each other write the poems.

Dear John,

Earnest helped me write this poem about nature.

> *I see a road to somewhere*
> *One winding long and blinking.*
> *There is a big brown grizzly bear*
> *It's dead and wow it's stinking.*

Dear John,

I gave the nun that poem and I'm gonna help Earnest write another one. We like writing about nature and roads. But then when I got to Earnest's house he already got his poem done. I jist helped him look up some of the words so they got spelled right. This is Earnest's poem.

> *I see a road to nowhere*
> *One twisting dark and hairy*
> *Most roads lead to somewhere*
> *But this one's too darn scarey.*

Dear John,

Me and Earnest got our poems back. The nun wrote the same thing on both. She wrote, "Assignment completed."

Dear John,

Earnest don't like being a pigeon. He says, "The pigeons are defnitley on the *Road to Nowhere.*"

Dear John,

Miss Donnelly jist sits in the back of the room and she don't ever smile or nothing. One day she wears the grey dress and the next day she got the brown one on.

Dear John,

Earnest told me he seen Mrs. Cornwall and the nun talking on Maujer Street today.

Dear John,

The nun and Mrs. Cornwall became like instant friends. Mrs. Cornwall came to the nun's classroom after school. I hadda stay for a punchiment out in the hall. So I move my chair close to the doorway and listen.

They was talking about Miss Donnelly. Mrs. Cornwall told the nun that Alice Donnelly's family's one of the poorest in Sacred Heart parish in Red Hook. They saved for her education and they're very proud that she's going to be a teacher. It was jist terrible the way Miss Donnelly disappointed them by failing student teaching.

Mrs. Cornwall said, "That girl must learn to do what she is told. She must learn to follow the straight and narrow road."

The nun says, "Shocking disobedience! And to think she's a Catholic girl."

Dear John,

I told Earnest about what the nun and Mrs. Cornwall said about Miss Donnelly not following the straight and narrow. Earnest said he's been thinking more about that and now he is certain that it's stoopid to stay straight and narrow when the road curves. He said, "It makes no sense to go straight on a winding road. Every road is winding."

Dear John,

Today Miss Donnelly got up and walked over to the window and jist looked out for a long time. But then the nun keeps looking at her. Then the nun says, "Miss Donnelly, stop looking out the window and return to your seat."

Dear John,

Earnest told me he's been thinking more about what Mrs. Cornwall and the nun was talking about. Earnest says, "Bugs! Bugs!"

I aks him how come he says that but Earnest don't say nothing. He jist walks away with his head down. I don't know why he said that but I figger he don't like the nun and Mrs. Cornwall all that much.

Dear John,

Miss Donnelly's gonna start teaching next Monday. Maybe she'll smile then cause she smiled a lot when she was teaching us at P.S. 18.

Dear John,

Miss Donnelly was teaching the eagles and Christine Carney's says "the" when the word is really "a." Miss Donnelly stops her and explains that all the words must be read exactly as the author wrote them and that is the only correct way to read.

Christine Carney looked like she was gonna crawl into her ink well and die.

Dear John,

Me and Earnest made up a poem and we wrote it big with chalk in the school yard so Miss Donnelly can see it when she looks out the window.

The Fish and the Bee

Fly little fish,
said the bug.
Fly like me.

Swim little bug
said the fish
swim if you wish.

Then the bug swam the air
and the fish flew the sea.

We wrote on the bottom in big letters, For Miss Donnelly.

Then me and Earnest laffed all the way home about Christine Carney getting corrected for reading the wrong word. Miss Donnelly's gonna get Christine Carney with her own medsin.

Tomorrow Miss Donnelly's gonna teach science. Last year she showed us expeerments and made it real inneresting.

Dear John,

Today Miss Donnelly don't show us no expeerments. She jist called on kids to read up and down the rows in the science book. I sit in the fifth desk and Johnny Paizano's reading. I turn the page so I can see the words in the fifth pargraph but Miss Donnelly cort me and tells me to keep my place. Then I try it again when Jimmy DeAndro's reading but she cort me again and then she tells me to read where Jimmy DeAndro left off but I don't know where he left off. I gotta write a hundred times. "I must pay attention."

Miss Donnelly says, "There's only one way to do anything. Boys and girls, what is that way?"

"THE CORRECT WAY."

Dear John,

After school today, me and Earnest went to the school yard and we rubbed our shoes all over the poem and we rubbed it out. Then we walk home together but we don't say nuthing. We jist take the shortest way home. Then we get to Earnest's apartment house and Earnest's dad is washing his new truck, what ain't so new.

Earnest's dad aks us, "What's going on? You gloomy guys look like it's the end of the woirld."

Earnest tells his dad the whole thing about the nun and how Miss Donnelly changed and all.

But I guess Earnest's dad don't care all that much about anything except his truck and the axcident. I mean we was telling him about Miss Donnelly and the nun and all but Earnest's dad looks at me and Earnest and he says, "I learned a lot from crashing my truck. My advice to you guys is to keep your eyes on the road, don't keep going straight when the road turns, pay attention to where you are going and pay no attention to bugs on the windshield."

Chapter 4

Victoria's Manshun

Fifth Grade

Dear John,

They sold the big old house across the street and the two old people what lived there are moving. My mom says it used to be Victoria's Manshun. I figger Victoria musta been rich and she musta had lots of money. It's the biggest and prettiest house in Brooklyn. But now it's real old and run down. But it musta been real pretty a coupla hundred years ago.

Dear John,

I been reading Treashur Island. I like Hawkins. He's a good guy. It'd be fun going treashur hunting with him and his crew.

Dear John,

Carpenters and painters are working on the old house what used to be Victoria's Manshun. I aks them, "Can I go

97

inside and look around?" The painter said, "O.K. but be real careful. The place is a mess."

He ain't kidding. I walk all around. It's about as big as the whole partment house what I live in. It's got about a hundred rooms. It musta been pretty a coupla hundred years ago but the paints all coming off and there's wall paper curling down from the gigantic high walls. The doors are all real heavy dark wood. There's red and green and yellow glass in lots of the windows and some ceilings got these big pieces of fancy decorated metal squares but some of them are on the floor and udders are gonna fall any second. Somebody could get killed in that house. I was real careful and I didn't get killed or nuthing.

Dear John,

I told Earnest about the old house and what it looks like inside. Earnest said it'd be fun to play hide n seek in. Lots of places to hide.

Dear John,

Victoria's Manshun would be a great place for pirates to hide out. I can see them fighting with sords and they can run up and down the stairs swishing the sords and dooling. Then they can stop fighting and open treashur chests what they got hid under their beds and they can count the loot and smoke cigarettes and drink beer.

Dear John,

The nun told us about when she was young and she loved adventures. At first I figgered we was gonna hear about a real adventure like about pirates or something. But her idea of adventure ain't exactly the same as mine. The nun says she had a thrilling adventure shopping in New York City. She bought shoes, two of them. But then she says that was a long time ago. She gave up all the things of the world for her calling to be a nun.

Dear John,

The nun says we gotta write a short adventure story called, "The Day I Went Shopping in New York City." She says it's gotta be a great adventure like buying a new pair of shoes or a beautiful coat.

Dear John,

I never seen Earnest laffing so hard. He walks home from school laffing all the way and he keeps saying, "Adventure? Shopping? Adventure? New shoes? Adventure!"

Dear John,

I hate writing. I don't know nothing about writing a short adventure story. And I don't know nothing about shopping in New York City. Maybe I can write about buying some stuff at Freedman's candy store what's around the corner. The nun says we gotta write it perfect and she's gonna grade it for spelling and handwriting and grammar, and everything. But most of all we gotta write with stile, like the way the great books are wrote. I'm done for. I always do bad in writing. I hate writing.

Dear John,

I told my mom about how I got to walk in and around Victoria's Manshun and about the red and green and yellow glass. My mom said, "That's stained glass."

I don't tell my mom but the glass ain't stained. It's real pretty. Some of the windows are busted but nobody spilled stuff on the windows. After some parties, we gotta clean the rugs and chairs because somebody always spills wine and that really stains. The glass in Victoria's Manshun ain't stained.

Dear John,

It's been a long time since I wrote you and Victoria's Manshun is all spiffed up and looking swell. It looks like a new house, a really old new house. I seen the guy what let me look around and I aks him if I can see it again. He says I can't go in because I might mess it up. He told me the new owner was gonna move in tomorrow. I seen the green and red and yellow glass is all fixed like new. The guy told me they had a coupla old guys fix the stained glass. I guess red and green and yellow glass is called "stained glass." That's a new one on me.

Dear John,

The moving truck was just pulling away when I got home from school. I don't know what family moved in yet but maybe they gots some kids. Boys, not girls, I hope. We got enuff girls around here. But we sure could use some more boys and then we could have a club, maybe a pirate club. I like pirates and treashures and them are real adventures. I deafenitly don't like no adventure about shopping and buying pretty little shoes.

Dear John,

Me and Earnest are sitting in Randy's Restaurant eating the greatest, greasyest hamboiger with chopped roar onions.

We're sucking up a chocolate malted when all of a sudden Earnest falls right off the seat and flat on his face. First I think he got food poizoning because that happens about once a day to people what eat at Randy's Restaurant. But no. Earnest looks up and stares at the counter and then I seen what's happened. There's a lady standing at the counter and she got long blond hair and she's tall and thin. She's wearing a bright red dress. Just Earnest's type. He's fallen in love again. He always falls off chairs or crashes to the sidewalk when he sees a beautiful girl. I take a look at her. Yeah, O.K. she's real beautiful but she's old like maybe twenty-one. But then she looks right at me and Earnest but mostly she looks right at me and she smiles. She is really beautiful for an old girl. I ain't blind. Then she pays for a pack of Camels and starts to leave but what do you think? She turns right around and throws me a kiss. Earnest thinks she throws him the kiss. He was jist getting to his feet but he's flat on the floor again.

Then Earnest gets up and says, "Let's follow her."

Well, I still got half of my great greasy hamboiger and most of my malted ain't sucked up yet but I wraps the hamboiger in a napkin and drinks a mouthful of the chocolate malted and I follow Earnest out. No tip from Earnest. So I leave two extra pennys. Earnest just pays for his stuff and leaves half a great hamboiger and most of his malted. Earnest gotta really be in love.

Well, we don't gotta follow her far because where do you think she lives? Right across the street in Victoria's Manshun. She lifts her dress up pretty high and she walks up the stoop to the front door. Me and Earnest hide behind some garbage cans and watch her take out the key and unlock the door. She opens the door and fast—she turns around and looks right at the garbage cans and throws another kiss. Well, you shoulda heard the noise from all them garbage cans what with Earnest falling all over them. The garbage cans and Earnest go rolling out into the street. A taxi's coming and screeeeech. I close my eyes. The taxi's sideways in the street with Earnest's head about two inches from the left front tire. The cabby's shouting lots of words what I don't write here. Earnest gets up dizzy but he's still looking at the front door of Victoria's Manshun. The cabby's out on the street, shouting more of them words and shaking his fist. He's gonna knock sense into Earnest. But Earnest sees the cabby coming at him. He runs home. Earnest's gonna get killed someday if he don't stop falling in love.

Dear John,

See, I don't really mean to see nothing sinful. See, it's like this. I look out my bedroom window and I can see Victoria's Manshun right across the street. My bedroom window's in the front next to the kitchen what has the firescape. So last night I'm looking right out across the street at Victoria's Manshun and it really is beautiful now, all painted and the roof fixed and new shudders on the windows. Well, I didn't mean nothing sinful but I was just looking at the window on the second floor of Victoria's Manshun when a bedroom light goes on and I can see that beautiful old girl from Randy's Restaurant in the room. Well, then she unbuttons her shirt and takes it off. She got this short undershirt on. And then she loosens her skirt and it drops off and she got underpants on. Earnest's right. She is really beautiful for an old girl. I ain't blind. Then she pulls down the shade. My heart was beating really hard. I wish she didn't pull down the shade. But I don't mean to see nothing sinful, really I don't.

Dear John,

Last night I'm looking out my window and I seen her again. But this time she was with her husband. He helps take off her shirt and skirt and then he starts taken off his shirt but then she goes over and turns the lights real low. But I don't mean to see nothing sinful. Besides the lights were so low I didn't even get a chance to see nothing.

Dear John,

I wish I lived in olden days when there was pirates and treashures. Me and Earnest was talking about how great it'd be to be on a sailing ship and go after buried treashur like they done on Treashur Island. I been telling him the story because he don't read so good.

But Earnest says, "I don't trust that Long John Silver."

I told Earnest, "He ain't bad. He talks real nice to Hawkins."

But Earnest says, "You gotta watch out for him cause he's real sneaky and I don't trust him none."

I say, "Earnest, maybe you're right but I figger on giving the guy a chance."

Then Earnest says, "Pirates sometimes steals beautiful ladys and keeps them til somebody pays a grandsum to get them back,"

I ask, "Grandsum? What's that?"

Earnest splains, "That's a aweful big amount of money what somebody gotta pay to get somebody back when they get kidnapped."

But then I say, "If somebody around here gets kidnapped, nobody in this neighborhood ain't got no grandsum to pay."

"Grandsum ain't the only ways to get beautiful ladys back." Then Earnest ups and grabs a stick and makes like it's a sword and he dools with his shadow and says, "You evil scoundrel, I will defend my love to the death." Then he stabs the air and says, "Take that you landlumber."

Earnest seen too many Errol Flynn movies.

Dear John,

I'm trying not to look in the window across the street because it's sinful to do that and the priest in the confeshion box sure is gonna be mad at me because it's a sin to look and it's against the Legion of Decency and all. We gotta take the pledge in church every year so we don't go to movies what are indecent and immoral. But that's about movies and it don't say nothing about the Victoria's Manshun across the street. So I ain't doing nothing against the Legion of Decency. But it ain't a sin anyways if I don't go looking on purpose. What I seen so far ain't much and besides what I seen so far was an axcident. So I don't gotta say nothing about it to the priest in the confeshion box.

Dear John,

That family what lives in Vicotoria's Manshun had all their friends over for a big party last night. Lots of cars, real spensive ones like Cadilacs, and Packards and real rich looking men. That pretty lady musta invited lots of people to celebrate because she fixed up Victoria's Manshun. I try not to look in the bedroom windows because I might see something sinful. But just by axcident I seen another real pretty lady in the room across from our kitchen window. It's probably the old pretty lady's sister. She looks real pretty too but not so old. So I just need a drink of milk from the ice box. So I hadda go in the kitchen and then after I turn out the light I just look out the window like maybe there's another spensive car driving up or something but I just see the bedroom window. So it was like an axcident that I seen the younger one and her husband. Well by the time I get to the kitchen she got the prettyest underwear I ever seen, all red and lacy and he got nothing on. Then I can't see nothing because they are under the covers going to sleep with the lights on. Just like me. When I was a little kid, I didn't like to sleep in the dark either. Then the lights go on in her older sister's bedroom. I can't see in it because it's across from my bedroom. I gulp down my milk because I gotta get back to bed. Getting late. But when I get to my bedroom and check the cars, the shade's down. I don't see nothing sinful or nothing much. Just two hugging shadows on the shade.

Dear John,

It's hard staying awake in school because I been watching partys for the last three nights and that's why I ain't got much time to write you.

Dear John,

Something funny's going on in this partment house what I live in. See, I live on the second floor front right above Randy's Restaurant which ain't exaktly your classiest place to eat except you want the greatest greasyest hamboiger with a ton of chopped roar onions. If that's what you want, then Randy's Restaurant sure is the place for you. Then there's the Ricardo's. They're the family what live in the back partment second floor. Mr. Ricardo's a taxi driver and he got some udder business what he does. Upstairs lives the Remsons and the Zizacks. The Remsons got just one kid, Skippy Remson, but he's all growed up and going to Brooklyn College. The Zizacks got no kids and ain't likely to get none because they're about a hundred years old and between them they're two hundred years old. I know about these things. See old people don't get new kids except they're in the Bible. On the top floor nobody lives. They can't rent nothing up there because it's too far up to walk and besides it gets wet in those apartments when it rains. Then on top of that there's the roof and that's a great place because you can see the sky all yellow and red when the sun goes down. The smoke and stuff in the air from New Joisey makes the sky look beautiful. It just don't smell too good but it's a good place to go if you like that sort of thing what some people call Tar Beach. Well, under all that is the front cellar where every partment got a little bin to store stuff like my bicycle, glasses for beer partys, and old broken furnicher what someday will be valuble anteeks. In the back cellar Randy keeps restaurant stuff. It's real greasy back there and all over the cellar but that's O.K. cause that makes the old furnicher anteeks faster.

Well, right in the middle of the night like 3 in the morning I wake up cause I hear noises on the stairs and voices. I sneak out of bed and tiptoe to where I hear the voices and I put my ear up to the door. I hear somebody saying, "Sh, sh, keep quiet." Creek, creek. "This thing sure is heavy." Bam against the wall. "Sh, sh."

Then it's quiet for a few minutes and then all the noise heads downstairs and I don't hear no more. Something funny's going on, John. When I waked up this morning, I figgered maybe somebody got robbed or murdered but nobody never said nothing about that. I wonder what's going on. Don't you?

Dear John,

All day in school I'm thinking about all that noise last night in the hallway. I think something reel suspishus is going on. I don't learn much in school cause I'm thinking about important stuff like adventures, and the noise on the stairs, and the pretty lady. I'm going home and I feel something big in my pocket. So I put my hand in the pocket of my jacket and there's the rest of that greasy hamboiger from about a week ago. But it wasn't so greasy no more. Most of the grease ran out or got hard. But it tasted pretty good for a hamboiger what's cold and old.

Dear John,

I went to sleep real early before anybody showed up for the party. But then I hear some noises in the hall what wakes me up. So I check out Victoria's Manshion but it's too late and cars are driving away and the rooms are all dark. That family really likes partys.

Dear John,

It happens again last night. Almost the same thing. Creak, creak. "Sh, sh, be quiet." Bam—against the wall. The noise starts way up like maybe on the third floor, where nobody lives, and footsteps go all the way down to the cellar. I told Earnest all about it and he's coming over after supper. We're gonna check this out tonight.

Dear John,

Me and Earnest checked out the third floor. No problem getting into the empty partments because they just got old skeleton key locks and Earnest got plenty of skeleton keys and one of them fits. We've been up there in both the front and back partments a lot. The back partment is almost empty except for lots and lots of roaches and a coupla rats what we surprised but they run away before Earnest can catch them. Then we go to the front partment. We listen first. Nobody. So we unlocks and opens the door real slow but the front partment ain't empty no more. It gots an old table and 2 chairs and lots of matches and used cigarettes stamped out on the floor. Nothing valuable except one half pack of Lucky Strikes. I don't never smoked before but Earnest says he knows how. Earnest says Camels are better than Lucky Strikes. Then Earnest lights one of the Lucky Strikes and puffs on it. Then he starts coffing. He shakes his head and says, "I never coff with Camels. They're better." Earnest knows a lot about lots of stuff. But then we figger we gotta get outa there in case they come back. Besides if anybody's around, they'll hear Earnest choking to death.

Dear John,

Something funny's going on, John. It's suspishus. I think it's bad. Maybe sumbody's doing sumthing sinful.

Dear John,

I aks Earnest if he thinks it's a sin to look in windows of Victoria's Manshun. Earnest says that depends on why you are looking. He aks me if I looked on purpose to see something sinful or was there some udder reason. I told him I don't wanna see nothing sinful. I look at the pretty cars what come and go all night long. Earnest says then it ain't no sin. He says it's no sin if you see something sinful on axident.

Dear John,

The noise in the hallway was going on again last night but this time I wanna see what all the noise is about. So open the hall door just a little crack. I seen these two guys wearing suits but with their jacket collars up and their ties loosened and their shirts open at the top. They're both smoking cigarettes what dangles out of the sides of their mouths. Lucky Strikes I bet. They're grunting and cussing because they're pulling and pushing and lifting a big heavy machine. It's a thing what looks like something what I seen in the movies. I think it's a movie camera. They don't see me and they just go down the stairs. I open the door and creeps out onto the stair landing and peak between the banister railings and I seen them go all the way down into the cellar. Then the noise stops and they come up to the first floor and go out the back door.

Dear John,

Earnest came over to my partment last night because he wanted to investigate all the pretty cars what come and go all night. My mom and dad are watching Kate Smith singing about a moon coming over a mountain. It takes about an hour so they don't know we're investigating all the pretty cars. I turn out the lights and we kneel on the floor and peek out the window with the shade up jist a little. A big Packard drives up and four men get out and jern the party. In a coupla minutes the lights go on in four bedrooms and each of these guys are in each room with one of the sisters. I wisper to Earnest I never seen these guys before. Earnest figgered maybe they was the girl's brothers visiting. Three shades go down but one stays up right across from my bedroom. Let me tell you sumthing. They don't act like no brother and sister what with the kissing and all. Earnest figgers this is really suspishus. But then I hear my mom coming and we get up and pull the shade all the way down and put on the light. Me and Earnest are playing cards when my mom opens the bedroom door and tells Earnest it's time for him to go home. Earnest looks real sad because he figgers there's more pretty cars to look at and something real suspishus going on. The moon came up over the mountain a lot faster than we figgered.

Dear John,

The bad guys was up there in the partment on the top floor tonight and I creep up the stairs real quiet and all and then I peek in through the key hole. I seen the two bad guys looking out the window at Victoria's Manshun. The two bad guys are looking with binoculas and one taps the other and he gets behind the camera and it starts and I get out of there fast. I gotta tell Earnest about this new stuff. This is reel suspishus! I think the bad guys are sinful. They ain't making no movies of the beautiful cars.

Dear John,

First thing this morning I tell Earnest all about what I seen last night. I tell him I think the bad guys are doing sinful stuff what with making a movie of the lady's taking their clothes off and all. But Earnest figgers it's even badder than that. The husbands gotta be real rich what with them Packards and Cadillacs. These bad guys are gonna steal the pretty ladies and grandsum them.

But I don't think that. I think the guys upstairs are real sinful and they like to look at pretty ladys naked and all and that's a sin espeshally when it ain't a axident. It's a mortal

sin when you do it on purpose. Well one way or the udder
we know it's a bad thing what these guys are doing and we
figger on helping out the pretty ladys. Only thing is we don't
know how we're gonna help them yet.

Dear John,

Earnest says we gotta make a conspiracy. He says it's a
word what means to be against pirates and that's why it got
piracy in it and cons means against. We gotta be against these
bad guys what are doing bad things like what pirates do.

For a guy who don't read and write all that good, Earnest
shore knows a lot about big woids.

Dear John,

Earnest says he's been thinking about if it's sinful for
us to see sinful stuff in the windows. He figgers it ain't
no mortal sin because we're investigating all the suspishus
stuff what's going on. We really only wanna figger out if the
pretty ladies are gonna be kidnapped and grandsummed.
If we see the sisters and their husbands naked and all, it's a
axcident. It probably ain't even a venial sin because we ain't
looking at that on purpose.

Sometimes we look and it ain't no axcident but that's
O.K. We're jist looking because it's suspishus. It ain't no sin
to try to figger out how to help them pretty ladies.

Dear John,

I been worried about this important stuff so much that I
forgot all about the adventure story I gotta write for school.
I gotta have it done by this Friday. Earnest says he'd write
the adventure story for me for a dollar. I said thanks but I'll
shop around a bit. Earnest got good idears but he don't spel

good and nobody, not even him, can read what he writes. I'd pay Christine Carney fifty cents. But I already found out that ain't a good idear. Sometimes my sister, Maggie, does my homework for me but only if I scratch her back. But then she writes real slow and my hand and arm get real tired. But the worse thing is that her writing is too good and the nun's gonna know it ain't me what wrote it.

Dear John,

Earnest aks me to write down a story for him if he tells me what to write. Earnest don't write all that good. He aks me because I spel reel good and gots good grammar. I was gonna tell him about Maggie scratching my back but I decided aganst that. I don't want Earnest scratching nothing on me. I ain't gonna write no story for Earnest.

Dear John,

I wrote my story myself. It took me about a hundred hours to write just 200 words. The nun said the story gotta be 200 words and 200 words exactly is what she gets. I figger the story wouldn't take so long except I kept counting the words all the time. I hate writing adventure stories about shopping in New York. But if I hadda write a story anyways, I used imajination and wrote about something the nun and God are gonna like. So I stretched things a little and wrote about the day I went shopping and bought a prayer book because it's the most important thing in the world for me to say my prayers right. It's mostly the truth except I never went shopping in New York City and I never bought a prayer book.

Dear John,

The nun gives me back the story what I wrote. In the beginning she got red marks all over the place because I'm jist writing about the subway to New York but then when I say I'm gonna buy a prayer book, all the red marks stop. I got A+.

Dear John,

The nun says the story what I wrote was real truthful and full of sinseerity and she's gonna write it over for me and make it right and then I can copy it in my own writing. But that's O.K. It ain't cheating for her to write it over for me cause it's called editing.

Dear John,

The nun's writing my story so it don't got no mistakes.

Dear John,

I told Earnest about the nun writing my story for me and Earnest says she got sumthing up her sleeve. He aks me if I know her angle. But nuns don't got no angles. They just got straight and narrow yard sticks.

Dear John,

The nun told us the Brooklyn Diocese is having a writing contest and each class gotta be in the contest. Each class gotta have two kids in the contest and they each gotta send in two stories. Then the nun says I write sinceer and truthful stories so I gotta be in the contest. Now I gotta write another story for the Brooklyn Diocese contest. She tells me to write about somebody saving the soul of a pagan. She says I gotta write it with sinceerity.

Dear John,

I ain't got much time to write another story. Besides I hate writing. Too much important stuff to do. I shoulda wrote that first adventure story about buying binoculas. That's what me and Earnest need for investigating.

Dear John,

The St. Vincent de Paul thrift store on Metropolitan Avenue got binoculas for two dollars and fifty cents. I gotta tell Earnest.

Dear John,

Earnest got the binoculars at the St. Vincent de Paul thrift store. See we hadda collect money in are mission mite boxes for the pagan baby girls in China. Well, Earnest walks around the whole of Williamsburg and collects five dollars for the pagan girls in China and he told people about the Chinese pagan baby girls what get dumped in the garbage because they don't want no more girls in China. Lots of people give money for that story. Earnest says he even got some people crying over it. Well, Earnest figgers it's a real good thing to help pagan girls so far away and all but we got girls right here in Brooklyn what need help. So he splits the take and gives two fifty to the Chinese pagan girls and the other two fifty goes to help the American girls in Victoria's Manshun. Earnest thinks that's fair and he says it was the right thing to do.

Dear John,

Now there's a whole big family of pretty girls living in Victoria's Manshun. That pretty lady got lots of sisters. Maybe some of them are cousins.

Dear John,

Me and Earnest tested out the binoculars up on the roof.
I can see the Umpire State Building real good and the top
of the Brooklyn Bridge. And when the sun goes down, it's
jist the most beautiful thing I ever seen what with the pink
and yellow clouds coming from New Joisey. But when it got
dark, the binoculars went right for a bedroom window just
by axcident. Well it was a different lady but real pretty in a
bedroom up at the top of the house. I never seen no one in
that room before. So me and Earnest said it's O.K. to look
because it's suspishus. But she's all alone and just sits down
and puts on lipstick. She puts her head down across her arms
on a table. She just sits that way for a long time. Then real
slow she gets up and turns out the lights. In about a minute
we see her downstairs at the party.

Dear John,

The pretty girls don't look like sisters or cousins. Me and
Earnest figger they are all real good friends. Maybe they all
went to the same high school.

Dear John,

Me and Earnest seen why that pretty lady's sad. We
was up on the roof and we seen her and her husband and
we seen he gives her the allowance money for the week and
then she takes his tie off and unbuttons his shirt. The he
unbuttons her shirt and puts it on the bed. Then she takes
down his pants and then he takes down her dress and she
got red underwear too. Then she starts to open his belt and
he stops her and she smiles and takes off her top underwear.
But we don't see nothing sinful much because all we see
mostly is her back. Then real slow she takes down her red

115

underpants. Me and Earnest fight to investigate with the binoculars because that's really suspishus. Then the husband looks at his watch. Like he's late for a pointment and he fast puts on his clothes. But then he bends over and picks up her red underpants. Then he grabs her red underpants and rushes out into the hallway and slams the door. She just stands there looking at the door like she don't know what's going on. That's why she's sad. Her husband steals stuff from her like her underpants and he ain't given her no attenshun. He's a real mean guy.

Dear John,

Earnest says he's been thinking about that husband who steals under pants and ain't paying attenshun to his wife. Earnest says some men got so many worries about business and other stuff that they don't take good care of their wives. Earnest figgers when he grows up, he's gonna be real good to his wife all the time and he ain't never gonna steal her underpants. We can learn about important stuff by looking at what's going on in Victoria's Manshun. Earnest says it ain't no sin to learn important stuff, espeshally when it's suspishus too!

Dear John,

Remember the first pretty lady me and Earnest seen in Randy's Restaurant? I seen her coming out of the A & P store today. She got a big bag and it slips out of her hands and falls on the sidewalk. Lucky Strikes and Camels all over the place. So I run over and help pick them up. She smiles and says, "Thank you very much." She really likes me a lot.

Dear John,

Earnest's right about Long John Silver. Hawkins is hiding and hears Long John Silver talking about being a bad pirate and he wants to kidnap the whole sailing ship and do a lot of bad stuff. Earnest is gonna be real happy that he got Long John Silver figgered out from the start. Earnest ain't too good at figgering out words and school stuff but he's pretty good at figgering out lots of udder stuff. What's more important?

Dear John,

I can't get nobody to write that story for me about saving pagans. I figger I gotta do it myself. The nun says I gotta have it done by this Friday so she got time to edit and then I gotta copy what she wrote next week so she can send it to the Brooklyn Dioceses writing contest. She told me that it's gonna have sinceerity if it starts with a guy praying in church and God taps him on the shoulder and wispers that he has to go save pagans.

Dear John,

I wrote the story and gave it to the nun. It's about this guy named Parkins praying in church and he's real sad cause he don't have a good life and he's been real sinful and feeling guilty and all. So God taps him on the shoulder and appears as a vishon floating right in front of him and God talks to him like in a real low voice so nobody else can hear and God tells him to go to a pagan place and save a pagan or two.

Well this story is about what happens a long time ago. So the guy gotta get a sailing ship and a crew but he don't got no money. So he tells them that there's a treashure buried in this pagan place what's an island in the middle of some big ocean. He even shows them a treashure map.

Parkins even burns the edges and crinkles it to make it look old and genuwine. It shows where jewels and dimonds and gold are berried in this pagan place. He tells them about the treashur because he knows darn well they ain't gonna go on a dangerous adventure just to save a pagan or two. Parkins can't exactly tell them about God talking to him and all cause they're gonna think he's funny in the head and that it's a hallucination and not a reel vision.

So they get going and sailing for about a month and this bad guy named Short Harry Gold starts trouble and is gonna kidnap the whole ship because he wants to grandsum the treashur all for himself. Then the ship comes to the pagan island and Short Harry Gold sneaks into Parkin's cabin and steals the map. Parkins ain't worried at first but then Short Harry Gold shows the crew the map what they all think is real. Then Short Harry Gold takes over the ship. But first there's lots of duling with sords and knives and stuff.

Then they land on the pagan island. The place is loaded with pagans. But then Parkins and Short Harry Gold both see a pagan girl what is beautiful. Right away they fall in love with this beautiful pagan girl. She don't wear no undershirt like I seen in National Geography but I don't say nuthing about that in the story what I'm writing for the nun. The pagan lady's name is Dfgtre. I made that up so it sounds like a pagan girl's name what ain't English. Parkins learns to say her name. Short Harry Gold don't. He jist calls her Pagan Sweety. Dfgtre likes Parkins and she don't like Short Harry Gold.

Then Short Harry Gold and the bad guys can't find the treashur and they get Parkins and tie him up to a tree and they stab him ten times and leave him bleeding and all.

to be continued

Dear John,

I ain't finished the story for you because I ran outa time and there was another party in Victoria's Manshun what I gotta investigate. It was very suspishus. There was a big white Rolls Royce with a driver in a black suit. It was parked for a long time in front of Randy's Restaurant. The driver went in and got one of Randy's great greazy hamboigers and a malted. He sat in the car and ate. I watched him because he was suspishus. I didn't look in any of the bedrooms and that was a good thing not to do. Besides all the shades was pulled down.

Dear John,

I'm gonna tell you the rest of the story what I wrote about saving pagans.

The bad pirate guys look at the map and they walk two step this way and ten steps that way and they keep digging for the treashur and don't find nothing. Some bad guys get mad at Short Harry Gold. Some others are still for him. So they all fight and they all get dead. Blood all over the place. Only Short Harry Gold don't get dead. He goes and gets Pagan Sweety. Only she don't wanna have nothing to do with him. So he takes her and ties Pagan Sweety to a tree right across from Parkins. She's naked like most pagan girls but I don't say nothing about that in my story. Parkins looks at Dfgtre cause he ain't dead yet. Then Parkins prays. He says Hale Mary's and Glory Bees and lots and lot of ejaculations like, "God help me" and "Familys what pray together stay together." But he don't look at Dfgtre cause praying and looking at pretty ladys don't mix good, speshally when they're naked and all but I don't write nothing about that. Then Parkins is just about dead but he

119

don't give up. He can't say long prayers no more. So he just keeps ejaculating.

Then his head goes down and he's dead. Dfgtre screams and says, "Dtimrst tpanneoiu!" Then BOOM! Lightining hits the tree what cracks in half and breaks the rope and Parkins falls to the ground. Dfgtre screams again, "Dtimrst tpanneoiu." Boom another lightning and her tree cracks in half. Dfgtre runs over to Parkins and falls on him and kisses him right on the lips and he ain't dead no more. Them ejaculations done the trick.

So Parkins goes after Short Harry Gold and they duel up and down the hills and in and out of Manshuns, jumping up and down stairs for hours and hours. Then Short Harry Gold jumps right at Parkins and Parkins cuts right through Short Harry Gold's heart. Blood all over the place.

Then Parkins and Dfgtre hug. Then Parkins smokes a Camel and puts his shirt on Dfgtre. The shirt got blood on it but they don't care cause they're in love. Then they look where her tree got cracked in half and the roots made a big hole and down in the deep hole there's a treashure.

Then they get in the sailing ship with some of the good crew what ain't dead cause they staid on the boat. They sail home and Dfgtre ain't a pagan no more. She gets converted and baptized in a big church with holy water over her head. Her name gets changed to Mary and that's a real good Catholic name. They live happy.

The moral of the story is that Short Harry Gold got greedy and he got nothing but dead. Parkins saved a pagan girl and got lots of treashur and every night they have a big party. Great Story!

Dear John,

I told Earnest the story and he agrees, "Great Story!" Earnest and me think alike.

Dear John,

After school me and Earnest go down to the cellar to investigate. You should see all the roaches in Randy's part of the cellar. Roaches love grease. Then we seen one of the bins what use to be empty but now it got something big in it. It's all covered up and there's this big lock on the door. Earnest tries them all but he ain't got no skeleton key what fits that lock. So we find this long pipe and push it between the bars of the bin and lift the cover. It's the camera all right and there's other machines what look like radio stuff and microphones. Somebody's coming so we gotta go out the back door. Roaches running everywhere. Some don't run fast enough. Crunch, crunch.

Dear John,

The nun don't like my story. She says it ain't a good adventure and it don't got enuff sinseerity and it ain't worth her spending her time editing. But its O.K. because now I don't gotta copy over the two stories. I don't got no time for this stuff anyways. I got really important stuff to do. Sumthing bad's going on and me and Earnest gotta save them ladies.

Dear John,

Last night me and Earnest are investigating that front partment on the top floor again. Earnest is smoking a Lucky Strike what he found in the room.

I says, "Sh, sh, listen." Then I gotta put my hand over Earnest's mouth to stop him from coffing.

Creek, creek, footsteps up the stairs, key in the lock, doorknob turning. Quick cigarette out the window, run for the closet, get down, hide.

Voices whispering, "You smell that?"

"Yeh, maybe we ain't alone. We better check the other rooms."

We peak through a crack, nobody in the room, run for the door, sh, sh, run, run, out in the hall, somebody coming up, turn around, run upstairs, push the door, on the roof, run, run, over the side, down the firescape, climb down, rattle, rattle, open the window, climb into my kitchen, close the window, into my bedroom, under the bed, out of breath, sh, sh. Noise on the firescape, noise out in the hall, then all's quiet. Except for Earnest. He's under my bed trying not to coff. When it's all clear and all those shades are down, Earnest goes home.

Dear John,

I been thinking about it all day but Earnest aks, "You see that guy upstairs? You ever seen him before?"

"I think so," I says. Then we look at each other and shake our heads. The guy chasing us last night is the husband who steals underpants and don't pay good attenshun to his wife. But Earnest thinks maybe he's not her husband but a bad guy who makes her do bad and sinful stuff and all. Now me and Earnest know we gotta save them ladys.

Dear John,

It's bad. Real bad. Them poor ladys. This is what happened.

Me and Earnest was investigating with our binoculas from my bedroom last night and we seen that same guy. He's the guy what steals the sad lady's underpants. He was in another lady's room. Well that done it. He's a bad guy and he probably ain't nobody's husband. It's very suspishus! We gotta do something before the ladys all get kidnapped. So I say odds or evens, one takes it. Earnest says evens. Once twice, three, shoot. Both me and Earnest puts out two fingers. Earnest wins. He goes down stairs and I seen him cross the street and walk right up to Victoria's Manshun. He pushes the bell and the door opens. It's the pretty one with the Camels. Earnest goes in. Then I wait. Nothing. Then all the lights is going out in the house. In the top floor bedroom I seen a shade go up fast and then down. All of a sudden the husbands are all coming out of the house and getting into their Cadillacs and Packards. Then all the wives are coming out with suitcases. They all get into two cars and drive away real fast. Then sirens far away. Getting closer. Getting louder. Then police cars coming fast from all sides. They stop in front of the house. Cops all over the place. Crash. Break down the door. Lights on all over the house. Cops in all the rooms, turning beds over, knocking furnichure over, breaking down doors. Then they come out and look all around the street and the backyards. Then what do you think? The two bad guys are right down there with the cops. They're really sneaky making like they're helping and all. Then these two guys get in a car and drive away and some cops drive away. Some keep looking around. Then they all drive away. Then it's all quiet.

I forgot. Where's Earnest? So I go downstairs, cross the street, through the broke down door, into the house. What a mess. Everything's broke, smashed, thrown all over. I call real loud, "EARNEST WHERE ARE YOU AT?" Nothing. I walk through the back kitchen, crack, crack, walking over smashed plates and glasses, into the back yard. Then I hear something. Then crash. Garbage cans rolling all over the back yard and a bag of cement falls on the ground and I hear Earnest yelling like far away but it's coming from the garbage can. I open the top and there's Earnest stuck inside the garbage can.

He says, "Help me outta here."

I help him out and he tells me that all he done was tell the pretty lady about the guys with the camera and then one of the husbands takes him out the back and shoves him tight into the garbage can and tells him to keep his mouth shut, a thing what he does till he hears me calling him. Then I tell Earnest about the husbands and pretty ladies driving away and the cops coming and smashing everything up and all.

Dear John,

This is what happened. Earnest and me figgered it all out. See those bad guys was gonna kidnap and grandsum the pretty ladys but when Earnest tells the ladys, they call the cops and take off. When the cops get there, they go looking for the bad guys but they don't find them hiding no where because they was right in front of the cops' eyes and making like they was looking for the bad guys but they was the bad guys looking for themselves. Pretty sneaky!

I told Earnest we should tell the cops about the bad guys but Earnest says, "No, there's no sense in getting any deeper into this. We don't care none about the bad guys. The main thing is that we helped the pretty ladies and we done enuff good."

Dear John,

When I got home from school, I checked upstairs and the camera and radio and stuff are all gone. Just some camels squished on the floor.

Dear John,

It's real boring around here now. No more pretty ladies. Victoria's Manshun's getting real run down because everybody just goes in, takes things and messes it up more. Kids play hide and seek and stuff and they break things. All the stained glass is all smashed. Some bums and drunks stay in there at night and it smells real bad now.

Dear John,

Me and Earnest went into Victoria's Manshun today. We walked around real quiet like we was in a church or liberry. In the pretty lady's bedroom we look up way in the top of her closet way in the back and there's two cartons of Camels. I take one carton and Earnest takes the udder and we're gonna keep them forever in a real safe place. Just keep them and think about all the good we done for the pretty lady and her friends.

Dear John,

I finished reading Treashur Island. Earnest aks what happens at the end. I don't tell him. I just give him the book and says, "Find out for yourself." Maybe sometimes it ain't such a good idear to help.

Dear John,

I seen Earnest going into Victoria's Manshun. I followed him and stepped over the broken down front door and looked around inside and then I went up the stairs. I found Earnest sitting in the pretty lady's bedroom on the floor. I sat down next to Earnest. Earnest took a pack of Camels out of his pocket and tore open one end. He tapped the pack on his left hand. I took one and put it in my mouth. Earnest lit a match and then he brings the match up and lights my Camel and then with the same match he lights his Camel. Then we jist sit there and smoke and think.

Chapter 5
Watching Radio

Fifth Grade

Dear John,

Bombs explode. Ocean waves spill over the side. That Japanese battle ship's heading right for the P.T. boat. It's gonna ram!

Don Windlow shouts "Fire when ready!" But they wasn't ready.

"Captain, Captain, we ain't gonna make it. The engine's dead and they're gonna ram us."

"Well, boys, we gave them a good fight but this looks like the end. So jump boys and remember God is with you. But swim real good anyways."

One after the other, sailors plunge into the choppy sea. Don Windlow of the Navy stays with his P.T. boat and looks up at the bow of that Japanese battle ship. Closer, closer. Don Windlow looks up like into like the jawrs of a giant whale. BOOM! Don Windlow gets blown to pieces . . . to be continued.

I love these Saturday afternoon cereals at the movies. And you gotta come back because you gotta find out what's gonna happen next. Poor Don Windlow of the Navy got blowed up, definitely got blowed to pieces. I seen him sailing through the air jist before the—to be continued. What are they gonna do with Don Windlow of the Navy all blowed to pieces? Ding it, dang it! I can hardly wait for next Saturday.

Dear John,

I like the kind of story what ends with—to be continued. Sometimes I write stuff like that. They're called cereals.

Dear John,

We got a new victrola what gots a radio in it. A Philco. It's really big and sounds swell. Last night Inner Sanctum was on, really spooky and scary. First an organ makes a deep and then a screeching sound and then a doorknob turns and then the door creaks and squeaks open. I close my eyes and I can see that big heavy dark door opening and I don't wanna see what's on the other side. That squeaking door drives me nutty, so scary.

Dear John,

Fibber McGee and Molly live on 79 Wistful Vista. Every week Fibber McGee forgets about the hall closet. He's always looking for something and thinks it's in the hall closet. Molly McGee says, "No, Fibber don't open that closet" but Fibber McGee goes and opens it. He does not listen but I do! Crash, crash, tinkle, plop, tinkle, ping! It sounds great. I can jist see all the stuff falling out of that hall closet and there's Fibber McGee buried and crawling out from under all the mess. Every week that happens. Fibber McGee don't ever remember but that makes it lots of fun. I really like listening to all the stuff falling.

Dear John,

I don't think I ever told you about my Uncle Bob. I'm named after him. He works for the Brooklyn Union Gas Company and he's real good at fixing everything. But yesterday he had an axcident. He's in the hospital because he was stopping a gas leak in somebody's cellar and the place blows up. The explosion was so big Uncle Bob went flying across the cellar and right up the cellar stairs and landed in the backyard. The doctor told my mom it was real good the cellar door was open. My mom says it was a miracle that he lived and that God was watching over him and all.

Dear John,

Tonight I get to listen to Baby Snooks on the Philco. It hurts my rear end when Baby Snooks gets a spanking and she gets one every single week.

Dear John,

I got a problem. Baby Snooks is on the same time as Mr. and Mrs. North. I like Baby Snooks and my mom and dad like Mr. and Mrs. North. We got two radios only the old one don't work no more. I hope my mom don't wanna listen to Mr. and Mrs. North. The old radio what I use to listen to Baby Snooks on burned out a tube or something. Put it on and it goes ZZZZZZZZZZZZZZ real loud.

Dear John,

I told Earnest about Uncle Bob and about the miracle what saved him because God was watching over him.

But Earnest asks me if God was watching over Uncle Bob, how come God let the place even get blowed up?

I told Earnest maybe God was busy with lots of other people to save but then when He hears the explosion he looks down and saves Uncle Bob.

Dear John,

My mom and dad listened to Mr. and Mrs. North on the Philco. I went to my room and put on the ZZZZZ radio. You can hear the talking and stuff jist a little and you can hear Baby Snooks pretty good when she gets that spankin but the ZZZZZ gives me a headache. I aks my mom, "Can we get that ZZZZZ noise in my radio fixed?" She says, "I'm afraid we can't budge it for this month." That means we don't got enuff money. We gotta wait.

Dear John,

I ask my mom how come if Uncle Bob got saved by a miracle, how come God let the cellar blow up?

My mom says we can't know God's will and He had a good reason and that it was part of his plan because what's not part of God's plan either don't happen or the devil done it.

Dear John,

I get to listen to Captain Midnight on the Philco. Some radio programs are on during the day like The Romance of Helen Trent and Ma Perkins. Cereals are more fun than regular stories like Mr. and Mrs. North. Everytime in a cereal the people get themselves into a real tuff jam and then when things are jist about as bad as anything can be—to be continued. Then you gotta figger out how they're gonna get outa the jam they're always getting in. But you gotta wait to find out, sometimes a whole week. They always figger a way out. Then you listen to see if you figgered it out right. Sometimes I get it figgered out real good but sometimes I don't. One time I seen a real old cereal in a movie and this pretty farmer's daughter was tied to a railroad track because the guy named Villain wants her to marry him but she don't go for his type. So the train's coming and he sits next to the track and says, "Mary me."

"No."

Choo, choo.

"Marry me."

"No, never."

Choo, Choo.

"MARRY ME."

"NEVER! NEVER!"

CHOO, CHOO, WOOO, WOOO.

She Screams. "AAHHH. Ahhh."

CHOO CHOO, WOO, WOOooo.

"to be continued."

You don't see the blood and stuff but you know the train got her because there jist ain't no way out.

But then the next time the cereal starts jist before it left off and Villain's sayin, "Marry Me." She's yelling, "NEVER! Never!"

Choo, CHOO. And the train switches to another track and goes right by without even a little woo woo. It never touches her. Cereals get pretty tricky, John.

Dear John,

I wish we had good stories in our school reader instead of the dumb ones. Maybe when I grow up, I'm gonna write real good cereals for kids like me and then they'll wanna learn to read.

Dear John,

My Uncle Bob got out of the hospital today. He got bandages all over him because he got burned on his face and hands from being blown out of the cellar and all. He looks like a mummy what they got in the Museum of Natural History.

My mom told Uncle Bob God was watching over him and it was a miracle that he was not killed or seriusly hurt.

Uncle Bob says it was good that God was watching over him but he wishes that God was paying a little more attention before the place blowed up.

Dear John,

Uncle Bob and Earnest think the same way.

Dear John,

A really long long time ago, maybe about two years ago, I was at the movies and it was a cereal about this cowboy what's named Gene Autry and the Radio Ranch and he gets shot right off his horse. Then—to be continued. But I figgered he's gonna be up and runnin in the next cereal. But no. He's shot real bad and gets taken to the secret cave what's in the mountain. The bad evil queen got him. Them cereals are real tricky sometimes. You jist can't always figger them out.

Dear John,

When bad things happen, it ain't because God wants them to happen. It's because of bad people what are doing the devil's deeds. My mom told me that when I ask her about God letting bad things happen. My mom says that good people always do God's will and they don't stray from the right road. And even when something happens that seems bad for good people, it always works out for the best.

Dear John,

I love garbage pickin. I'm walkin down the street checking out the garbage and I seen across the street there's a real interesting pile. Lots of great stuff! Somebody musta moved outa the apartment house and left some pretty good stuff, mostly broken but that don't mean it ain't real good anyways. So I see this machine way down at the bottom of the pile. Well I tugs it out and it looks something like a radio only it got two spools and wire running arown from one to the other and it got a microphone but no wire to plug it in. I don't know what it is but I'm definitly glad I got it. I always find fastenating great stuff in the garbage.

Dear John,

My uncle Bob seen my machine and says it's a wire recorder. I told him I don't need to record no wire. But he says it uses wire to record somebody's voice and you can sing into it and talk and all. He fixes stuff like that too. Maybe he got a lectric cord for to plug it in. But it's kinda hard for him to fix stuff now because his hands and face still got bandages.

Dear John,

Don Windlow of the Navy don't got blowed up. I kinda figgered he don't, even if I did see his dead body blowed to pieces and flying up into the air. At the beginning of the cereal this Saturday it don't show nothing about Don Windlow's dead body pieces flying through the air. That was jist a trick. Remember I told you about the BOOM at the end of the cereal just before _to be continued? Well they made me think it was Don Windlow's boat what got blowed up. It wasn't. The Japanese boat got blowed up instead. Remember the torpedoe launncher wasn't ready on the P.T. Boat? But then in this one, after all the sailors jump over the side, Don Windlow of the Navy pulls something on the cannon one last try and it works. Lucky for Don Windlow, unlucky for the Japanese. It was a Japanese guy what got blowed to pieces. This time the cereal ends when a suicide plane's coming for them. It's a Kamakazee plane. It looks really really bad for Don Windlow of the Navy . . . to be continued.

Dear John,

Another lucky day at garbage picking. I got a broke lamp, a broke chair, a broke table and a victrola that ain't broke. Well the victrola ain't exactly broke but it ain't exactly working right either. I put on this record of Doris Day singing Senta Mental Joiney but she sounds a lot like Humphrey Bogart. The record turns round too slow. Other than that the victrola works jist great.

Dear John,

I told Peter Ackerman about the great stuff what I find in the garbage all the time. I told him it's better than going to a store and buying stuff. I get to make lots of fun stuff outa garbage. But Peter Ackerman rolls his eyes and says, "It's all junk. It's below me to pick junk from garbage."

O.K. Peter Ackerman but you don't know all the fun you're missing.

Dear John,

I told Earnest about all the great stuff what I find in the garbage and he thinks it's jist great. He says he gets things outa the garbage sometimes but he don't never go looking. Earnest says, "I don't look for it. Garbage looks for me. It jist sort of jumps right out at me." Earnest says he's gonna go looking from now on.

I shoulda kept my mouth shut. Now Earnest is gonna be big competitshun for all the best stuff in the garbage.

Dear John,

No problem with Earnest being competitshun. We look for different stuff. Earnest don't look for broken lamps and chairs and tables and radios and stuff. He looks for strange stuff. Like today he's walking down the street and smiling and swinging a big paper bag.

"What's you so happy about, Earnest?"

"I found something great in the garbage. Wanna see it?"

"Definitly."

He opens a bag and I look in. It's real smelly and hairy inside. I ask, "What's that?"

Earnest looks at me and says, "A perfectly good dead cat."

Dear John,

Me and Earnest went to the movies and now Earnest likes Don Windlow of the Navy too. Earnest says me and him got lots in common. We both like some of the same things and we both don't like some of the same things. Now we both like Don Windlow of the Navy and picking garbage and we both don't like school.

Dear Jphn.

Don Windlow of the Navy got real lucky again. The kamakazee plane missed blowing up an aircraft carrier because Don Windlow of the Navy shot a hole in the bottom of his plane. Earnest said, "The Kamakazee pilot got it in the end."

Dear John,

The Japanese Kamakazee pilot musta felt real bad because his plane crashed into the ocean and he don't blow nothing up. He died for nothing. Kamakazee pilots try to kill themselves because they think that's what God wants and they'll go to heaven right away. I wonder if maybe God gets confused in wars, which side to help and all.

Dear John,

My Uncle Bob got all the bandages off and he looks good, but kinda sunburned and blistery and all. He gives me a cord for to plug in the wire recorder and it works great. You can talk into the microphone and the wire goes round and round the spools and then you rewind and play it back and you can hear yourself saying what you jist said. It even plays back at two different speeds. One speed makes me sound like Humphrey Bogart.

Well I figgered that if I record Doris Day sounding like Humphrey Bogart at a slow speed and then play her back at a fast speed, she's gonna sound like Doris Day, not Humphrey Bogart. I done it and it works kinda. It don't exactly sound like Doris Day but more like a sick Doris Day with a real bad cold and real tired from her senta mental joiney.

Dear John,

Mr. and Mrs. North won last night. I gotta do something about this or I'm never gonna hear Baby Snooks again. Now my little radio don't work at all except if you like nothing but ZZZZZZZZZZZZZZZZ.

Dear John,

I ask, "Mom can we get that old radio fixed because I wanna listen to Baby Snooks when you wanna listen to Mr. and Mrs. North?"

She says, "We can't budge it this month."

"Can we like maybe take turns? You got to listen to Mr. and Mrs. North for the last two weeks. Can it be my turn to listen to Baby Snooks?"

Mom says, "I'll talk to your father about it."

Dear John,

Uncle Bob is all O.K. now and he went back to work at the Brooklyn Union Gas Company. My mom told him he should sue them for his getting hurt and all. But Uncle Bob says that ain't a good idea because he needs to keep working there and they don't like people what sue them.

Dear John,

I ask my mom why she told Uncle Bob to sue the Brooklyn Union Gas Company. Maybe it was jist part of God's plan that the cellar got blowed up. God don't let nothing bad happen without it being part of His plan, except for the devil's stuff. My mom says maybe it was part of His plan but maybe it was also part of God's plan that Uncle Bob sue the Brooklyn Union Gas Company.

Dear John,

I showed the wire recorder and victrola to Earnest. He thinks its swell but aks, "What good is it?"

I told him, "Better than a dead cat."

Then Earnest tells me that a dead cat is a real good thing and then he starts telling me all the stuff what he expeermented with the dead cat and I almost throwed up.

Dear John,

My dad said, "Nothing doing. Baby Snooks is a little brat and she's not a good example for kids."

Dear John,

Earnest promised me he won't tell me no more about his dead cat. But he says he's gonna be a doctor when he grows up. He likes cutting and he don't mind blood and guts and smelly stuff.

"STOP!" I almost throwed up again.

Dear John,

Every year the priest says it's time for us to take the Legion of Decency pledge. That means we don't go to see no bad movies what are on the bad list. My dad thinks Baby Snooks is on that list.

Dear John,

Roy Rogers kissed his horse in the movie me and Earnest seen today. Me and Earnest almost fell outa our seats from laffing and people sitting all around us gave us dirty looks and one guy said, "Shhh." Anudder guy said, "Shut up!" They got mad at us but we don't care. We couldn't stop laffing. I can't believe they showed Roy Rogers kissing a horse right in the movies.

Earnest said, "It's against the Legion of Decency."

Dear John,

Earnest ain't real practical. You gotta be real smart in school to gets to be a doctor. I tell him, "Earnest maybe you better think about being a butcher."

Dear John,

I got more practical idears than Earnest. When I grow up, I'm gonna be a cowboy like Roy Rogers. Only problem is I don't sing good. You gotta sing good to be a real cowboy.

But Earnest asks, "How come Gabby Hays is a cowboy? He don't sing."

But then Earnest thinks and he answers his own question, "Maybe that's because he got a beard. That's it. Cowboys what got beards don't gotta sing. It's probly in their cowboy contracts. You either gotta sing or grow a beard."

Earnest knows a lot but what he don't know he jist figgers out.

Dear John,

School starts tomorrow. I'm gonna be in 5B grade and even Earnest got promoted from 5A. The nun said he got promoted for social reasons.

Dear John,

In singing class we hadda sing by ourselves for Miss O'Rourke, the music teacher. When she heard me sing, she put me in the Bluebird group. Bluebirds can open and close our mouths but we can't let nothing come out. Bluebirds don't sing. I gotta grow a beard.

Dear John,

We gotta write a composishun. The nun gives us three titles. They are trees, the wind, or mountains. We gotta write a composishun about one. I can't think of a thing to write about any one of them. I hate writing.

Dear John,

Peter Ackerman likes Gene Autry better than Roy Rogers. Now ain't that the stoopidest thing what you ever heard! Peter Ackerman don't know much about real cowboys. Real cowboys don't drive jeeps and have radios and they don't got no underground caves like on Radio Ranch with people what look like they come from Mars. All that stuff's jist make believe.

Dear John,

Me and Earnest don't got everything in common. We like to take things apart but for me they gotta be things what was never alive.

Dear John,

Don Windlow of the Navy ended last Saturday. Don Windlow won the war.

Dear John,

Me and Earnest are listening to the Philco and I put on the wire recorder and it copies *The Captain Midnight* show. We listen to it back and then Earnest says "We can do that."

I get his idear and I say, "Shore, why not? We can make our own radio program."

So we try it out. Earnest says into the wire recorder, "Them rustlers jist robbed the bank, Sherif, and we gotta round up a possee and go after them.

I say, "O.K. Depyoutee Earny, get the guns and I'll kiss my horse." (We can't help but laff at that one and it runes the show but we picks it up again.) Depyoutee Earny, you got the guns?"

"Yeh, I got em. Help me find some bullets and stop kissing your horse."

Well we went on like that and it was great fun and when we play it back, it was swell. But Earnest says, "It don't sound like the real thing but it's OK cause we laff a lot."

Dear John,

I ain't even started writing that composishon about trees and stuff yet. I hate writing. But the nun's gonna want it pretty soon.

Dear John,

Sound effects! That's why it don't sound like the real thing. Mel Blank makes all the sound effects on the radio. That's why it sounds real. I was listening real hard so I can figger out what they done what we ain't done. It's sound effects what does the trick. You can hear the horses galooping and the gun shots and bombs blowing up and everything and when you hear them, you can see them in your head just like with Fibber McGee's closet.

Robert S. Pehrsson

Dear John,

Christine Carney goes and tells the teacher that Earnest is making disgusting sounds at her. The teacher jist gives Earnest a dirty look and shakes her head. Earnest was jist practicing the sound effect for horse kissing.

Dear John,

But where we gonna get a horse and how we gonna carry the wire recorder to get the sound of him galooping? Earnest says we need a real long electric cord.

Dear John,

I know it's like pretty sinful to brag and all but I'm a geenyus. I put on the wire recorder and then first I walk arown my room, footsteps, but they don't sound real good. So I'm thinking and tapping a pencil on the table, the wire player's going. So I turn it off. I play it back to hear the footsteps. But at first they ain't real good, don't sound real but then I hear really good footsteps. It's gotta be the real thing but how'd I do that? It was the pencil I was tapping, the pencil on the table. Do it again, tap, tap, tap, tap. Do it slow, do it fast, taptaptaptap. Listen to the recorder. First somebody's walking, then running. Great. Next I take my fingers and tap all of them one after the other right on the microphone. Listen. Sounds jist like a horse galooping. We don't need no long electiric cord!

Dear John,

Earnest listens to the galooping horse and ask how'd you do that? I tell him I took the wire recorder on the subway to Prospect Park where they got all them horses and I ask the man if I can record a horse galooping. He says shore so

142

I plug it in but it don't work good because the horse don't stand still when he galoops so I got on the horse with the wire recorder and then I kick him and he starts galooping and I lean over and put the microphone right near his feet and then I'm slipping and the recorder is slipping and the horse is gonna jump a fence.

Then I stop talking and Earnest's eyes are wide open. So's his mouth and he ask, "What happened?"

I say, "I fell off the horse right on my head and all blood and brains was coming out and then I died right there. And now it's my ghost you are talking to."

He don't know what to say at first. But then he smiles and hits me on the head. It don't take Earnest long to know when he's been tricked. Then I showed him how I really done it. He thinks it's swell.

Dear John,

We expeermented with lots of sound effects. It's great. You don't gotta go out in a rainstorm to get the stormy sounds. You jist take a bucket of water and slosh it around. You jist gotta be careful not to get the microphone all wet. You can make the sound like fire if you crumble a piece of paper. If you drop some metal on the floor, you get breaking glass and you get a exploshon if you jist blow into the microphone. Now we're gonna do our own cereal. I'm gonna write the story. Earnest will read what he can and make sound effects.

Dear John,

We tried it out. It works pretty good. It's a story about these bad guys what rob a bank. It's called The Sherif and The Bad Guys. First I'm the Sherif and Earnest is the bad guys. But then we start getting real mad at each other because we was on different sides. So we changed it and me and Earnest was both good guys and as for the bad guys we changed our verses to sound like we are mean and nasty. We both done the sound effects. It sounds good. Now we got another idea to try.

Dear John,

It works! We got my victrola and put on my favorite cowboy song, *Don't Fence Me In*. We play that in the beginning before we start the show. Well we done the first part and Sherif Bob is riding out after the robbers. But first he kisses his horse . . . mmmmmmmmmSMACK. We really think that's funny. You can hear the galooping horse and men running and then the sheriff is in the hideout cave and the bad guys set off dynamite. BOOM! . . . to be continued.

Dear John,

I wrote most of the story but Earnest told me what the other good guy is sposed to say and I wrote what he told me because that's his part and then I hadda read it to Earnest a couple of times and then he could read his part real easy. I made two of them, one copy with carbon paper so Earnest could read along and come in with the sound effects and even read his parts. Sometimes Earnest don't read the exakt words what I wrote but he gets it close enuff. Earnest says it's O.K. because he was adlibing. It went real good. Then after to-be-continued we played *Don't Fence Me In* again. It sounds almost like a real radio cereal.

Dear John,

Peter Ackerman and Patrick Garino ask where me and Earnest been for the last week. I told them we're making a radio show. They laft.

"Well come on up to my room and I'll show you."

They come up and they're still laffing but then they hear it and they don't laff no more.

Peter Ackerman says, "It's really good."

They ask can they be in the show.

"Maybe the next one."

They wanna know what's gonna happen next. I tell them it's a secret. It's a secret because I don't even know what's gonna happen next. Only thing I'm shore about is that Sherif Bob ain't got blowed up. We'll be sneaky about that.

Dear John,

I ask Earnest about Peter Ackerman and Patrick Garino wanting to be in the radio show.

He says, "It's O.K. so long as they pay the dues."

"What dues?"

"The cereal actor union dues. If we get the dues, then we can class up our equipment or maybe buy another wire for the recorder."

We got only one wire and we gotta erase it and play over it. We can get better if we got dues.

I ask, "How much dues?"

"A dollar a year."

"O.K. Hey, I don't got a dollar."

"No problem. We don't gotta pay no dues for 20 years because we started it. We got what's called the Introductory Twenty Year Free Membership."

Dear John,

I told Peter Ackerman and Patrick Garino and they say
O.K. if they can pay 25 cents a month for 4 months. I got
out a piece of paper and figgered it out. It's the same as one
dollar. O.K. So they're gonna be in the cereal.

Dear John,

Marie Magatarino and Delores Granowski wanna be in
the story now too. O.K. if they got a dollar. They are gonna
pay 50 cents for two months. I don't need no paper to figger
that out. I added that in my head. O.K. Now the story is real
good because Peter Ackerman and Patrick Garino are two
bad guys and they get throwed in jail. Patrick Garino is one
of the bad guys and he kidnaps Delores Granowski which
fits him jist fine because he likes her. Only there was almost
a fight because Peter Ackerman wants to kidnap her. But we
flipped a penny and Patrick Garino won her. So we got the
second cereal done. It's called Epeysode 2 and it ends with
Patrick Garino leaving a note for the Sherif that he's gonna
kill Delores Granowski if he don't let Peter Ackerman outa
jail. Then you can hear Delores Granowski screaming. To
be continued.

Dear John,

All the kids in our class and almost all the kids on the
block listened to our story. First I let a coupla kids into my
room to hear it. They told other kids and more come. Then
it gets too crowded and my mom throws us out. Then I take
the wire recorder down stairs and I plug it in the cellar where
there's lots of room. They all wanna know what's gonna
happen next. Who knows?

Dear John,

We got about ten more kids what jerned the cereal actor union and paid the first installment dues. For now on anybody what ain't in the union gotta pay a penny to hear the story.

Dear John,

We finished the cowboy story with Sherif Bob saving everybody and then kissing his horse, mmmmmmmmmsmack. Now we're gonna do the next exciting story about a lady what gets tortured.

Dear John,

Earnest tells all the actors "We gotta make the first epeysode real exciting speshally at the to-be-continued. That way we got them hooked."

Earnest told me that's what the movie people do to get you to come back.

I told him. "You're getting smarter all the time, Earnest."

He says, "I think real good when I got somethin interesting to think about."

Dear John,

Marie Magatarino is the lady what gets tortured. She's a great screamer. Marie Magatarino is kidnapped by a bad guy. See she's out galooping on her horse and this biplane comes swooping down outa a cloud and the pilot reaches out and jist grabs her right off her horse. Then he brings her to a dungeon where he got a great big buzz saw to cut fair maidens in half if they don't get grandsomed first.

Dear John,

Patrick Garino is the bad guy and Earnest is the sound effects man. Earnest is real great with the galooping horse but the airplane and the buzz saw jist sound like Earnest with a sick stomach. Marie Magatarino got most of the parts in the epeysode. She don't say much. She mostly screams.

Dear John,

I put on the radio to listen to Baby Snooks because my dad gotta work late tonight and they say Baby Snooks ain't gonna be on no more because she died last Tuesday on May 29. At first I thought they was kidding because they kept saying, "Rockabye baby." My mom says Baby Snooks wasn't a baby. She was lots older than she sounded. I can't believe it. She was really old. She was 59. Baby Snooks is a baby and she's dead of old age. You never know what's gonna happen next.

Dear John,

We're practicing in my partment and all a sudden, Bam, bam, bam. "Open up. It's the cops."

It's really really the cops, the real cops! It ain't part of the cereal.

Two seconds flat, Earnest's under the bed.

Bam, Bam, Bam. "Open up or we're gonna knock down the door."

"O.K." I open the door and two cops with guns pointin at me. We all got our hands up.

"What's goin on here?"

"Nothing."

"We got complaints about somebody screamin."

"Oh that's jist Marie Magatarino."

"She still alive or somebody kill her?"

Then I tell them the hole thing and they see it's jist our radio cereal. "O.K. kids but keep that girl from screamin so loud."

And they leave. We laft and got back to work but where's the sound effects man? Still hiding under the bed.

Dear John,

Earnest was real scared when the cops bang on the door and come in with their guns ready to shoot. Earnest probly got lots of good reasons. I think he done some stuff what makes him worry about cops.

Dear John,

Almost everybody what is in the union got in trouble with the nun because we ain't been doin our homework. None of us wrote the composishun. Too busy with our cereal.

Dear John,

I told Earnest about Baby Snooks dieing of old age and all and he says he knows about it but it wasn't old age what got her. He says she was really about our age but she got so many school problems that she died from being worried about school. Then Earnest says, "That's why I don't worry much about school. It can kill you."

Dear John,

When people die like Baby Snooks, is that God's plan? Sometimes I think about old men and soldiers dying but I didn't ever think about girls dying. Fanny Brice, that was her real name.

149

Dear John,

I got the best sound effect in the whole world. It's the ZZZZZZZZZZZZZ radio. When you turn it low, it sounds like an airplane. When you turn it loud, it sounds like anything you say it's supposed to sound like. If you want a buzz saw because some lady's gonna be sawed in half by a bad guy, you jist say the big blade of the buzz saw is coming close, Closer, CLOSER, the ZZZZZZZZZ gets louder and Louder and LOUDER because you turn up the dial on the radio. Then Marie Magatarino screams. She's a great screamer, too bad now she gotta scream low. Then we all say, to-be-continued. After that we put on a record.

Dear John,

The nun wants to know how come none of us done our homework composishon about trees, the wind, or mountains. I hate writing about trees, the wind, or mountains.

Dear John,

Some of the kids told the nun about our radio cereals. She asks if she can hear them. O.K. I'll bring the wire recorder in. We already got some of a vampire story done. It's a perfect story because it got horses galooping and Marie Magatarino screaming lots.

Dear John,

The nun listened to our cereal story. She says it's great and she absolves all of us and says that the radio program can take the place of our composishun because it's got trees, the wind, and mountains in it. But we gotta let everbody in our class hear it free. No writing no composishuns? O.K. It's a deal!

Dear John,

The nun edited our story so the spelling and grammar was real good and then she even types it on a stensil. She makes mimeograph copies so all the kids can read along and listen. She says it's a great way to help kids use their imajinashuns when they read. I ain't never seen a teacher like this before. She's a good teacher.

Dear John,

Earnest is getting to be a pretty good reader. He keeps reading over his part and then he remembers the words and knows them when he sees them in other stories. I think he's doing good too because he gotta read along what others read because he gotta know when to make the sound effects at the right time. He jist keeps practising reading the epeysodes over and over.

Dear John,

The whole school thinks our cereals are great. They wanna know what's gonna happen next. I never seen the liberry so crowded after school. Then they always ask how'd you get the horses on the recorder and what buzz saw did you use and how'd you get the airplane to come outa the cloud?

We say, "It's a secret" and all the union members swear never to tell.

Dear John,

Everybody in the class wants to write a cereal. So the nun says we can work in groups and we can write cereals and now she got three other recorders from the convent. They're a lot better than the wire recorder I found in the garbage. They got a little piece of tape runnin from reel to reel and they're called tape recorders. Me and Earnest are gonna buy one with the union dues. Everybody says it's a good idear for us to buy a tape recorder because it ain't likely I'm gonna find one of them in the garbage for a long time.

Dear John,

One of the union members squealed. I don't know who but somebody told how we done the sound effects. But it's O.K. because it's the most fun thing we ever done at school.

Dear John,

Baby Snooks was on the radio last night. They played a tape of what they recorded before she died. My dad says it was O.K. for me to listen to Baby Snooks for the last time and my mom and dad missed Mr. and Mrs. North.

Dear John,

Earnest loaned the tape recorder from the school and put the microphone in front of his radio and recorded Baby Snooks for me. It was jist great. Now I can listen over and over again to Baby Snooks. This way it's kinda like she never died. Maybe I won't miss her so much.

Dear John,

The nun says we can write our stories and practice them and make the sound effects and everything during our reading time. She says we don't gotta read the reader. YEAH!

Dear John,

We got ghost stories, war stories, vampire stories, cowboy stories, outer space stories, racing car stories, all goin on at the same time. You should hear the sound effects. Great! But all the stories are gonna be better when I bring in my radio that goes ZZZZZZZZZZZZZZZ. It makes the really greatest sound effects. I told everybody I'm bringin it in tomorrow.

Dear John,

I figger God let that radio get that noise because He knowed that it'll work out for the best and it did!

Dear John,

We are real lucky because we got a great teacher. Her name is Sister Everesta.

Dear John,

I got home today and my mom says, "I got a suprise for you. It's in your room."

I go in. Nothing different. Then I hear it. My radio's workin. I think, Oh, Great. Now I could listen to Baby Snooks but then I remember she died. Ding it. Dang it! But then uh, oh. No ZZZZZZZZZZZZZZZ sound effects.

I walk slowly into the kitchen and my mom's smiling and real proud that she got that radio all fixed for me. I think how hard it was for her to budge it.

I look at her and smile real big and hug her and say, "Thanks mom, thanks." Then I give her a big kiss with sound effects, mmmmSMACK!

Chapter 6

The Power of Prayer

June, 1950s, end of Fifth Grade

Dear John,

This is the greatest day in my life. The last day of school.
No more pencils. No more books. No more teachers' dirty
looks. Me and Earnest sang that song all the way home
today. Free for the whole summer. I'm going write you every
day during summer.

September, Sixth Grade

Dear John,

Sorry I don't write you all summer. I got sent to a
summer camp what is known as Send this Boy to Camp
Fun. This camp upstate is someplace north of the Bronx.
It was a big surprise when I found out about my going to
camp and I got pushed into a bus so fast that I did not have
any chance to take you with me. When I got back home,
I looked all over my room and finally found you. You got
lorst in the bottom of my closet again and my mom jist

says, "Clean your closet." I tell her it don't need cleaning and she says, "Clean it or you are going nowhere, grounded for a week."

"Why mom?"

"Because I said so!"

You was way under the dead socks, Phew!

Dear John,

Another summer's all gone and I got a new nun and the very very first thing she does is to tell us to write about are summer vacation. I seen Earnest shaking his head, rolling his eyes and whispering, "Not again!" She says we got two weeks to get it done.

Dear John,

The nun says we gotta get rosary beads and keep them with us all the time. Prayers don't count none if you don't got no rosary beads to pray on. I got a problem. I don't got no rosary beads and I ain't got no money to buy no rosary beads either.

Dear John,

I hadda stay after school. This time it's because I don't got no rosary beads. I told the nun I got no money and she says everybody has enuff money for rosary beads.

"It's of the utmost importance," she says. "We must all sacrifice and pay a price for salvation."

It's a buck fifty.

Dear John,

We're learning all about the rosary and the nun says that Mary appeared to some kids in Lourdes and some other kids

155

in Fatima and those places are in France and some country nearby. Mary told them kids to tell us to pray and make sure you do it with the beads. We can save the world from the communists if we pray but without the beads it don't count much.

Dear John,

The nun says the hole world will be saved by the power of prayer.

Dear John,

I ask Maggie who is my sister if she got rosary beads to borrow me but she says she got only one rosary and she needs it because she's in high school and she ain't doin so good. She's gonna use them to pray so she passes algae bra.

Dear John,

The rosary got three kinds of mystries. They are sorrowful and joyful and the glorius. The sorrowful ain't no fun. It's all about the agony and thorns and carrying a cross and getting whipped and nailed and hung up on a cross. Sorrowful defnitly ain't no fun.

Dear John,

The nun says that God will always answer our prayers. But Earnest says he ain't so sure about the power of prayer. Earnest told me he prayed once and asks God for just a little favor or two and God never answered his prayer. I told Earnest maybe God wasn't listening at the time because He's very busy what with the communists and the problems in the world and all. Then I asks Earnest if he prayed using the rosary beads and he says no. Well there's the problem right there. If they ain't said with the beads, prayers don't count all that much.

Dear John,

I'm not going to ask Earnest what he prayed for. It's probably not the sort of thing God wants anybody to have or even talk about.

Dear John,

Today's Friday and there is one thing I like lots about Fridays and one thing I hate. I like Fridays because the week is almost over and tomorrow's Saturday and we got no school. And for that reason I like Friday afternoons better than Friday mornings. But what I hate about Friday is the way the school stinks all afternoon. Most of us bring our lunches in bags and lunchboxes. Well on Fridays it's a sin to eat meat like bolognee what don't smell all that bad except for the fried bolgnee sandwiches what Earnest eats sometimes at Randy's Restaurant. But on Fridays when the lunch boxes all get opened, the school stinks of tuna fish and peanut butter. And that mixture don't smell pretty. No, no, not at all! Most of the time I get peanut butter sandwiches because tuna is kinda spensive and we don't got much money. I hate the smell of tuna and peanut butter Fridays.

Dear John,

Earnest told me he ain't bothered by the smell of tuna and peanut butter because it means the next day is Saturday. Besides he likes peanut butter so long as it's got lots of jelly and it's all on smoothed out on top of Wonder Bread and then anudder piece of Wonder Bread gets mushed on top.

Dear John,

I've been thinking about Earnest's prayers not being answered and all. I think God always answers prayers but God's answer to Earnest's prayers is No!

Dear John,

I got some old pearls what Maggie don't want because the string got busted and they rolled all over her bedroom floor and a couple went into the holes in the floor where the wood is rottin because the termites got hungry and all. They ain't real pearls but Maggie gave me a good idear. I can use them to make my own rosary beads. All I gotta do is put a string through them.

Dear John,

First that string thing don't work. I can't get it through the holes. But then Maggie showed me how I can use thread and a tiny needle and that done the trick.

Dear John,

The nun says Rosary beads work best because Mary listens to them and then she tells God to do what you ask for. It's better to ask Mary because she interseeds and gets God to do what she says. That's because she's his mom and he gotta do what his mom says. If he ask how come, she says, "Because I say so!"

Dear John,

Earnest asks the nun, "How come my mom always prays for lots of money but we don't got enuff to pay the rent? It don't look like God's answering my mom's prayers."

But the nun says, "God works in strange ways. He always answers prayers but He knows what's best for us and maybe money is not what your mother really needs."

Earnest told me, "I bet Mr. Pitsacola don't agree with the nun." Mr. Pitsacola is Earnest's landlord.

Dear John,

The nun walked around the classroom and everybody hadda show that they got rosary beads. I strung together ten of Maggie's pearls. So when the nun got to me, I held them tight and jist showed the ten beads and it kinda looked like the rest of the beads are in my hand. That way I showed the nun my ten pearls and she fell for it. Those ten pearls done the trick.

Dear John,

My beads don't work because the nun says they gotta be blessed by a priest. No priest is gonna bless my ten pearls.

Dear John,

I told Earnest his mom's gotta stop going direktly to God. She gotta get to Mary and she gotta use them rosary beads. I figger it's gonna woik better if it's mom to mom talk.

Dear John,

Maybe what the nun says is right. I'm gonna pray to Mary with my ten beads and ask to get me money to buy real rosary beads and maybe Mary can tell God to get me a buck fifty.

Dear John,

I borrowed my sister's rosary beads and said a real Sorrowful Mystery because it's the only one I remembered. It wasn't no fun but it might do the trick.

Dear John,

It's another peanut butter Friday and the place stinks. It never use to stink so much at P.S. 18 because a lot of them public school kids ain't Catholic so they can eat real good food like bolognee sandwiches on Fridays. Even Randy's bolognee sandwiches smell better than peanut butter and tuna fish. But nothing smells as good as Randy's greasy hamboigers.

Dear John,

I found some more pearls but I got only fifteen pearls and a rosary bead takes about sixty beads and one cross what's called a crew see fix. But I strung them pearls all together and tied them up real strong. The nun comes arown again to check everybody's rosary beads. I closed my hand like most of the rosary was in it and showed her just the part what I had. This time she don't fall for it. She says, "Open your hand." She shakes her head and tells me that they are not rosary beads. The nun says to pray on those beads is blast for me. I hadda stay after school again.

Dear John,

Beads gotta get blessed by a priest to make them real rosary beads. Mary don't listen to no beads what ain't got blessed. Praying on beads what ain't blessed don't do a bit of good.

Dear John,

I hadda stay after school again because I don't got no rosary beads. Gets boring. I got stuff to do, important stuff. I don't gots no time for staying after school.

Dear John,

I got some idears about getting money to buy rosaries but I can't do it because I gotta stay after school every day because I ain't got no rosary beads.

Dear John,

I told Earnest about my problem with the rosary beads.

Earnest says, "No problem. You shoulda told me before. You can have my rosary beads."

Then he reaches down into his pocket and pulls out his rosary beads and gives them to me.

"But what about you? Now you don't got no rosaries. You're gonna be in trouble," I said.

Earnest says, "Don't worry about me. I can get rosary beads. I'm real good at finding things."

Dear John,

The nun's right. Money ain't what I really needed. I just needed a friend what gives me rosary beads. Mary answered my prayer and it all woiked out in a strange way.

Dear John,

Peter Ackerman seen my rosary beads and said they look just like his what got stoled off his desk.

"Was your name on it?" I ask.

"No, he says, "But there was a scratch on the back of the cross and I know exactly what it looks like. I marked it just in case they got lost."

I turn the cross over. Lots and lots of scratches on the back of the cross.

Dear John,

Today I was worried all day because I left my rosary beads in my other pants. Lucky the nun don't check.

Dear John,

Earnest says he ain't got no problem about leaving his rosary beads in the other pants. He don't got no other pants.

Dear John,

I'd like to get a thousand of them rosary beads and keep them in both my pants and shirts, and coats, and in my desk. I don't wanna do no more time after school.

Dear John,

Earnest ain't takin no chances. He keeps finding more rosary beads. Today he gives me an extra rosary beads what he found. Now I can put them in both my pants. No problem about staying after school now.

Dear John,

They knocked down a building over near P.S. 141. That's near Broadway where the elevator train goes. Me and Earnest walked over there and the basement and foundashun is all that's left. We climbed all over it and had real good fun.

Dear John,

The nun says that God always listens to Mary and does what she says just like at some wedding what they went to. They was having a real good time because of the wine and the music and dancing and all. So they're laffing and joking and being real happy and all. Like my mom says nobody was feeling no pain. But then the wine is all run out and it's gonna sperl the party if they can't get no more wine. So some of the people are putting on their coats and probably thinking of going to some other party what still got wine. But Mary's having a good time and she don't want the party to stop. But they can't get no more wine because the wine stores are all closed. So Mary asks Jesus to make some wine but he don't wanna show off and all. So she like nags him and keeps asking and all. He ask her why he should do a miracle. His mom tells him, "Because I say so." So he gets some water and says some stuff over it and it gets changed to wine. So if you want something, you just gotta ask Mary because God just don't say no to her.

Dear John,

Earnest found five rosary beads and gives me two more.

Dear John,

Five kids gotta stay after school because they don't got no rosary beads. They told the nun they lost them.

Dear John,

Me and Earnest took toy guns over to that building what got knocked down. It's great to play soljers or cops and robbers. We was like in Germany and fighting the commies.

Earnest says "I'm a war hero because I shot two hundred emenies."

"I shot two douzand. I'm the better hero."

Then Earnest turns and makes like he shoots me and says, "Posthumorous hero."

Earnest says a posthumorous hero is a guy what don't got nothing to laff at no more.

Dear John,

The nun made a rosary beads inspection and Earnest told me that first he couldn't find none of his. But then he felt way down in the bottom of his pocket and there they are, real small ones stuck all in the threads and stuff in his pocket. He tried to get it out before the nun gets to him. But it was all stuck. When she got to his seat, he told her, "I got my rosary beads, really I got them. They're stuck in my pocket and I'm gonna rip my pants if I get them out."

He can see the nun don't believe him because she puts her hand on her hip and glares like only a nun can glare. They all got special God given glarin powers that see right through you. She don't believe him.

So he pulls out his whole pocket backwards. Keys, bolts, nuts, screws, two small screw drivers and a rabbit's foot roll all over the floor. Kids laff. But stuck to the threads, his rosary beads.

She says, "O.K. leave them there. Don't rip the pocket."

He hadda say the sorrowful mystries with his hand in his pocket.

Dear John,

The sorrowful mystries defnitly ain't no fun.

Dear John,

Earnest told me, "When we said the sorrowful mystries, I just keep my hand in my pocket and played with my keys, my bolts and my nuts." Then Earnest starts laffin so hard he falls on the ground. I can't see nuthin funny about the Sorrowful Mysteries.

Dear John,

Earnest says a rabbit's foot works better than a rosary and a lot faster. He says he never goes no where without the rabbit's foot. I told Earnest I need a rabbit's foot. Earnest says he's gonna try to find one for me.

Dear John,

Earnest says that a cat's foot is just as lucky as a rabbit's but a cat's foot is real easy to get in Brooklyn.

I told Earnest, "A rat's foot is even easier."

But he says, "They ain't lucky. I tried it."

Dear John,

Earnest says a rabbit's foot costs money but a cat's foot don't. He got lots of them and gives me one. I gotta think over and over again what I want and rub the foot at the same time. The cat's foot ain't pretty but if it brings luck, I'm gonna try it.

Dear John,

Me and Earnest went over to that building what got knocked down and they're putting up this fence all around it.

Earnest asks a man what got a helmet on, "What're you doing?"

165

The man says, "This here's gonna be a park for you kids to play in."

Earnest says "What a stoopid idear. Right now it's the best place to play with all the stuff to climb on and jump off. So they fence up a real good place and build a stoopid park that ain't half the fun."

Dear John,

I'm runnin out of rosary beads. Kids keep stealing rosary beads off my desk. I told Earnest about kids stealing rosary beads off my desk and Earnest shakes his head and says, "You jist can't trust nobody around here."

Dear John,

The nun tells us we only got two days to get the report done on our summer vacations.

Dear John,

Earnest says he seen this beautiful girl walking down Maujer yesterday. He says, "Hubba hubba, she's a real knock out."

Dear John,

Earnest says he keeps trying to forget about that report on summer vacation and hopes the nun does the same.

Dear John,

My sister Maggie and her friends, Patsy Jane and Joan Dillon and Barbara Williams, got a club and it's called the Polly Pigtails Club. The club's going to Radio City Music Hall. That's a swell place and all. They got music and dancers called Rockets and a movie. I used the rosary beads and said a prayer so Maggie will take me.

Dear John,

I ask Maggie if maybe I can go with her to Radio City Music Hall.

She says, "No!"

Dear John,

I rubbed my cat's foot so Maggie will take me.

Dear John,

I ask Maggie again and she says, "No."

Dear John,

I said two Sorrowful Mystries and I went up the beads in my right hand and rubbed a cat's foot with the udder hand. It was easy to think sorrowful stuff because I can't go to Radio City Music Hall. The rosary and the cat's foot gotta do the trick.

Dear John,

Maggie says I can't go because this is only for members of her club. I ask her if I can join but she says no boys can be in the Polly Pigtails Club.

Dear John,

Earnest says, "I figger the sorrowful mysteries don't work so good. I can't see no good in getting Mary all reminded of the sad stuff. If you wanna get a favor off me, it ain't real smart to make me remember all the bad stuff what happened. That puts me in a bad mood. It just ain't real smart to put Mary and God in a bad mood when you want them to do you a favor."

Dear John,

I told Maggie that girls what belong to the Polly Pigtails Club gotta wear pigtails but none of them girls what are in the club got pigtails. Maggie says they don't gotta have pigtails because they got acceptions. I told her I should get acceptions for being a boy.

Dear John,

I said another rosary and rubbed the cat's foot for Maggie to take me to Radio City Music Hall. But this time I said the joyful mystries and that's happier stuff than all that nailing to the cross and all. The joyful mysteries is about happy things like Jesus getting born and I made it speshally strong because I went to church to say them and I said the prayers with two rosary beads, one in my right hand and a nudder in my left hand. Mary gotta listen and get God to get Maggie to let me go to Radio City Music Hall.

Dear John,

Maggie still says, "No." The joyful mystries ain't working. I wish I had three hands.

Dear John,

Maybe them rosary beads ain't blessed. Praying on beads what ain't blessed don't do a bit of good.

Dear John,

Christine Carney's the only one in the class what done the report on summer vacations.

Dear John,

Earnest gives me the biggest rosary I ever seen. It's about a mile long with beads the size of grapes. I can't fit it in my pocket what with the cat's foot and other valuble stuff.

Dear John,

I got the big rosary beads at home and I said another rosary on them big beads. Only this time I said the glorius ones because Earnest agreed with me about the glorius mystries gotta be the best when you want God and Mary and all them saints to get in a real good mood. The glorius mystries are all about swell stuff like Jesus coming out of the grave after He was dead and going to heaven and then Mary got to go to heaven where she got crowned.

Dear John,

I ask my mom if I can go with Maggie to Radio City Music Hall.

She says, "Yes."

The glorius mystries done the trick.

Dear John,

Maggie's real mad because my mom says she gotta take me to Radio City Music Hall with the Polly Pigtails Club. Maggie says I can't go to Radio City Music Hall because I ain't a member of the club.

Dear John,

My mom says Maggie can't go if she don't take me to Radio City Music Hall.

Dear John,

I think the nun forgot about the report on our summer vacations. I'll say a glorius mystry on them really big beads so the nun don't remember. That's gonna woik real good.

Dear John,

It takes a long time to say a glorius mystry but it takes a lot longer to write a report about my summer vacation.

Dear John,

I'm going to Radio City Music Hall next Saturday. They made me a ornery member of the Polly Pigtail Club. God works in strange ways.

Dear John,

I figgered out what done the trick. Father Smott was in church the other day and I ask him to bless my rosary beads. He was real surprised to see me with such big rosary beads what don't even fit in my pocket. He hadda use up almost all the holy water to do the job. Then I seen Father Murphy last night and I ask him to bless them. Then I took the rosary beads and stuffed them in the holy water fountain in the back of the church. They got a real good soaking. But they put too much holy water in the fountain and when the rosary beads went in, the back of the church got kinda flooded. Them two blessings and one dunking done the trick.

Dear John,

I figger everybody's trying to get something all the time but then they don't do nuthing when they get it. Well you know it's always a real good idear to say thanks when somebody does you a favor. It's just good thinking because the next time you ask, they are going to remember that you said thank you the last time. So I said the glorius mysteries with the beads what got two blessings and one dumping and that jist gotta make Mary real happy and all. I figger it was a real good way of saying thanks. I hope she remembers the next time I ask for something.

Dear John,

I told Earnest about my going to Radio City Music Hall with the Polly Pigtails Club next Saturday. Earnest says I'm gonna feel real funny going on the subway to the Radio City Music Hall with all them girls. Then Earnest says he can solve my problem. He ain't doing nuthing special next Saturday and maybe he should come with me as a favor and all.

Dear John,

I ask Maggie if Earnest can be a ornery member of the Polly Pigtails Club and go with us to Radio City Music Hall next Saturday. Maggie says, "No!"

Dear John,

I told Earnest that Maggie don't go for the idear. He ask me what time Maggie gets home from High School. I told him and he says he wants to talk to her.

Dear John,

Me and Earnest are going to Radio City Music Hall tomorrow. Earnest splained to Maggie that she's gonna look funny with her kid brother hanging on to her and he knows his way around New York City real good. So it's better for her if he comes to take care of me and she can be more with her friends.

Dear John,

Earnest told me he's in love. A new girl moved into the neighborhood and he says she's a knockout. I remember seeing her around too. Earnest is only eleven and this girl what Earnest says is a knock out gotta be at least fourteen.

I told Earnest, "You should be interested in girls what are your own age."

Earnest says, "I like older women. They're so grown up."

Dear John,

Those gigantic rosary beads work better than any of the others. Earnest smiles and says bigger is better. I guess it's because gigantic rosary beads are more powerful than the small ones. Maybe the prayers are louder and easier for Mary to hear them.

Dear John,

I took the cat's foot and all the other stuff out of my right pocket and put them in my left pocket and I put the gigantic rosary beads in my right pocket. My pockets are bulging out but I keep the gigantic rosary beads with me because they work so good. Earnest keeps saying, "Bigger is better."

Dear John,

I seen what Earnest is talking about. That girl is really pretty. I was in the A&P getting some Hostess cream filled cupcakes and I seen her. I was hoping she'd see me and maybe I'd smile at her. And then she looks at me and stared at my pockets bulging with the gigantic rosary beads in one and the rabbit's foot and other stuff in the other. Then she smiles at me and winks. It's a good thing Earnest ain't there because he'd want those rosary beads back. They are really powerful rosary beads. Bigger is better.

Dear John,

Earnest told me it ain't a good idear for me to carry big rosary beads around. He told me to leave my big ones home and don't bring them to school no more because the other kids will be jellus and all.

Dear John,

Earnest and me are walking down Maujer and we seen that girl what's a real knock out. Earnest tells me to check out her sweater. He says, "When a sweater looks like that, real tight and bumpy, that's when you know a girl is real grown up and all."

I don't tell Earnest about what happened in the A&P. But this time she don't even look at me. It's because I left the gigantic rosary beads home.

Dear John,

The nun got real small rosary beads now. Maybe she lost the big ones. I figger that's good because God's gonna have a harder time hearing her and she won't remember about the report about our summer vacation.

Dear John,

Most of the time Christine Carney got her blue and white school uniform on. But today me and Earnest seen her and she got a sweater on and it's tight with two bumps.

Earnest said, "Sometimes it ain't because a girl's growed up. In Christine Carney's case it's just fat."

Dear John,

Tomorrow is the day me and Earnest are going to Radio City Music Hall. After we come back, I'll tell you all about the Rockets and all the music and the movie.

Dear John,

Me and Earnest had the swellest time at Radio City Music Hall but we had just one little problem or maybe two or three. Maggie and ten of her Polly Pigtails and me and Earnest all left together at ten in the morning and we all walked down to Broadway where we got onto the elevator train. Me and Earnest walked about a block in back of the Polly Pigtails and then we follow them on the elevator and subway so we don't gotta worry. Earnest says he knows all about the subways and he knows how to get anyplace in New York. But he was watching the Polly Pigtails anyways. Earnest says it's good they know the way other wise he'd hafta lead the way and they'd be embarrassed and all. So we change to another train in New York City and then we all get off at the station what's named Rocket Feller Center.

Then we get on the end of a long line what starts right there at Rocket Feller Center. Earnest had a real good time showing me all the women and girls what got tight sweaters. I tried to talk to him about Christine Carney but he says to stop because he don't wanna throw up and embarrass all the Polly Pigtails.

After a long long time we get inside Radio City Music Hall and it's beautiful and gorjus but it's so crowded we can't all sit together. So Earnest and me get two seats together way down in the front. Maggie and the Polly Pigtails sit all over the place. We hear music from an organ what's a little peppyer than the one at St. Mary's. Then there's this band coming up from the floor and then gorjus girls with long legs jumping all up and down together on the stage. Earnest told me they're called Rockets because of Rocket Feller Center. There was singers and jugglers but Earnest says they wasn't worth a darn. Then the movie comes on but Earnest says this one is the B movie and it's real boring so Earnest says we got time to case the jernt. So we get up and check out the whole place and then we find this door what says Emergency Exit on it but Earnest says it's just a trick to keep us out because the Rockets are on the other side practicing for the next show. So we open the door but the loudest alarm you ever hear goes blaring and guys in red and blue uniforms are yelling and running at us. So we run out the door and down the street and hide in a great big building. But Earnest says he seen a cop looking for us so we got on an elevator and push the top floor button. The doors open and there's a swell restaurant what's called the Rainbow Room. It was closed for cleaning but the cleaner said we can look around. It's a swell place and we seen the menu and it costs tons of money to eat there. Things what I can't even read cost $5 and Earnest says it's a swell looking place but he ain't never gonna eat stuff what he can't pronounce. Then Earnest told me people come to a swell place like this and pay lots of money and they don't know what they're eating so the restaurant tricks them and gives them terrible stuff like snails. Well we left and it was safe to go back but a whole new bunch of people are going into Radio City Music Hall and we can't find one Polly Pigtail. Earnest says we don't gotta worry because he knows all about traveling in the subways and all. So we get on a subway train and then switch to another train and then switch to another train and then switch to another train and then switch to another train. When we got home, it's 2 in the morning and the police are there and so are Earnest's mom and dad. They're real happy to see us and they're all thanking God for answering their prayers and getting us home safe.

Dear John,

Earnest says first his parents are real glad he's not dead and then they wanna kill him for not being dead.

Dear John,

When we was coming back from Radio City Music Hall, we got off the elevator train and walked past the park what they're making. There's a little house in the middle of the park. It was dark at 2 in the morning and we can't see all that good in the dark. Me and Earnest are gonna check it out.

Dear John,

Earnest says those Rockets at Radio City Music Hall are really, really grown up.

Dear John,

Earnest says them Nazies and Commeys are building up the fort what's in that new park and we gotta go and make a reconnoiter.

I ask Earnest how we gonna make a reconnoiter but he says he don't know exactly how we are gonna do that but it sounds like a real good thing to do.

Dear John,

The nun remembered she forgot about the report on summer vacations because Christine Carney asks her if the rest of the class still needs to write it. The nun says, "Yes."

Dear John,

Thank you Christine Carney! I don't believe it. Teachers sure think summer vacations are important. I gotta write that summer vacation report. Ding it. Dang it! Darn!

Dear John,

Me and Earnest was having a 2 cent plane at Friedman's candy store. We're sittin in one of the booths across from the counter. Do you remember what happened when Earnest seen the pretty lady what lived in Victoria's mansion? So I'm looking at my soda and sipping and I hear this bang on the floor. I look up and Earnest ain't in his seat. He's on the floor. Earnest falls out of the seat right on the floor. I think he's sick. But he opens his eyes and says, "I'm in love." He points to the front of the store and there's that girl standing there staring at Earnest flat on the floor.

Dear John,

Earnest says that girl likes him because when he was sitting on the floor at Friedman's candy store she smiled at him. He says he likes her because she's so grown up.

Dear John,

I hadda write the thing about my summer vacation. Here's what I wrote.

My Summer Vacation

Last summer I went to my Uncle Bob's farm in Pennsylvania. We went fishing everyday and I helped him milk cows and fix his truck. I like Pennsylvania better than Brooklyn in the summer because in Brooklyn if you go fishing you catch mostly dead beer cans. In Pennsylvania you catch live fish. I had a good time in Pennsylvania and I hope I can go back there again next summer. The End.

Dear John,

Earnest found out her name and even where she lives. He followed her home and talked to her kid brother. She lives way over in Greenpernt way on the other side of Metropolitan Avenue. Her name's Irma.

Earnest borrowed the big rosary beads back. He says he got a miracle to ask for and a gigantic double blessed, double dosed, holy water soaked rosary is just the thing to do the trick.

Dear John,

My Uncle Bob don't live anywhere near Pennsylvania. He really lives on a boat in Brooklyn. He got it docked in Canarsie. It's a real nice place except for two times a day. When it's low tide, the water really stinks.

I kinda hope Uncle Bob lets me stay with him for a little while. My mom and dad and me are gonna go see him tomorrow. Maybe I'll say a prayer he invites me to stay. I don't mind the stinky water none. It's not all that more smelly than Newtown Creek when the wind blows from the north.

One problem! I don't got that big rosary.

Dear John,

I already told you about my Uncle Bob working for the Brooklyn Union Gas company in the daytime but at night he's a Captain on his own ship. He got this really big boat what got sunk in the Hudson River years ago. He got it floating and patched it and now he lives on it right next to a dock in Canarsie.

Last summer I stayed with Uncle Bob and his boat for two days and I really liked it. I made like I was captain steering the big wheel and all. Uncle Bob took me to a diner two times where all the waitresses know him real good and one time I had meatloaf and the next time I ate hot rolls with gravy on them. The waitress was real friendly and when we was leaving, she gives Uncle Bob a kiss on his cheek.

The boat don't go nowhere because Uncle Bob don't got enuff money to buy gas. I changed what I wrote about Uncle Bob and my summer vacation because the nun ain't gonna like my real report about Canarsie. It ain't a thing what a teacher likes to hear about.

Dear John,

It's pretty and smells great when the tide's high but when the tide's low, Canarsie got the ugliest water what with dead things floating all around and it's a smelly place. Now I know what my mom means when somebody farts. She says, "Canarsie at low tide."

Dear John,

I told Earnest about the report what I wrote about my summer vacation. Then I told him about Canarsie and my uncle Bob really living on a boat and all. Earnest asks how come I wrote about my uncle Bob living in Pennsylvania. I said, "The nun don't believe real stories like that." Earnest says, "You probly had more fun making it all up."

I did!

Dear John,

I don't believe it. Earnest and Irma was walking across Grand Ave. and he was holding her hand. That gigantic rosary musta done the trick for Earnest.

Dear John,

I ask Earnest, "How'd you get Irma to hold hands with you?"

Earnest says, "The nun's right."

"About what?" I ask him.

"I prayed with them big gigantic rosary beads so that Irma's gonna like me. Then I even went to St. Mary's church to pray and there she was right in front up near the altar talking to Father Smott. He's always talking to girls and I hadda wait a real long time. So I kneel down in the back of the church and watch and said a whole glorious mystery with the gigantic rosary beads.

Then she leaves but first Father Smott gives her a blessing and a real big hug. Then I stuff the gigantic rosary beads in my pocket and genuflect just as she's coming and I axidentally bump into her. Well after I say sorry and all, I exsplain that I'm praying for my grammar cause she's reel old and sick and all. So I gotta go over to a special farm place in Greenpernt to buy some medsin for my old sick grammar. She says that's where she lives. I acts real surprised. I ask if she can show me where LaPatto's farm is and she says O.K. but it's LaPatto's farm a see and she smiles real big and I can see she really likes me. She keeps looking at my pocket with

180

the gigantic rosary beads stuffed in them. When we get to Grand Avenue she takes my hand and we hold hands til we get to her house. Then she looks at my pocket what got the rosary beads and she asks if she can touch it. I says, sure, and I take out the rosary so she can touch it but she just starts laffing and goes into her house. Then I see LaPatto's what turns out to be a drug store but I don't need no medsin because my granma died before I was born."

Dear John,

Them big rosary beads are real powerful. Earnest says it definitly works better than the cat's foot.

Dear John,

My Uncle Bob asks me to spend the weekend on his boat. I ask, "Is the tide gonna be real low this weekend?"

Dear John,

I told Earnest about my uncle Bob axing me to come to his boat in Canarsie. Earnest told me he ain't never been to Canarsie and he ain't got no plans for the weekend.

Dear John,

I'm gonna ask my Uncle Bob if maybe Earnest can come with me. Earnest never been to no exciting place like Canarsie.

Dear John,

Me and Earnest went to my Uncle Bob's for the weekend. Like I told you, the boat don't go nowhere because Uncle Bob don't got enuff money for gas. But me and Earnest done some exploring. The boat ain't going nowhere even if it got gas. It got no motor. You can't fish off the side of the boat because there ain't nothing alive in that water except mosquitoes. But we had fun because Earnest showed me how to run back and forth across the Belt Parkway. Breaks screeching and horns blowing. Earnest almost got hit by cars three times. It was really really fun.

Dear John,

I ask Earnest if he was scared when cars almost hit him. He said he ain't scared because he got that gigantic rosary and ten other ones around his neck. He says the nun told us that when we have rosary beads Mary is always with us. He says, "Mary don't wanna be hit by no car."

Dear John,

Earnest says my uncle Bob is a real good guy and all but it ain't exactly normal to be living in Carnasie on a boat what don't go nowhere. Christine Carney hears him say that and she asks, "By what standard could you possibly measure normal?"

Dear John,

Earnest and me are sitting in Friedman's candy store across from each other in a booth. We're sipping on 2 cent plains and in walks Irma. Well anyways, after Earnest almost falls on the floor, he innerduces me to Irma. Then she sits down next to Earnest. Earnest looks real proud to have this older woman paying him some real good attentions.

Irma says, "I'll have a malted if you're buying."

Earnest says, "O.K. Irma, drinks are on me." Then he checks his pockets for loose cash. At first he looks worried but then he checks his back pocket and settles down.

Then this gigantic guy, looks like Atlas, comes over and slides in next to Irma. He puts his arm around her. Now there really ain't enuff room for three in the booth so Earnest is getting all strangled against the wall, getting crushed to death. Then Irma whispers somethin to Atlas who looks at Earnest and says real slow, "Get out of here and stay away from Irma, creep."

Earnest twists his neck away from the wall and looks at Irma half smiling like asking her "Atlas don't really mean that, right?"

She looks up at Earnest and says, "I think you better leave."

Earnest hadda scrape himself off the wall and slide and crawl under the table. Atlas kicks him twice and Earnest yells, "I'm going. I'm going."

We ran real fast. When we was outside, Mr. Friedman comes out and says Earnest owes him for the malted. Earnest gives him thirty cents.

We walk down Maujer and Earnest says, "I don't love her no more."

I never seen nobody fall in and out of love so fast.

Dear John,

Earnest says he's done with women. He says you can't trust none of them. He ain't never gonna fall in love again.

We're talking in the school yard and I seen Christine Carney stretching her neck to hear what Earnest is saying. Then Christine Carney comes over and tells me and Earnest that she remembers both of us in her prayers everyday. She prays for the sake of the world that we will grow up to be normal.

Dear John,

Earnest says, "Them rosary beads and them prayers what I said in St. Mary's caused me more problems than good. I ain't gonna put much stock in them no more. I'm going back to the rabbit's foot."

Dear John,

Earnest says there ain't nuthin speshal about being normal.

Dear John,

It takes a lot to make Earnest get into praying and falling in love and all but it don't take much to get him out of it.

Dear John,

My uncle Bob says I gotta learn a trade because I don't know enuff to make it in the real world. So he gives me a box of tools. Two screwdrivers, a hammer, a plyers and other stuff what got names I don't know.

Dear John,

Uncle Bob's a real good guy and he ain't normal living in Canarsie on a boat what ain't got a motor and all. He always got sumthing he's fixing. He says he finds lots of stuff in basements. He says stuff what's in a basement is stuff what nobody else wants. He's just helping them get the stuff out of their basements and he don't charge nothing for the cleaning.

Dear John,

Me and Earnest go to the movies and seen a great war movie about prisoners of war and Nazis and stuff. Them prisoners are so brave and they just keep telling the Nazis their names and ranks and cereal numbers. They say, "We don't gotta say no more on account of the Jenovese Conference."

Dear John,

Them prisoners of war said some prayers just before they made the excape and it worked mostly because of them prayers. I tried to tell Earnest about how the prayers got them freed but Earnest says it was that they had a real good exscape plan. He says, "Prayers only get you into trouble."

Dear John,

I'm real worried about Earnest and his not believing in the power of prayer helping and all. Earnest says, "God ain't fair."

Dear John,

I ain't gonna walk near Earnest when we got any thunder and lightning around.

Dear John,

It was a sunny day so me and Earnest walked down to the park what they're building and seen it's almost finished. They even got swings up and monkey bars and sand in the sand pit. They made lots of stuff what kids can climb on and jump off. Earnest thinks that's real funny because they spent all that money for nothing. It was a more fun place before they went and mest it all up.

Dear John,

The nun says God helps those who pray. Earnest says God helps them what helps themselves.

Dear John,

I told Earnest maybe he should put a lightning rod in his apartment.

Dear John,

Earnest said, "Them prisoners of war excaped from the prison what had wires all around it. That park what's being built looks kinda like the prison."

This is gonna be fun. Me and Earnest are cooking up some exscape plans.

Dear John,

My Uncle Bob's in the hospital again because a gas pipe blowed up in somebody's basement.

Dear John,

I said lots of prayers for my uncle Bob.

Dear John,

Earnest says he's real sorry about Uncle Bob getting blown up and all. But then Earnest says, "I said some prayers for him to get better."

I was real happy about Earnest getting back to praying again. I'm gonna worry less about lightning.

Dear John,

My Uncle Bob's gonna be O.K. I saw him in the hospital. He said, "I'll tell you how it happened but you gotta keep it a secret."

I promised but that wasn't good enuff. He made me swear which is a thing I never do under normal conditions. So he told me when he's in that basement, he knows there's a leak because he can smell the gas but there's no light bulb in the basement and his flashlight's in the Brooklyn Union Gas Company truck. The smell is called fumes and its getting worser and the leak is getting worser. So Uncle Bob gotta fix it real fast. But he can't see. He lights a match.

Dear John,

I'd wonder if fumes from all them peanut butter sandwiches can blow up the school.

Dear John,

I saw Uncle Bob again today. He's getting out of the hospital tomorrow. I told him he gotta be more careful about lighting matches to find gas leaks. Uncle Bob told me that he lights matches hundreds of times because it's a real fast way to find gas leaks. This was only the second time he got blowed up.

Dear John,

My mom says God was watching over Uncle Bob and that's why he don't get dead in the explosion. She remembers him in her prayers every day espeshally since he got blown out of the last cellar.

Dear John,

Me and Earnest like playing war. Last night we went over to this new park what ain't even open yet but it got a wire gate all around it just like the prisoner of war camp. We're soldiers going to break in and help all the Americans excape. And we're gonna blow up this ammyounition dump what's in the camp. But the dump is guarded by Nazis and Commeys. We get down on hands and knees and crawl real slow. The guards don't see us. So we get to the fence and pull out wire cutters. Earnest holds the first wire and I snip. Nothing happens. Dull cutters. The soldiers gotta wait in the prisoner of war camp til tomorrow night.

Dear John,

We go over to the park again tonight but we bring out the plyers and screw drivers what my uncle Bob gave me. We open up the two screws and bolts at the bottom of the fence and Earnest pulls the fence back just enough. No Nazi or Commey guards around but we keep low. I crawls through the fence first and Earnest comes through and rips his pants. I never heard such a loud rip. We get down to listen. No Nazis. No Commeys. Up and run for the brick building and up against the wall.

Commando Earnest whispers, "You got the dynamite?"

"Yea," and I show him the firecracker, a cherry bomb with a real long fuse. The door to that little house opens easy—no lock yet. So I light the match and we throw the dynamite in the ammyounishun dump and we run back to the fence.

But then this big cop's jumping the fence and saying, "Stop or I'll shoot." Bang, the firecracker in the park house goes off and the cop swings around and shoots the door to the little house. Earnest and me run and try to get through the hole in the fence but it's too small for both of us at the same time. We're stuck. We can't move. The cop is standing over us with his gun pointing right at us. We surrender. I'll tell you more in the morning. I'm real tired. It's been a real busy night.

Dear John,

I was telling you about how me and Earnest got taken war prisoners. Well after we surrendered, we got searched. The cop finds tools in Earnest's pocket. Then the cop ask us a million questions but all we said was our name and school locker number. The cop was mad mostly because he ripped his pants too and wasted one bullet.

Well, when he drives us to the police station with the car windows open, Earnest reaches in his pocket and then puts his hand out the window and dumps all our spy tools all over Brooklyn. I can hear them bouncing off the sidewalk and streets but the cop don't hear a thing.

He drives us to the precinct and we go up long stairs and get to a great big desk. The cop tells the desk Sargent, "O'Reilley, I caught these two breaking into the park with these burgalar tools."

"Let's see the evidence, Potter," says O'Reilley.

And then Potter checks Earnest's pockets. Empty. Now he's real mad.

Potter tells me to go into this small room. It got a chair, a table and a big floor lamp. He tells me to sit in the chair and don't move but then I hear Potter talking to Earnest and I get up and sneak over to the door. I can see just a little through a crack in the door.

Earnest's telling him about the Jenovesee Conference but Potter don't pay attention just like in the movie. I hear slap, slap. Then I seen him punch Earnest in the gut. He asks, "Where are them burgalar tools?"

Earnest tells him his name and locker number.

But then Potter says he's gonna send Earnest up the river. I think maybe that's like the concentration camps what got a gas chamber.

189

So Earnest tells him something what ain't true just to get the cop off his back. He says, "In the sand pit in the park. I throwed them in the sand pit."

So Potter stomps out of the precinct and gets back into the patrol car and goes lookin for tools what ain't there.

Then I hear Sargent O'Reilley walking across the squeaky floor and he opens the door. By then I'm back sitting in the chair. Then Sargent O'Reilly comes in and says, "Empty your pockets and put everything on the table."

Bolts and screws and nuts and a cat's foot roll all over the table and then my regular rosary beads are in the bottom of my pocket. So I pull them out. He looks at the stuff and then talks real nice and tells me wait in this here room.

Then another cop comes in and says, "Put everything back in your pockets. I'm taking you home."

The cop takes me home in the patrol car and tells me not to go near that park again and to stay out of trouble. I just shakes my head and says, "O.K."

I don't know what happened to Earnest. Maybe they gassed him.

Dear John,

Earnest's face is swollen and blue under both his eyes but he's still alive and he told me what happened. He says that he was looking through the crack in the door when the Sargent O'Reilley tells me to empty my pockets. Well, he seen the look on the sargent's face. So he got a good idear.

When the desk Sargent comes in Earnest got his rosary beads out and he's saying a real sorrowful mystry. Earnest acts it out with tears and all. He puts his hands together and says, "Hail Mary, full of grease, the lord is with knee . . ."

"What are you doing, kid?" O'Reilley ask.

Earnest opens his eyes and looks up real sad like and says, "I know sir that Mary, the Mother of God, will ask Jesus to help me get out of this fix what I'm in. I just gotta ask."

Well the desk sargeant looks at him and says, "I'm sure He will, son."

Earnest tells me, "When he says 'son,' then I figger it's gonna be O.K. The Lord helps them what prays."

But then Potter comes back in the patrol car with no tools. Earnest figgers maybe he'll get another rap on the ears. But then he hears low talking . . . mumble . . .

"You're kidding. I got them for burgulary."

The low voice . . . mumble . . . "No. Absolutely not. They go down town tonight." More mumble . . . The door slams. It's all quiet. Wait. Wait. The front door opens and Earnest hears Potter and Sargent O'Reilly talking again . . . mumble . . . mumble.

Earnest says, "Now I really do start praying, Please God, I ain't foolin now. You gotta get me out of this jam and if you do, I'll do something real good for you. I'll become a priest or a monk or a nun or something! Anything you want, just give me a sign."

Potter walks into the room and sees Earnest got five rosary beads now and praying for real on all five of them. He walks real slow and smoke is almost coming out of his ears.

"Put them beads away. They're taking you home. But first put them beads away and stand up."

Earnest puts them back around his neck. Slap! Punch! Potter gets him on the left side of his face and it sends Earnest onto the floor. Earnest says, "I was gonna stay down for the count. But then O'Reilley comes in and gives Potter a real dirty look."

By this time the other cop is back from taking me home and he takes Earnest home.

Dear John,

Earnest believes in prayer again. He told me, "The power of prayer, it done the trick."

Chapter 7
Rules

Sixth Grade

Dear John,

I didn't really mean to find it. I was just looking around for a pair of socks in my sister's room. Maggie always gets mine and hers mixed up. So here I am looking in her dresser drawer and I give it a pull but it's stuck. So I pull harder and harder and then WAM I'm sitting on the floor with the drawer on top of me. But I look up into the place where the drawer comes out and I see something stuck way in the back in there. Well maybe it's something real important. So I reach all the way in and I grab it. It's says Diary. She had it hid pretty good.

Dear John,

The nun brings in the big chart and it got 15 rules on it. She says when we brake a rule we gotta write the rule maybe a hundred times, maybe five hundred times. I hate stuff like that.

Dear John,

I get home from school about twenty minutes before Maggie cause she goes to Eastern District High School. So I got just a little time each day to keep up with things in her diary. Maggie hid it pretty good but she shoulda hid it better. There's stuff in there what nobody should know about. But it's OK for you to know about it, John, because you ain't gonna tell nobody. I just gotta remember to hide this notebook real good—speshally I gotta hide her diary back in the eggsact same place where Maggie hides it. Well you're probly dying to know what Maggie's up to, right? Well so far I can tell you she really goes for this guy in her high school and his name is Joe Volare. I didn't know she even likes him but she wrote that he really sends her. Tingles her up and down just by thinking about Joe Volare. Anyways she goes for him because he sends her. That means she's in love. My mom ain't gonna like this because my mom don't like Joe Volare none. My mom works in the high school cafeteria. She always says bad things about Joe Volare because him and his friends are real loud and rowdy. I ain't gonna snitch. It ain't right. I ain't no blabber mouth. I ain't no stool pigeon. Besides Maggie would kill me.

Dear John,

There's a new kid just moved in next door. His name's Johnny Volare and he just moved to Brokklyn. He's from Queens. I ask him if he knows Joe Volare who goes to Eastern District High School and Johnny Volare says, "Sure, I know him. He's my cousin."

Dear John,

My mom's real upset. She don't like the way the block's changing. The neighborhoods going down. Too many Italians moving in. But then my Mom stops talking and she puts her finger up to her chin, a thing what she does when she's thinking about serius stuff, and then she says, "It could be a lot worse. What if Jews moved in?"

Dear John,

I don't know about my Mom. I think she's got some predjudishes.

Dear John,

My mom and dad was up in the Remson's partment real late last night. This morning I ask how come you was up there so long. Mr. Remson works for Schaeffer beer company and he got promoted and transferred to Albany and that's real far away. They gotta move. So they was talking about the good old days. They said that they laffed a lot when they remembered the block party after the war when I was just a little kid. When they played the Star Spangled Banner, me and Diane Williamson danced in the street. You're supposed to stand still when you hear the Star Spangled Banner. That's a rule. Well I know that now. I guess everybody on the block thinks me and Diane Williamson was real jerks. I remembered all about that but I been trying to forget about it. It's embarassing. You better not tell nobody else about that, John, because everything I tell you is a secret and the same goes for all the secret stuff what Maggie writes in her diary.

Dear John,

My dad likes lots of beer. Every night he drinks a big bottle and he let's my mom have a glass. My dad says, "Schaefer is the one beer to have when you're having more than one."

Dear John,

The moving truck's here when I get home from school today. I thought it was moving the Remsons out but they was gone this morning. The truck was moving another family in. I see this girl probly about my age.

So I innerduced myself to her, "Hi. I'm Bobby Anderson. What's your name?"

"Barbara Zuccaman."

"You moving in upstairs?"

"Yes."

"Where you from?"

"Manhattan, Lower East Side."

"How come your moving here? Don't you like the Lower East Side no more?"

"Sure but my dad's a cantor and he's gonna work in the Synagogue."

"You mean you're Jewish?"

"Yes. Why?"

"Uh, nothing, no reason, It's just there ain't many Jewish peoples around here. That's O.K. and all. It's just that this ain't a Jewish neighborhood. Mostly Irish and Italians live around here. Mostly everybody is Catholic and goes to St. Mary's except for maybe a couple of Polish peoples what go to their own Catholic church in Greenpernt.

I thought she needed to know more so I told her. "There are some Jewish people what live near the Williamsburg

Bridge but they dress funny. They got long black coats and the men got long hairy curls on the sides of their head and big black hats. They're real strange looking, real weird."

She said, "Well here's my dad. Dad, this is Bobby Anderson."

Barbara Zuccaman's dad got a long black coat and long hairy curls on the sides of his head and a big black hat. Barbara Zuccaman is looking at me and she smiles.

Dear John,

The nun says that if you ain't Catholic, you can't go to heaven. God made that rule along time ago. That's tuff for Barbara Zuccaman. She's pretty and nice. I told my mom Barbara Zuccaman's nice but my mom says she got a Jewish nose and her father dresses real strange. My mom says their moving in is not good for the neighborhood.

Dear John,

Joe Volare's Catholic but he don't never go to church. Maggie wrote that she don't care. He really sends her anyways.

Dear John,

I'm not exactly up to date with reading Maggie's diary. I gotta be real careful so she don't suspect nothing.

Dear John,

My sister and Joe Volare kissed about a week ago. They was in the school basement and nobody was around and he kisses her right on the mouth. Her diary's getting real inneresting. She really goes for him.

Dear John,

Me and Earnest was going to church, the nine o'clock Mass, on account of it's being Sunday. But we was going by the candy store and Earnest says he needs a two cent plain because he's so thirsty.

"O.K." I told him. "but you can't go to communion if you drink a two cent plain."

He says he can't go to communion anyways because he ain't been to confection in about a hundred years.

I watched Earnest drink his two cent plain and got real thirsty too. So I got a black and white which cost three cents. But then we hear the bells at St. Mary's ringing and we know we're late. So we run to the school yard where all the classes line up to go to church. Gone. They're all in church. Well it's real bad if you walk in late. The nuns get real mad and give those terrible looks.

Earnest says it would be wrong to walk in late because it ain't right to get the nuns mad. It's probably a big sin to get nuns mad espeshully in church.

I figgered he's right. It ain't right for us to get the nuns mad in church. So we jist sit on a stoop across the street and talk some more.

Dear John,

Barbara Zuccaman goes to P.S. 18 where I use to go. She can't go to St. Mary's because she's Jewish and all. I think she's nice. Too bad she can't go to heaven.

Dear John,

We learn that you gotta go to church every Sunday and if you don't go just one Sunday, you can't go to heaven. Joe

Volare ain't going to heaven. I just remember something. Me and Earnest ain't going up there neither.

Dear John,

You gotta keep lots of rules to get to heaven.

Dear John,

Barbara Zuccaman is sitting on the stoop when I get home from school today. I figger I better tell her the bad news. "You can't get to heaven because you're Jewish."

She don't say nothing. She just gets up and walks into the apartment house. I figger I'm doing her a favor telling her about it. But she don't act like I done her a favor.

Dear John,

Maybe it was the wrong thing to tell Barbara Zuccaman. Maybe I gotta learn to keep my big fat mouth shut.

Dear John,

Me and Earnest and Nicholas and Peter Ackerman and Patrick Garino and Johnny Volare are playing stick ball and it's tied, 3 to 3. Johnny Volare is up at bat and he swings and misses. Well, he's out. In stick ball one swing and you're out. Right John? That's the rule. Everybody knows that rule. You get three swings in baseball but one swing in stick ball. So it's three out and we start coming in and Johnny Volare swings again and hits the ball over our heads and then he runs around the bases and he says he got a home run.

"NO, you're out."

"No I ain't. I got a home run."

Well me and Earnest and Nicholas get real mad. But Peter Ackerman and Patrick Garino just stand there and don't say nothing. They know the rules but they just keep their mouths shut because they are on Johnny Volare's side. Johnny Volare says that the rule is three swings just like in baseball. But in baseball you got a pitcher. In stick ball you throw the ball up yourself. If you can't hit the ball the first time, tuff!

Johnny Volare says, "That's the rule in Queens."

Earnest says, "Well you ain't in Queens no more, Toto. You're in Brooklyn now and the rule in Brooklyn is one strike and you're out!"

We spend the rest of the time fighting about the rule and then Patrick Garino gotta go eat supper. So they say they win. They win? That's a lot of foney balognee! It's a tie.

Dear John,

Earnest and me are talking about that stick ball game and Earnest says Toto don't know where he is at and he better work at fitting into Brooklyn or he ain't gonna make it to the Emerald City. I ask Earnest, "Why are you talking about Toto when the new kid's name is Johnny Volare and what's the Emerald City?

Earnest says, "Everybody gotta figure out the rules when you are in a real strange place like Brooklyn."

Dear John,

I've been thinking about the rules that you gotta keep to get to heaven. If you miss going to Mass just one Sunday, you can't get into heaven. That's a pretty tuff rule. Sometimes me and Earnest are on our way going to church but you know how it is. We don't always get there on time so we don't get there at all. But today I told Earnest the bad news. We ain't going to heaven. He's real surprised.

"Who says?"

"The nun says so. You was in school when she told us that."

Well it is news to Earnest but that figgers. Sometimes Earnest is in school when his brain ain't. Well Earnest ain't all that upset because he figgered it ain't worth it. Too much trouble, too many rules. It ain't worth it speshally when you gotta sit around and do nothing when you get there anyways. Heavens gotta be boring.

Dear John,

We got so mad about Johnny Volare that we forgot to get the ball what he hit down the street. It was my brand new Spalding. Gone forever!

Dear John,

We can get another chance to go to heaven but you gotta tell the priest in confeshon what you done. Our class went today. So I go in the box and the little door opens and the priest says something and I smell his cigar breath.

After I stop coffing, I say, "Bless me father for I have sinned. Coff, coff. Me and Earnest don't go to 9 o'clock mass last Sunday and once last month and two times the month before and a cupula more times what I forget about."

The priest says I should try to go every Sunday and he asks will I try to go regular like?

Oh, sure. I ain't gonna miss it no more because I wanna go to heaven and all. Then the priest says that God forgives me and then stuff in Latin what I don't understand but it's O.K. because God understands. Latin is what God talks.

Dear John,

Earnest went to confeshon but he don't tell the priest nothing about not going to Mass on Sunday because he says he don't snitch on nobody, not even on himself. I told him you gotta snitch on yourself or you can't go to heaven. It's a rule. But he says when he gotta go to confeshon he don't tell nothing bad about himself. I ain't telling Earnest but it's O.K. He can still get to heaven because I told the priest for both of us.

Dear John,

Barbara Zuccaman don't talk to me no more.

I seen her coming down the stairs and I say, "Look I only said that about heaven because I figger you should know just in case you wanna go. I hear it's a real swell place."

She just goes by but she don't say nothing. I gotta learn to keep my big fat mouth shut.

Dear John,

We're eating dinner tonight and my sister says that Joe Volare is a nice boy. My mom drops her fork and my dad gives Maggie an evil eye. I figger he knows Joe Volare too.

He don't because he says, "That's an Italian name. Is this Joe Volare Italian?"

My sister says she don't know. She knows. She wrote it in her diary—something about Joe Volare being a red hot Italian lover. I keep my big mouth shut real tight. It ain't easy but I'm learning to keep my big mouth shut.

Dear John,

We're learning about heaven and all about the rules what you gotta do to get there and how you know everything in heaven and you just sit around and don't gotta do nothing but be happy forever and ever and eternity.

So the nun ask what eternity means.

Peter Ackerman says it means forever.

I think about my Spalding ball, a brand new one, nice and pink. It don't even flook when you bounce it. I paid whole dime for it and now it's gone forever.

"Master Bobby Anderson," My name, she just called my name.

"Uh, yes, Sister?"

"Well answer my question."

Think fast. What was she talking about? Don't remember. Oh, eternity.

"Yes, sister, well, it's like my Spalding ball."

She don't like my answer. Now I gotta write rule number three, I must pay attention a hundred times.

Dear John,

Now the nun says, only perfect people can go to heaven. That leaves me and Earnest out. It leaves out almost everybody I know, except maybe Christine Carney. Earnest says if she's going to heaven, he'd rather wait outside. I told Earnest that if Christine Carney's there, she'd hafta be in another room. If she's in the same room with us, we ain't gonna be happy. If it ain't happy, it ain't heaven.

Dear John,

Maggie and Joe Volare are sure doing a awful lot of kissing. They kissed three times in the school basement, two times in the hallway, three times behind a wall in the school lunchroom. I'm court up all the way to yesterday.

Dear John,

The nun tells Christine Carney to take the attendance record to the Principal's Office. Christine Carney always gets to be a monitor because all the teachers think she's just so wonderful.

Then the nun goes out of the room to talk to the nun next door and lots of us are talking and throwing paper and she walks in and sees this paper airplane landing on her desk. Perfect landing. Earnest is getting good at lots of things.

She says, "Who is responsible for this outrageous behavior?" What she really wants to know is who throwed the paper airplane but she got a strange way of asking that.

Well, nobody snitches. That's mainly because Christine Carney ain't there. Then the nun says it matters nothing to her because God knows who is responsible for such outrageous behavior and God will tell her who misbehaved when she gets to heaven and then she'll know. She says God is watching us all the time and is gonna tell her when we break rules and commit sins.

Dear John,

Earnest said something so bad that I don't wanna even write it but being that you ain't gonna tell nobody, John, I'll tell you. Earnest says, "God's a snitch."

Dear John,

Ring, ring, ring. The door bell. My mom answers it. It's Ronny Hayes. He works for the florist and he got a big package.

My mom asks him, "What's this?"

"A plant for you, Mrs. Anderson."

Then she says, "Thank you."

Ronny Hayes keeps standing there with his hand out. It almost got squished when my mom closes the door. She brings the big package into the kitchen and takes off the paper. It's a gigantic plant with big leaves. She says, "It's a Philadelphian. Oh, isn't this nice."

"Thank you Alfred." She thinks my dad sent it.

But he's just as surprised as her. Then she finds this card and reads it. She turns white. It's from Joe Volare! Hey, John, Joe Volare either got rocks in his head, or he's trying to get around my mom so he can go out with Maggie.

Dear John,

It's Sunday and it's dinner time and we're having southern fried chicken what I love most of all in the whole woirld and everything is real nice and peaceful. Then out of the blue Maggie says Joe Volare asks her out on a date. That was the end of a very nice peaceful southern fried chicken dinner. Lots of yelling and tears and Maggie runs into her room and SLAM goes the door. Nobody's hungry no more. My mom and dad get up and leave and here I am sitting at the kitchen table with four plates of chicken. Well, no sense in letting it all go to waste so I change seats and move around the table so I can better eat some of the southern fried chicken what nobody else wants.

Dear John,

I got all court up with reading the diary. Maggie is gonna go out with Joe Volare anyways. I read it. Maggie and Joe Volare are going to a party. She's gonna meet him on the corner at 8 tomorrow night. I don't know how Maggie's gonna pull this off. But it's gonna be fun to watch.

Dear John,

She done it and she don't even know how much of a help I am. I'll tell you about it. Tonight Maggie says she ain't feeling good so she's gonna go to bed. It's only 7:30. So she goes in her room and I check about half an hour later. My mom and dad are watching *I Love Lucy* and they're laffing pretty loud.

I open her door real slow. I whisper real low, "Maggie, you ain't in there are you?"

I see the covers all wrinkled and a big lump in the middle of the bed. Tip toe over to the bed.

Whisper, "Maggie."

Nothing. I check the covers. Pillows. She ain't there. Then I go into the kitchen and check the kitchen window. It ain't locked. She got out down the fire scape. I go back in the living room.

My mom says, "Wake up Maggie and tell her Rock Hudson is on. She likes him and she'll be real mad if she misses him."

"O.K."

So I go into her room and say, "Maggie, wake up, Rock Hudson's on."

Then I say, like in her voice but kinda sick, "Don't bother me, Bobby. I don't wanna see no Rock Hudson. I'm sick."

Then I go back to the living room and I says, "Maggie don't wanna see Rock Hudson. She's sick."

My mom says she gotta be real sick not to wanna see Rock Hudson. He's the kind of boy she should be wanting to date.

I figger it's because Rock Hudson ain't Italian.

Dear John,

I was just going to the bathroom and I got this terrible feeling. I remembered what the nun says. God's watching all the time. I like privacy when I go to the bathroom.

Dear John,

I hear the T.V. just got turned off. Maggie still ain't home. I'm going to bed.

Dear John,

Maggie forgot last night that my dad always checks and locks the windows before he goes to bed. Speshally the window with the fire scape. He puts two chains on the door too. But I remembered. So I staid awake until I heard snoring, one loud and one soft. I got up and went to the kitchen and unlocked the window. Then I went back to bed. This morning everything was just as usual. It's Saturday and Maggie always sleeps late on Saturday. I'm eating some left over southern fried chicken for lunch by the time Maggie's door opens. She walks out rubbing her eyes and yawning. Joe Volare should see her now. She looks like a squirrel with curlers. It ain't a pretty sight. But she pulled it off real good. I'm real proud of her.

Dear John,

Just me and Maggie were home today and I was in my room and I hear Maggie talking to somebody in the living room. I went in to see who was there but there ain't nobody there. Maggie's talking love stuff to the philadelphian.

Dear John,

Good thing for Maggie I been reading her diary and keeping up with things. She's gonna keep needing my help.

Dear John,

It snowed last night and this morning the radio says the schools in Brooklyn are all closed. I love snow days especially when it's Friday and that means a long weekend.

We had a big snowball fight this morning so me and Earnest and Nicholas figgered it would be a good idear to eat lunch while our coats and gloves are drying out on the radiator in my apartment. It's Friday so you get two choices, tuna or peanut butter. I'm having a peanut butter and jelly open sandwich, no top piece of bread. It tastes better that way.

My mom's standing there in the kitchen cutting a piece of bread and Earnest comes right out and says, "I seen your sister out with Joe Volare Friday night."

I drops my peanut butter and jelly open sandwich right on the floor. PLOP! They never land with the bread down.

I leave it there and say, "No, you didn't. She was sick in bed Friday night. It was somebody else"

And Earnest says, "YOW! Ouch!"

He says that because I kick him real hard on the shin. "What the . . ." He stops what he's gonna say because my mom's there but she ain't really listening. "I seen them going to the party at . . . YOW!"

Then I take a piece of paper and write SNITCH on it. He gets the pernt and keeps his big mouth shut.

He's rubbing both legs when my mom turns and says, "What did you say? Something about Maggie with Joe Volare?"

Earnest don't know what to say but it don't matter none because Nicholas is walking around the table and he starts saying, "YOW!" Nicholas slides right past the table. His legs go flying up into the air and he lands in the kitchen closet upside down. Me and Earnest turn Nicholas right side up and get out of there before my mom has any more questions. My peanut butter and jelly open sandwich saved Maggie's life.

Dear John,

I seen Maggie kissing the philadelphian on one of its big green leaves.

Dear John,

Me and Earnest and Nicholas and Johnny Volare are playing Ring-O-Leeveo. It's like tag but you got this jail and you can free another guy what's on your team. So I'm "it" and I got Nicholas and Earnest already in the den and I'm looking for Johnny Volare. I gotta keep one eye on Nicholas and Earnest so Johnny Volare don't come sneaking around and touch them and yell Ring-O-Leeveo, 1-2-3, 1-2-3, 1-2-3. The jail where Nicholas and Earnest gotta stay is on the stoop of my apartment house. So I'm walking down the street about four houses down and I'm passing a big pile of empty garbage cans and I hear a noise. I stop and listen. It's either a cat, a rat or a Johnny Volare. I back up on tiptoe and pick up a little rock and toss it right on the other side of the garbage can. BONK, OUCH! It wasn't no cat. It wasn't no rat. They don't say ouch. Then crash the garbage cans are falling right in front of me. Rattle, Rattle, crash bang. And Johnny Volare comes running out from behind them garbage cans. He's heading right for the stoop but he's got three houses to go. I gotta tag him before he gets there and frees the prisoners. All of a sudden he trips and slips on his shoe lace and falls. I'm right behind him and ready to tag him when he reaches up and touches a fence and yells, "Safe base."

I tag him but he yells, "You can't tag me when I touch something and call safe base."

"What're you talking about? There's no safe base in Ring-O-Leeveo."

He says, "You can call safe base and then you can't get tagged."

"No."

"Yes."

"No."

"Yes."

"That ain't no rule."

"Yes, it's a rule. We play it that way in Queens."

"Well, it ain't no rule in Brooklyn."

"You cheat."

"You cheat."

Well, I'm about ready to slug Johnny Volare for calling me a cheat when Nicholas' mother comes along and says we gotta stop playing here because we're making too much noise and Mrs. Kresselmyer is sick and we're gonna wake her up.

So we all go home. Anyways it was getting dark.

They play with different rules in Queens. Queens gotta be a really stupid place.

Dear John,

Earnest says, "Toto's cruising for a bruising."

Dear John,

Maggie was kissing a big green leaf on the philadelphian today and my mom walks into the room. Maggie makes like she's just looking at the leaf but my mom seen her kissing it. My mom goes over to the plant and pulls off the leaf what Maggie was kissing and tells Maggie, "Young lady, you better learn to control yourself and be very careful where you put your mouth." Then she throws the leaf in the garbage. I seen the whole thing because I was hiding behind the player piano.

Dear John,

Now we're up to 20 rules and the nun writes them on the black board and when we break a rule we gotta write the rule hundreds of times. The nun says that's gonna help us be better and more responsible people and improve are handwriting at the same time.

Dear John,

Maggie and Joe Volare had a real swell time at the party Saturday night. It was romantic the way she wrote about it. I don't like that stuff for myself but it's O.K. for Maggie and all. He was waiting for her at the bottom of the fire scape and he even got a taxi to take them to go just 5 blocks and all the other kids were real impressed when the taxi drives up to the party. They danced every dance and then he walks her home to the fire scape. Then they kiss a lot. I guess she likes that kind of thing because he really sends her. When she goes up the fire scape, she tells him to stop looking up her dress.

Dear John,

Babies what are born and die right away can't go to heaven because they got sin all over them even if they don't do nothing wrong! They got original sin from Adam and Eve, what they done by eating a bad apple.

Dear John,

Earnest is gonna be in big trouble with God. Earnest says that it ain't fair that babies can't go to heaven. I think he's saying that God ain't fair and that's definitely not a good thing to be thinking about. But then I told Earnest that the nun said babies can go right to heaven if they get baptized and that cleans off that original sin what they got from Adam and Eve's bad apple. That don't make Earnest happy. I worry about Earnest's soul. I mean if I get to heaven and Earnest ain't there, heaven ain't gonna be all that much fun.

Dear John,

It'd be real bad for Maggie if mom ever goes looking for socks in Maggie's bottom drawer.

Dear John,

The nun told us that people what ain't Catholics sometimes can get to heaven anyways. But they gotta get burned to death and that's baptism by fire. If they don't know nothing about Catholics and if they never commit a mortal sin, and if they are real responsible people, and if they just wanna do good stuff, then they get baptized by desire. The other way is by water getting poured over their heads. The nun says anybody can baptize somebody. You don't gotta be a priest. You just gotta say "I baptize you in the name of the Father, Son and Holy Ghost" and you gotta pour the water at the same time.

Dear John,

That philadelphian ain't looking good.

Dear John,

The nun told us about a nurse what is a Catholic but she's a nurse at a Jewish hospital in New York City. The nun said the nurse sent a lot of babies to heaven. This is what she done. These babies were born real sick and this nurse would take some water and put it on their heads and baptize them and then even the Jewish babies got sent to heaven.

Dear John,

My Uncle Bob got me a real swell ball pernt pen but I can't use it in school. The nun says ball pernt pens ain't legal and you can't write checks with them and they are no good and they won't last long and everybody will be back to writing with fountain pens again and ball pernt pens mess up your handwriting and she got lots of reasons but the main thing is that it's against the rules to write with ball pernt pens. No ball pernt pens allowed. It's rule number 15.

Dear John,

My ball pernt pen is so good you can't hardly tell the difference except it don't smear and blot like fountain pens.

Dear John,

My ball pernt pen works better than my fountain pen. The nun don't know that because nobody never gives her free stuff.

Dear John,

I done my homework with my ball pernt pen and it done the trick. I made it look like a fountain pen. All I done was to take my fountain pen and write on top of a coupla letters here and there and I blotted them with my blotter so they smeared a little and the nun went for it. She says it's the neatest what I ever wrote.

Dear John,

I left the cap off my ball pernt pen and it stopped writing.

Dear John,

The priest is coming to talk to our class next week. The nun says he's gonna talk to all the boys first and then all the girls. I don't know what that's all about.

Dear John,

I told Earnest about my ball pernt pen what stopped writing. Earnest looks at it and then he takes a match and lights it and put the pernt of my pen right in the flame. Now my ball pernt pen writes again! Earnest got some pretty good idears.

Dear John,

The nun keeps telling us about how God is watching all the time and how he keeps real good records and he don't forget nothing what we do. She says when she goes to heaven, God will tell her everything about each one of us. Every time I think about it I stop what I'm doing because I don't want God to see me doing it. I definitely don't want God telling the nun about what I do. Sometimes I ain't even doing nothing bad. Sometimes I'm doing something good and I stop. Sometimes I'm doing something that ain't neither good or bad and I stop. I don't like being spied on. He probly knows about my ball pernt pen and He's gonna tell the nun when she gets to heaven. He's gonna say, "Bobby Anderson broke rule 15." That's creepy.

Dear John,

I gotta write rule number 2 and rule number 5 two hundred times each. At least they're short ones. Rule number 2 is, "I must not tell lies." Rule number 5 is, "I must not talk in school." See I can't bring my ball pernt pen to school. I was just asking Peter Ackerman for some of his ink because my pen runs out. When the nun walks in the room, she hears somebody whispering and says, "Who was whispering."

Nobody answers. Then THE BIG ONE. "If no one tells me who was whispering, everybody must write all the rules a hundred times."

Quick as a flash Christine Carney's hand is up. "Bobby Anderson was whispering." It's better when Christine Carney is a monitor and going on errands all the time.

Dear John,

Earnest told me not to worry about the punishment what I gotta write. He says he'll help me. I ask him how. Earnest tells me to come over his house later because he got a surprize for me.

Dear John,

I got my punishment done real fast. Earnest helped. Remember the writing machine I already told you about? Well Earnest's dad made one what's speshally made for ball pernt pens. Earnest puts ten ball pernt pens through the holes in the wood and lines them up. Then he puts a thick rubber band around all the pens and straightens everything out so that each pen pernt touches the looseleaf paper.

Earnest says the only problem with it is it looks too good. It don't look like a fountain pen. So I take a fountain pen and make some smears and blotter them. Earnest says we're a good team.

Dear John,

I know God's watching me all the time and that's a problem. He probly knows all about the ball pernt pens and He's gonna tell the nun about my breaking rule 15.

Dear John,

I told Earnest about my problem about God telling the nun about all the bad stuff I do and all.

Earnest says, "What you got there are two different problems. The first problem is that God is watching and that's probably O.K. because how else is He gonna know how we're doing and all? God's like the boss of the whole earth and he's responsible so he gotta see everything. But it's the second problem, the snitching part, that's the biggest problem. The nun thinks that God's gonna tell her everything what we do but I don't think God is gonna do that. God knows what ain't none of the nun's business. Maybe He is gonna tell her about the ball pernt pens but He ain't telling her nothing what's none of her business, like when we go to the bathroom and other stuff what I do there."

I don't ask Earnest about what that other stuff what he does in the bathroom. I don't ask because I don't wanna know.

Dear John,

The philadelphian looks real sick. The leaves ain't dark green no more. Most of them are getting yellow.

Dear John,

So Barbara Zuccaman is walking under my window and I pour some water on her head and say the holy baptizing words. She looks up at me with her hair all wet and says something like "Mushugana." She calls me that a lot. I think it ain't a good word. Anyways, now Barbara Zuccaman can go to heaven.

Dear John,

Maggie thinks my mom's spying on her in school. She wrote that she sees my mom sometimes up on the second floor. The cafeteria's in the basement. She told Joe Volare that they gotta be careful not to get court kissing.

Dear John,

They got court yesterday. They was holding hands in the stairway on the second floor and my mom opens the door and sees them. I feel sorry for Maggie. She musta wrote about it this morning before she goes to school.

Dear John,

Barbara Zuccaman don't unnerstand that I helped her get to heaven. I told her she's baptized now. I tell her maybe she don't appresheate it now but, when she gets to heaven, then she's gonna thank me. I followed the rules and she's baptized. She just looks at me, shakes her head and walks away.

Dear John,

The priest came to our class and talked to all the boys. All the girls had to go into the lunchroom and Father McNulty talked to them. The priest what talked to us is Father Smott. He told us now we are growing and our bodies are changing and sometimes we are gonna have some dreams, and they are called wet dreams but we should never ever touch arselves down there because it's very very sinful. Then he told us about what Eve done to Adam by tempting him to eat the apple what God said they shouldn't eat and he told us that girls sometimes tempt boys into being sinful because girls all got a little bit of Eve in them. So we should never get too close and touch girls even if they say stuff what can leave boys into temptshun and sin. We just gotta tell a girl to leave me not into temptshun.

Dear John,

Earnest said that Father Smott should know a lot about not touching girls because he doesn't just touch them. He hugs them all the time. Earnest is right about that. I see him all the time hugging girls. Maybe it's because priests can't get the temptshuns from girls.

Dear John,

They're having a great big fight right now in the kitchen. My mom says she don't want Maggie to go near Joe Volare no more.

Maggie is saying that Joe Volare is a real nice boy.

"No, he isn't," my mom just said.

Now they're both talking at the same time and I can't understand nothing what they're saying. O.K. Maggie just shut up.

But before she shuts up she said, "It's because he's Italian. You're predjudiced about Italians."

"No, that's not true. I like all people. It's just that he's not your type. Did you sneak out of here last Friday night and go to the dance with him?"

Maggie don't say nothing.

My mom says, "You can't go sneaking around and disobeying. This family has rules and your mother and father make those rules and you better learn to keep them if you intend to keep living with this family."

Maggie's crying, sobbing real soft, it's getting louder, and louder, now running, crying real loud. SLAM. She's in her room.

"Bobby. Bobby. Come here, right now."

Oh, Oh. That's my mom. I'm in big trouble.

Dear John,

My mom ask, "Did Maggie sneak out last Friday night?"

"How do I know? I was sleeping." I answered that way even though I know God is listening and watching everything. But I never did see her. Maybe she was under the bed. I don't know.

"Well you better never lie to me. Nobody can go out unless I know where they are."

Then she whispers to me, "If you see Maggie with Joe Volare, I want you to tell me. O.K.?"

I just shake my head up and down but when she turns around, I shook my head back and forth. So that wasn't no lie because I cancelled out the up and down with the back and forth head shaking and the most important thing is I had my fingers crossed all the time.

Dear John,

I asked Earnest, "Which is worser, to tell a lie or to snitch? It's one thing to know what's going on but it's another thing to snitch.

Earnest says, "That is a very good and deep question and I have to think of a real good way to get the right answer which is that the worser of the two is to snitch."

Dear John,

Maggie saved her lunch money and got some new fertilizer for the philadelphian plant but I think it's too late. It looks almost dead. Only five yellow leaves hanging on.

Dear John,

We was playing stick ball and I swing and missed and then I swing again and got on first base and Johnny Volare says, "You cheated. You can swing only one time and if you miss, tuff."

He plays Queens rules or Brooklyn rules, whatever works best for him.

Dear John,

Maggie's reading a book on how to get a nervous breakdown.

Dear John,

He done it again. Johnny Volare's gonna tag me and I touch a fence and yell, "Safe base."

And he says, "That ain't fair."

I don't know what rules he's playing with because he keeps changing them. Johnny Volare ain't playing fair.

Dear John,

Earnest and me walk home from school today. Earnest stops and pernts to Johnny Volare and he says, "There's Toto. He's cruizin for a bruising."

Dear John,

Barbara Zuccaman told me it's O.K. what I done. She forgives me. She says I don't mean no harm. I'm just ignorant.

Dear John,

Maggie's gonna quit Eastern District High School. My mom took her to the doctor because she's acting strange and nervous and the doctor says it's school that got her all nervous. So she's dropping out and going to work. Maggie wrote that she don't wanna be in school to be spied on. She wrote that my mom's got all the teachers spying on her and Joe Volare.

Dear John,

Maggie wrote that Joe Volare is real upset about Maggie dropping outta school. He says it's real important to get an education. He's gonna go to college and be an accountant. His dad don't want him driving no taxi like him.

Dear John,

Maggie got a job in Manhattan. She don't see Joe Volare much no more because she dropped out of Eastern District High School. She wrote that she's real sad and misses her friends at Eastern District. Specially she misses Joe Volare, but she's glad she ain't being spied on no more.

Dear John,

I got court writing with a ball pernt pen in school. Gotta write rule number 15 three hundred times. I'll use Earnest's writing machine and smear it.

Dear John,

The philadelphian plant died. I hadda bring it downstairs and throw it out. Funny thing. It was real dry. My mom watered it a lot but I don't think the way she done it helped. I seen her put lots of salt in the water.

Dear John,

Maggie wrote in her diary that she met another boy where she woiks. He's a janitor and he dropped out of high school last year. She's gonna go out with him. He's Irish and he's Catholic. It'll be O.K.

Chapter 8

Order in the Classroom

Sixth Grade

Dear John,

You gotta check out the garbage cans just about every day because you never know what good stuff people throw out. So this morning I am on my way to school and I check out the garbage cans just in case somebody throws away something valuabull. Well, I find this clock in a garbage can way down one of the alleys. I take it home and check it out real fast. The spring's busted. But it's a real good clock other than it don't work. I gotta get to school fast.

Dear John,

I was late for school today because of the clock and all. I got a tardy and the nun said I hadda stay after school and write I must not be tardy a hundred times. But then I waited after school and the nun never comes back. So I walked home. I ain't worried because she don't know my name. This nun forgets a lot.

Dear John,

Earnest told me when he walks into his kitchen at night and turns on the lights, it looks like the whole floor moves to the walls. It's the cockroaches running for cover. Earnest told me his mom and dad are thinking about moving out of the neighborhood because they hate all the cockroaches. My mom and dad are thinking about moving out because they hate the kind of people what are moving into the neighborhood.

Dear John,

Today I found a really good aquarium in the garbage. The glass got a crack but just only on one side. I tried putting water in it but it leaks. Other than that little problem it's a real good aquarium.

Dear John,

The nun told us a story about when she was a little girl in Ireland and about the fairy rings. The farmers take all the rocks from the land and puts them in the middle of the field real neat. They never plant potaters there or nothing because that's where the fairies live. It's a real interesting story except she told us that same story every day for the last week. The nun's kinda forgetful.

Dear John,

I told Earnest about the aquarium I found in the garbage and he asks me if we can trade because he needs an aquarium for an expeerment and he don't care if it leaks. When Earnest wants to trade, he really means he just wants me to give him the aquarium. Earnest don't got nothing I want.

Dear John,

This is the last week with this nun in 6A. Next week I get promoted to 6B and we get a different nun. I liked the nun in 6A because she's old and she forgets a lot. I don't care if she tells us the same stories over and over. The kids in 6B say that nun is O.K. She forgets a lot too.

Dear John,

All morning I been thinking how to fix that busted spring in that really great clock what don't work. I got an idear.

Dear John,

Everybody got promoted to 6B, even Earnest and Nicholas!

Dear John,

Earnest wanted to trade me something for the aquarium so I go to his apartment and look around his room. He don't got nothing I want so I just give him the aquarium. Besides Earnest already gives me lots of stuff like the rosary beads and all. I don't need no aquarium what leaks.

Dear John,

Two nuns are going to the old nun's home. The nun what don't remember too good in 6A and the nun we was sposed to get in 6B. A new nun what's taking her place came to our class today. She's new around here so she probably don't know much. She's kinda young. Maybe she just got ordained a nun or something.

Dear John,

Earnest says the nun is real young. So we gotta start her out good and help her learn about kids and how they always try to get away with doing bad stuff and all. He can teach her real good because he knows about that stuff.

Dear John,

Today was the first day with the new nun in 6B. She says we're going to take a spelling test every Friday and on every Monday we will take a pretest on the same words. We're going to be tested on Friday only if we don't get most of the words right on Monday. She says it's pretest on Monday and real test on Friday. I don't know what she is talking about.

Dear John,

I know what she is talking about. It means Christine Carney don't never gotta take a spelling test on Friday.

Dear John,

I seen Earnest looking in the garbage can in the alley behind Pepey's Butcher Shop today. I helped him look because we don't ushually like the same stuff. I figger I might find something I like in there but I don't mainly because I don't like stuff what got blood all over it. But Earnest found lots of empty cans and toilet paper rolls and egg cartons and he got a big bag of saw dust with lots of bloody stuff all over it.

Dear John,

Me and Earnest don't exctly go looking for the same stuff in the garbage. When I go garbage hunting, I find great stuff. When Earnest goes garbage hunting, he finds garbage.

Dear John,

Earnest told me, "You gotta see what I done with that aquarium."

So I go up to his apartment and there's the aquarium in his room. But his room's real dark. I can see the aquarium got 2 empty cans and 3 toilet paper rolls and 2 egg cartons and saw dust on the bottom with bloody clumps. But I can't see nothing else in the aquarium. Then Earnest says, "Watch this!" He puts on a light and the whole bottom of the aquraium looks like it's moving. The aquarium's filled with cockroaches.

Dear John,

Earnest is interested in really strange stuff.

Dear John,

Earnest told me, "There ain't nothing wrong with cockroaches so long as they're in the right place and our kitchen ain't the right place."

I agree with Earnest about that. The right place for cockroaches is Earnest's aquarium.

Dear John,

I really don't like to waste my brain on school. Boring. Too many important things to think about. I gotta think about stuff what I'm gonna do after school. When I get home, I don't waste no time thinkin about what to do. I just do it. Like this clock I'm gonna work on. The most fun is trying to fix stuff what's busted. I don't know why people throw stuff out just because it don't woik. But I'm glad they do because I love busted stuff.

Dear John,

Earnest says the new nun's kinda pretty but you can't really tell about nuns because they don't got no hair and you can't see what shape they're in.

Dear John,

Today's the nun's first day and she don't say much. She keeps looking for stuff in the closets and cleaning up from what the old nun left. She says she gotta get this classroom in order.

First she tells us to fold our hands and keep them on top of our desks. Then she puts her pencil inside her desk. Then she takes it out and puts it on top. Then she takes the eraser and puts it on the left side of the board, then on the right side. She looks at it again and then puts it right in the middle. She baby-foot walks in front of the board and meshures both sides of the blackboard to make sure the eraser's right exactly in the middle.

Dear John,

Peter Ackerman and Patrick Garino washed the blackboards three times. The nun still found some spots what are dirty. Then they washed it again. The rest of us did woikbook pages that the 6A nun forgot about. The new nun says every page gotta be done and they gotta be done right. This nun ain't likely to forget nothing.

Dear John,

Earnest says he's gonna give the new nun a test. He says it's a pretest to find out what she knows about kids and teaching and all.

Dear John,

It's the new nun's third day. The nun's writing on the blackboard and Earnest farts. She don't even turn around. It was Earnest's loudest fart ever.

Dear John,

Earnest says she kinda flunked his pretest because her face gets all red when he lets one go. It was only from under his arm pit but it sounded just like the real thing.

Dear John,

The nun's face turns red real easy. Today she's telling us that we gotta never touch ourselves and we gotta keep our hands on the top of the desk all the time. She tells us that our bodies are evil and our souls must control our sinful bodies. Her face keeps getting redder and redder and I don't know why. Earnest don't even make a fart noise.

Dear John,

I got a good idear during arithmetic about how to fix the clock. We was doing numbers and dividing. That's like times tables in a backward order. The nun draws this circle on the black board and it looks like my clock. I think I can fix it. I'll let you know, John.

Dear John,

The universe what with all the planets and stars and stuff is in perfect order. The heavens are in order but the world is out of order. That's what the nun says today.

Dear John,

I ask Earnest, "How do you catch so many cockroaches?"

He says, "They're real hard to catch because they run so fast. They eat almost anythng. They eat paper especially if it's wet. But then I found one in a jar what had some peanut butter in the bottom and it couldn't get out. So I got some more jars and put them on the floor with ice cream sticks for them to climb up. I put different kinds of food in the jars. The peanut butter worked O.K. They don't like the balogny all that much, too dry. They hated the piece of bacon. They like stuff what is wet and greasy. They loved the cinnamon buns from Randy's Restaurant the best. I got most of the cockroaches from Randy's buns."

Dear John,

Earnest says he's doing some expeerments with his cockroaches. He says it's all very scientific. But then he says that the nun don't got her science right. Earnest told me about a guy he knows what goes to college. The guy's name is Gus and he said that the heavens are not all that much in perfect order and that a scientist named Gail Leo found that the solar system and everything else is messy.

Dear John,

Now the nun's come up with another idear. She's gonna give us a test every Friday. All about the stuff what we learned during the week. Then she's gonna change all our seats every Monday morning in the order what we get on the tests. The smartest boy gets the first seat near the window and the dumbest gets the last seat in the third row. The girls all sit on the other side of the room, and the smartest girl is up front right near the door. I don't like this idear.

Dear John,

The nun told us we must study very hard for the tests each Friday.

Earnest asks the nun if she's gonna teach us how to study because he don't know the first thing about how to do it.

The nun looked at Earnest and said, "You should have learned that last year."

Dear John,

Earnest told me he asked the nun last year if she was gonna teach us how to study and the nun said, "You should have learned that last year."

Dear John,

The new nun says we gotta keep our hands busy doing good things because that way our souls will have more control over our evil bodies. She says our bodies are evil.

Dear John,

The nun tells us again about the heavens being in perfect order but the world is out of order. In that garden where Adam and Eve lived, nature was real good and there was order but Eve let the devil get things out of order when she got Adam to eat that apple. Now God wants help in getting the world back in order so it's as perfect as the heavens. So we all have to work hard at keeping things in order and that includes our books in our desks.

But then Earnest raises his hand and he says that Gail Leo proved that the heavens are not in good order and that . . .

But suddenly the nun is like right on top of Earnest and she's swinging her yard stick and she's screaming that Gail Leo was blastfeeming and that he was silenced by the Catholic Church for his errors. She shouts about how the heavens are where God lives and they have to be in absolute order because the heavens are beautiful and that means they are in perfect order.

When she finishes Earnest is almost under his desk because he figgers that yard stick is gonna smack him on his head any second. But the nun is just staring at Earnest and then she walks away but she keeps saying, "Bastfeemy, blastfeemy!"

Dear John,

The clock's spring is all twisted at one end and busted off. I'm working at it but it ain't fixed yet.

Dear John,

Earnest told me that cockroaches are smart but he got one that's like a genius for a cockroach. I'm gonna go over to see what he means.

Dear John,

We took them tests today because it's Friday and all. I figger I flunked them all because I don't remember the nun teaching what was on the test.

Dear John,

The nun don't forget nothing. She gives us these tests last Friday and today she changes all our seats. Everybody had to stand holding our books and then she calls out the smart kids' names first. Christine Carney's name got called first and she got the first seat for the girls. Then the nun calls Peter Ackerman's name and he gets the first seat for the boys. Then Patrick Garino got the second seat. Almost everybody is sitting and my arms are getting really tired because we gotta hold all our books. Then it's just me and Earnest and Nicholas standing. Then she calls my name. I sit in the last row for the boys in the third seat from the back of the room. Earnest sits in back of me and Nicholas is in the last seat.

Dear John,

I showed Earnest my clock what's a real good clock only it don't work. I told Earnest how I'm trying to fix it and all. Earnest laffs and says, "Clocks take time."

Earnest is right. It's taking me a coupla weeks and the clock still ain't fixed.

Dear John,

I sit in front of Earnest and he sits in front of Nicholas and you know what that means. It means I'm the third dumbest kid in the class this week. I like sitting near my friends and all but I don't like being the third dumbest kid in the class, espeshually when everybody knows it. Besides I gotta sit next to the third dumbest girl in the class, Frances Bartino. Peter Ackerman is the smartest boy in the room. But he don't got so good a grade as what Christine Carney gets. He only got a 95 average. She got a 99 average.

Dear John,

Christine Carney was all broke up that she don't get 100. The nun smiles at her and tells her she should try harder next week.

Dear John,

I tried to fix the busted spring. I cut out the twisted part but I can't get my fingers to pull the spring around. I'll keep working at it.

Dear John,

I seen Earnest's genius cockroach. Earnest got a shoe box and made a maze out of it. I seen mazes on paper before and you gotta get from one end to the other with a pencil. But the one Earnest made is like a big room with lots of cardboard walls and the cockroach starts at one end and has to go fast and find Randy's buns what's at the other end of the maze. Some of the hallways got dead ends. Earnest put a dumb roach in and it just went down every dead end and never got to Randy's buns. Then Earnest put his genius cockroach in and it went right down all the right hallways and not one dead end. That cockroach loves Randy's buns.

Dear John,

The nun yells if she sees your hands under the desk. She says, "I know what you're doing. It's sinful to touch yourself."

Dear John,

Sometimes I get real itchy on my back but I don't never scratch myself when the nun's looking. She gets real red and mad about us touching ourselves.

Dear John,

She done it again. This Friday test stuff is driving me nutty. Last week I don't day dream so much and worked a little. Now I'm still the dumb row but I moved up to the second seat from the front. Nicholas is still holding down last place and Earnest is still in the next to dumbest seat. Peter Ackerman got first place in the boys again and you know who got champ of the girls? Right! Christine Carney. She got a hundred average and the nun and Christine Carney are real happy.

Dear John,

The problem with sitting in the second seat is that I ain't near none of my friends.

Dear John,

I miss sitting near Earnest and Nicholas but Earnest keeps in touch in his own way. He farts hello when I walk past his seat. The nun's face gets red but she don't never look up.

Dear John,

Tomorrow we get them tests again. I figger, if I study and stop day dreaming in class, I can get into the second row at the back and then I can sit next to Earnest and Nicholas in the third row. I figger I can hold my own in that place. That ain't so bad. At least it ain't the third row. That's the last row for boys. When you sit in the last row, you sit next to girls and the girls in that row are dumb.

Dear John,

I found some pliers in the basement and I think I can pull that busted spring around on my clock.

Dear John,

Girls what are dumb are ugly too. I mean if they gotta be dumb, you think they might at least look good. God should make dumb girls pretty so everything is like fair.

Dear John,

I told Earnest about some girls being dumb and ugly too. Earnest figgers that when babies line up to get born, some get more good stuff and others get bad stuff. But it should be even. If you're dumb, you should get good looks but it don't always work out that way. It's like God gets some good and bad things out of order.

Dear John,

Earnest says some cockroaches are smart and some are dumb. But every one of them of them is definetely better looking than Christine Carney.

Dear John,

God got that one right. When Christine Carney was getting born, God gave her brains. It woiked out fair.

Dear John,

I blew it! I aimed wrong. I overshot the mark. I got into the first seat in the second row. I don't study at all but I do pay better attention. It's easy because I ain't near Earnest and Nicholas. But it ain't so bad. I sit right next to Patrick Garino. He got the first seat this week. Peter Ackerman sits right in back of Patrick Garino. Peter Ackerman ain't never gonna be far from that first seat.

Dear John,

Earnest is really getting to like his cockroaches. He's been looking at them real close with a magnifying glass. He says roaches got three parts to their bodies and six legs.

Dear John,

Earnest and me were going past the used book store on Metropolitan and we heard the owner telling a friend that cockroaches were eating some of his older books. Earnest figgers that's how his genius cockroach got to be so smart, all them books he digested.

Dear John,

It's kinda nice not being in the dumb row. This week I'm the smartest in the next to smartest row. That ain't so bad.

Dear John,

I fixed the clock's spring. Simple. It's twisted at one end so I just take it out with the pliers and cut out the twisted end and connect the bigger half up. It'll work but I'll just have to wind it every day. It sounds real pretty when the chimes ring. That's the best part, the chimes. They sound like a church.

Dear John,

Earnest told me, "Some cockroaches learn real good one day and the next day they forgot everything. One day they learn to run right to the Randy's buns but the next day I put them back in the maze and they go into all the dead ends and take a really long time to get to Randy's buns."

Dear John,

Nicholas is like some of them cockroaches what forget. He learns stuff one day and the next day it's all gone.

Dear John,

Almost everybody's getting a cold in my class. We're sneezing and coffing and blowing our noses all the time. Nicholas started the whole thing and he got the worst cold of all but he don't never stay home. It don't matter if Nicholas stays home because he don't learn much and whatever he learns, he forgets the next day.

Dear John,

The nun's got this thing about hands always gotta be on top of the desk. When she sees your hands under the desk, her face gets red and she shouts, "I know what you're doing. Put your hands on your desk."

Dear John,

I'm holding my own in the second row, first seat for three weeks now. Peter Ackerman and Patrick Garino really compete. That's a new word what we learned in vocabulary. It's a real good word. I heard it before because the Brooklyn Dodgers compete against the Giants for the pennant. But now I figger people can compete too. Patrick Garino and Peter Ackerman compete for the first seat and it's just like the Dodgers and Giants when they compete for the pennant. It's O.K. to compete in school like in baseball. Maybe it's even fun. I dunno.

Dear John,

Earnest made two new mazes out of shoe boxes what he found in the garbage. They're the same size and he put the walls in the same places. He made the walls by cutting them from the top and taping them to the bottom. He puts a cockroach in each box and they race. It's almost as good as watching the horse races.

Dear John,

I think it's fun for Peter Ackerman and Patrick Garino but it ain't no fun for Nicholas or Earnest. Everybody knows they can't compete for nothing but last place. I figger they know they can't compete and they just give up trying. It's like the Pittsburgh Pirates. They are always in last place. I don't wanna be on no last place team.

Dear John,

It ain't good for the cockroaches what always lose their races. Earnests flushes them down the toilet. He keeps the winners and they get treated real good. Earnest says he don't give them Randy's buns most of the time because they are in training and gotta eat right. He gives them some dog food because it's got good vitamins. Earnest finds empty cans of dog food but they ain't all empty. Earnest scrapes out the left overs and the cockroaches like it real good. But not as good as Randy's buns.

Dear John,

Earnest made a big sign for his cockroach boxes. It says, "Cockroach Racetrack."

Dear John,

That clock runs real good and chimes every twenty five minutes.

Dear John,

I don't wanna be on any team in baseball. Now Patrick Garino, that's all he wants to be. He says he won't do nothing else but be a major league baseball player. I seen him play and he's O.K. but he ain't exactly no Peewee Reese or Gil Hodges.

Dear John,

Nicholas' cold is going away but now he's always picking his nose. I don't care on account me and Nicholas don't never shake hands.

Dear John,

Earnest got five mazes all the same and he paints little dots on the cockroach's backs and he got names for his smart roaches. The smartest one got a red dot and his name is Red Barron. The next smartest one got a blue dot and is Blue Knight. Then there's a Robin Hood with a green dot, Yellow Fellow, and Fred with a white dot.

Dear John,

Tomorrow's First Friday so today we gotta go and tell all our sins to the priest in the confectional. The confectional is a big box what the priest sits in and you gotta go in and tell him all your sins. But before we go over to church the nun gives us a long letcher about our sins. She says "Boys and girls, I know you are sinful because your hands are always under your desks. Don't forget to tell the priest about the filthy things your evil bodies do."

Dear John,

Earnest told me that Red Barron likes Fred and that Red Barron and Blue Knight had a big fight over her. They stood up on their rear legs and slugged it out for a couple of minutes. If you listen, you can hear them hissing and then Blue Knight cried uncle and ran away.

Dear John,

The nun changed our seats first thing this morning. Now I can see everything what Nicholas does because now I sit in the last seat in the first row. Nicholas and Earnest still sit in the last seats in the third row.

Dear John,

Earnest had two shoe boxes on his desk in school today and he kept watching his cockroaches. So after school I ask Earnest how come he don't pay attention and do good on the Friday tests. He says he don't care about the Friday tests and he don't care if everybody thinks he's as dumb as Nicholas.

Earnest said, "I don't care what people thinks about me. It just ain't important."

Dear John,

Nicholas figgered what to do with his snot. He flips it with his finger and it goes shooting across the room. I found out about it because I seen Rita Borgisi touch the back of her neck like all of a sudden. She pulled some snot off her neck and she gagged. She turned green and almost throwed up. I ask Nicholas at lunch why he done that to Rita. He got no reason to shoot snot at Rita Borgisi. She's real quiet and nice. And snot shooting is disgusting. But Nicholas said his aim was bad. He was aiming at Christine Carney. Oh, that's O.K.

Dear John,

I was over at Earnest's apartment and I see Fred and Red Barron in their own box with saw dust and all. Earnest says Red Barron is a red hot lover. He keeps giving Fred presents what he makes but then when Earnest starts telling me about this stuff what Red Barron does to make Fred love him, it's time for me to go home. Some things what Earnest thinks are fastenating, I think are digusting.

Dear John,

Earnest took Fred and the Red Barron to school and watched them all day. The nun don't care much what Earnest does so long as he keeps his hands on the desk.

Dear John,

It's gotta be a real challenge for Nicholas to hit Christine Carney with his snot. Christine Carney's a long way from Nicholas.

Dear John,

The clock runs O.K. if you look at the numbers and don't listen to the chimes. The chimes ring out of order. Any time they feel like chiming that's what they chime. It can be three o'clock and they'll chime nine or ten or two times. The clock does whatever it feels like doing. Just like Earnest, it don't care. I like that clock.

Dear John,

Maybe Nicholas ain't too smart but he don't give up easy. He's getting closer all the time at shooting snot at Christine Carney.

Dear John,

Earnest got a bloody nose today when he walks into the door because he got his eyes on what's happening in the cockroach box.

Dear John,

Today Father Smott knocks on the classroom door. The nun sees him and turns redder than Earnest's bloody nose.

The priest talks to the nun. Low voices but I hear because I sit in the first seat near the door. Father Smott ask, "Why did all the kids confess that they had dirty hands? Maybe you should tell them cleanlyness is next to Godlyness but it's not a sin to have dirty hands."

The nun don't say nothing but her face is redder than the red heart painted on the statue of the Sacred Heart of Jesus.

Dear John,

Nicholas is getting better aim at snot shooting. He got Christine Carney two times outta five shots today. She got long hair so she don't feel it but it looks real disgusting dripping down the back of her school uniform and all.

Dear John,

Even Nicholas can get to be good at doing something.

Dear John,

We had a fire drill today. The door is in the back of the room so when the bells clang, we get up and the middle rows go out first in order. Everybody gotta stay in order but like backwards. I'm near the end of the line because now I'm in the first row. Nicholas is the leader of the boys and Frances Bartino is the leader for the girls. I think that was bad planning on the nun's part but they was smiling and looking real proud to be first. Well, we get out onto the sidewalk and I seen the boys line making a big circle around something what's on the sidewalk. Then I seen what it was. Everybody's walking around this great big dog turd. And the nun stands near and keeps saying, "Watch your step" and pointing to it. She looks like she's gonna throw up because her nose is scrunched up almost to her bald head. I figger she don't want nobody stepping in it and stinking up the classroom for the rest of the day. Well, we all get around it without stepping in it. And then the fire drill is over so we turn around and walk back to school. Again the nun keeps pointing to the turd and is sayin "watch your step" and nobody steps in it.

But when we get back in the classroom Nicholas is in real big trouble with the nun. She got him in the hall and she's slapping him on his head what keeps bouncing off the wall, slap bam, slap bam. Sounds bad but Nicholas is real cool, slap bam, slap bam. I can tell the nun wants him to cry but Nicholas don't ever cry, slap bam, slap bam. Slap bam, slap bam. He walks into the classroom smiling just a little to let everybody know he don't break. The nun's real mean all morning but I don't know what happened.

Dear John,

At lunch I can't find Nicholas. I ask around but nobody seen Nicholas at lunch. Earnest told me Nicholas is still in the classroom getting tortured by the nun. I ask Earnest if he knows how come Nicholas got into so much trouble with the nun. Earnest says when Nicholas walks back from the fire drill, he's the last in line and comes to the turd what the nun keeps pointing to and saying "Watch your step." Nicholas bends down and picks it up and puts it in his pocket. It's a fake turd what's made from rubber. Nicholas put it right there on the sidewalk first time out the door. Nicholas and the nun ain't never going to be good friends.

Dear John,

We call Christine Carney Snot Head but we don't tell her that to her face. Nicholas's aim is getting better all the time. Earnest says, "It just goes to show you that everybody can get good at something."

Dear John,

Earnest says that Fred and Red Barron had baby cockroaches. Blue Knight went near the babies and Red Barron beat him up real bad. Blue Knight's leg is in bad shape. Too bad because Blue Knight was a real good runner but he's probly out of the races. Earnest says, like what they do with race horses what break their legs, he thinks he's gonna hafta shoot Blue Knight.

Dear John,

Today I seen Nicholas aim snot shots at Peter Ackerman. He missed and hit Patrick Garino in the ear. Patrick Garino ain't the kind to fool around with but he don't know who done it. Nicholas is gonna get creamed if Patrick Garino finds out. I won't tell because it's wrong to snitch.

Dear John,

We got our seats changed again and I sit right in back of Dennis Bowalski. Last Friday he done better than me by just one pernt. I think I'm gonna compete with him and beat him next week on the tests. I wanna get to sit in front of Dennis Bowalski.

Dear John,

Earnest went to the liberry and got two books about cockroaches. He says they've been around for about 300 million years and they're gonna be around for a long time. He says the atomic bomb what they dropped on Japan can't even kill them.

Dear John,

Christine Carney told Earnest that it's wrong to believe that cockroaches was around for over 300 million years because God created the world 6 thousand years ago. Christine Carney told Earnest he should get his facts straight before he goes shooting off his mouth like he's an authority on the subject.

Dear John,

Christine Carney is the teacher's pet. You probably figgered that out by now. But this morning the nun's talking to Christine Carney and because she likes her, the nun puts her hand around Christine Carney's head like giving her a little pat for being good and all. But the nun gets a real big surprise when she feels something gooey all over her hand.

You shoulda seen her face when she looked at her hand full of snot. She ran outta the classroom. I guess she went to wash her hands. She just leaves Snot Head Carney standing there in front of the room. First time Christine Carney looks dumb. We all start laffing.

The nun comes back in with clean hands and yells, "Who's that laffing? Everybody who's laffing stand up." Nobody moves. "O.K. everybody gets a punshment." We all gotta stay after school. Everybody except Christine Carney. She wasn't laffing.

Dear John,

Earnest says the nun gotta go to confection because she got her hands dirty.

Dear John,

Earnest don't flush the dumb cockroaches no more. He uses them to expeerment on how to kill them so his mom and dad don't move him out of the neghborhood. He says they don't die easy unless you step on them.

Dear John,

It don't make sense for Earnest's mom and dad to move out of the neighborhood because of all the cockroaches. Earnest is going to take his cockroaches where ever they move.

Dear John,

Earnest said Blue Knight exscaped. He was in a jar and just climbed up and out. I ask Earnest how he exscaped what with his bad leg and all. Earnest said his leg fell off and he just growed a new one. Some of the cockroaches got out of the aquarium. But Earnest spread some oily stuff around near the top of the glass and when the cockroaches climb up there, they slide down.

Dear John,

If Earnest cared, he'd get to sit in the very first seat. He could compete and even beat Peter Ackerman. He just don't care about it.

Dear John,

I'm in trouble now. See the tests we usually get are arithmetic, spelling and history and geography but now she's pulling the rug out. The nun says this Friday we're getting a writing test too. Big trouble. I hate writing. She says on Thursday she will give us a topic and we must write a research report. We can go to the liberry and look up stuff and then on Friday we must hand it in. We gotta write the report in good hand writing and neat and everything must be in perfect order. I got a bad feeling about this one.

Dear John,

I found snot in my hair right in the back of my head. That ain't one bit funny.

Dear John,

Earnest says he can trap lots of cockroaches every night and they don't get away. He puts Randy's buns in jars with little ladders going up and with oil around the edges on the inside. He says he catches about a hundred every night.

Dear John,

Me and Earnest seen Fred and Red Barron's babies hatch and they had lots of babies. Earnest found two magnifying glasses so we can see real good when the eggs hatch. Me and Earnest thought there were just 15 eggs but something funny happened. When the eggs opened there were smaller eggs in them big eggs and about 25 fat little babies popped out of each big egg. Their antennas and legs were wiggling. Fred and Red Barron had about 375 babies at one time.

Dear John,

The nun loves Christine Carney. That's because Christine Carney don't never put her hands under her desk.

Dear John,

If Fred and Red Barron had 375 babies at one time and if Earnest got thousands or maybe millions of cockroaches in his apartment, he ain't never gonna get rid of them all, not by trapping a hundred every night.

Dear John,

The nun gives us a letcher on neatness. She said, "Your desks are not neat. I went through each of your desks after school yesterday and your books are all out of order. Your geography book is the biggest and it is to be on the bottom and your speller is to be on top because it is the smallest book." And then she tells us what the order gotta be for all the other books in between.

Dear John,

Earnest done the arithmetic on the roaches too and figgers the traps ain't gonna do it. He ain't never gonna get rid of the cockroaches. Earnest is gonna start packing.

Dear John,

Christine Carney got a real short hair cut.

Dear John,

That clock is so funny. You can't never tell how many times it's gonna chime.

Dear John,

Earnest says he's been doing expeerments on his dumber cockroaches and he says they got small holes on the sides of their body what's called the abdomen. He says he put some salt in the holes and the cockroaches died. He's gonna put salt around inside one of his mazes and see if it kills the cockroaches.

Dear John,

I'm still sitting right in back of Dennis Bowalski. He says he's smarter than me. So I told him I bet I can get to sit in front of him after the seats change next Monday. We bet a quarter. I forgot about the report what we gotta write. I'm in big trouble.

Dear John,

The classroom's a little safer these days. Nicholas don't got a cold no more.

Dear John,

The salt don't kill the cockroaches. Earnest figgered out that it killed one because he poured the salt right into where it breathes but the salt don't bother them when they walk on top of it.

Dear John,

We gotta write a report and it's gonna count for seat order. The nun says, "Write a report about one of the planets." Then we gotta memorize them all in the right order and it's gonna be on our Friday test. I hate memorizing but most of all I hate writing.

Dear John,

Well I done my report and I wrote it all out. Tomorrow I'm gonna just copy it real neat. I wrote a really long report and I don't spell no words wrong. This is how I done it. I checks the ensiklopedia what the nun got in the room. It's Americana. Then I checks the school liberry. Britonika. Then to the public liberry and get the national one, a real old one. I copy out of that one but I don't copy every word. The nun says we can't do that. I copy every other sentence. I skip the first sentence and begin with the second sentence. It's a real long report and no words spelled wrong.

Dear John,

Just like old times. I'm back sittin in the dumb row with Nicholas and Earnest. I sit in front of Nicholas and Earnest sits in front of me. Your average ain't exactly high when you get a zero in writing. I really worked hard on that report but the nun said I copied it. She says I pagerized it. But she don't got no proof. She just THINKS I copied but she don't know where from but she gives me a big fat zero anyways.

She don't prove nothing. She just says, "You copied every word."

And I say, "No, I don't copy every word."

So she says, "O.K. read it."

Well naturly I can't read it good. Most of the words are too big. So I says, "I got the words from the ensiklopedia."

She says, "Which one."

Now I know her trick right off. I ain't telling what ensiklopedia. So I says, "The Ensiklopedia Brooklyna." I made that up. That stops her in her tracks. She looks at me.

I say, "It's the new one in the public liberry, very good ensiklopedia."

She told me that it's not a very new one because there are now nine planets, not eight.

She just looks at me. No more questions but she gives me a zero anyways. It ain't fair because I should get something for good hand writing and I spelled most of the words rite.

Dear John,

I looked in the ensiklopedia again and it says there are eight planets. So I ask Earnest how many planets are there.

Earnest says there are nine planets.

So I told him about the book what says there are eight planets.

Earnest says that if it's a real old book, the facts are real old.

Earnest told me, "That's easy to exsplain. God made a new planet after the book was wrote."

Dear John,

Earnest says Fred and Red Barron's babies are pretty big now and they learned how to get to Randy's buns in the maze real fast. They beat all the other cockroaches.

Dear John,

Fred died. She was upside down in the aquarium. Cockroaches live only about three or four months. Fred died of old age.

Dear John,

We did art today. The nun puts this pitcher of a saleboat on the blackboard and then she tells us to copy it. Earnest looks at my saleboat and says it looks like the Lucy Tanya after it got blowed up.

Dear John,

That Dennis Bowalski made me pay up the quarter. The only reason I paid him is because he's bigger than me but I told him it ain't fair about the writing test what I pagiarized. But then I tells Dennis Bowalski double or nothing for next week. O.K. from Dennis Bowalski. So we made another bet. We ain't gonna have no writing test so I figger I'll better him this time.

Dear John,

It ain't gonna be easy doing better than Dennis Bowalski. Earnest and Nicholas don't give me a chance to pay attention to the teacher. Earnest keeps showing me what Fred and Red Barron's children are doing. Cockroaches are more interesting than what the nun's teaching.

Dear John,

The nun gives us back our art pitchers of the saleboat. Earnest got a zero because he drawed a speed boat. It was a real good speed boat. She gives me "E" for effort. Good thing art don't count for Friday tests what with the seat changing and all.

Dear John,

Earnest came over to my apartment with a game board what he made. It got numbers up to 12 on it. Earnest says "Spin the clock to twelve and if it chimes 5 times, that's the winning number." I let Earnest borrow my clock and he says he'll bring it back and he'll give me 10 percent.

Dear John,

Earnest makes little boats out of paper and then puts the dumber cockroaches in them and then puts them in the toilet. Then he yells, "Fire torpedoe number one." Then he flushes.

Dear John,

Oh, No! The nun says she's gonna test us on all the planets and we gotta write them in right order starting at the sun. It ain't fair because I bet Dennis Bowalski before I knowed the planets was gonna be on the test.

Dear John,

Earnest done lots and lots of expeerments and tried lots and lots of ways to kill the cockroaches and he says he got it right this time. He put boric acid on the bottom of the shoe box with ten dumb cockroaches and in two days they was all dead. He looked at the dead bodies with his magnifying glass and they had the white stuff all over their legs and all their mouths is stuffed with dust from the boric acid. The cockroaches walk around on top but the dust goes up all over them and then they eat it when they try to get it off their legs. Boric acid ain't a healthy diet.

Dear John,

I done my best on the tests but there was lots of stuff about history I don't know. We hadda fill in the blanks. I filled in that Abe Lincoln got shot in his seat. He was killed by Shirley Booth. I think I got those right but I don't think I did good on the really hard questions.

Dear John,

The nun checked our desks after we went home yesterday and she found ten dead cockroaches in Christine Carney's desk. I looked at the cockroaches. They had little pieces of white dust on their legs. But I don't say nothing to nobody.

Dear John,

I go by Earnest's apartment house what with the window open and I hear kids yelling, "Come on number 2." One saying, "Number 10." Then I hear my clock chiming 8 and Earnest yells, "The house wins."

Dear John,

I could only think of eight planets for the test and I got the order all screwed up. I remembered the one God just made. It's called Pluto.

Dear John,

I hadda give Dennis Bowalski fifty cents. Good thing Earnest gave me the ten percent of his winings from the clock what chimes.

But it's good I don't sit with Nicholas and Earnest this week. I sit in the second seat dumb row again. I can pay attenshun better this week. Dennis Bowalski still sits in front of me. He keeps turning around and pointing to his brains. He thinks he's smarter than me.

Dear John,

I really did know the nine planets in the right order and all but when Friday came I forgot the order and I forgot all about the earth.

Dear John,

Earnest says Fred Junior is the smartest roach he ever met. He finds Randy's buns fast and even remembers for a coupla hours. He's still a little like Nicholas. Fred Junior gotta relearn everything all over again the next day but he learns it again real fast.

Dear John,

Earnest took Fred Junior to school today and he's in a little box and Earnest is looking at him under his desk. The nun makes Earnest put his hands on the desk and she hits them with the yard stick ten times. She keeps hitting them and saying "Filthy hands, filthy hands."

Dear John,

I checked out Earnest's hands. They're red and blue in places but they ain't no more dirty than any other kids. Maybe the nun knows he picks up cockroaches all the time because they're kinda dirty and all.

Dear John,

Earnest told me he learned a trick from Fred Junior that will help me beat Dennis Bowalski. Fred Junior don't ever forget so long as he practices running through the maze about three times a day. But if Fred Junior don't practice for a day, then he forgets. Earnest says I need to practice what I learn every coupla hours and then on Thursday night I gotta go over all the stuff and then get up early Friday and practice it all again. Earnest says I just gotta practice before I forget.

Dear John,

I ain't had time to write you this week because I been practicing so I don't forget what I learned. I bet Dennis Bowalski double or nothing and I gotta win because I don't got no money to pay if I lose and if I don't pay, I'll lose my nose or something else. Dennis is a ape. This Saturday and Sunday I think I'll pray a lot and maybe pack. But mostly I'm gonna practice what I learned. At least I'll give it a real good try.

Dear John,

Earnest says he thinks if I practice real hard, maybe I can get to be as smart as Fred Junior.

Dear John,

The nun court Earnest with his hands under his desk again and she turns all red and comes down to his seat. The nun says, "Put your hands on your desk."

Earnest puts his hands on his desk but they ain't open. His fists are clenched.

The nun tells Earnest, "Unclench your fists."

Earnest looks up at her and says, "You don't really want me to unclench my fists."

The nun says, "Unclench your fists right now."

Earnest unclenches his fists and two big cockroaches run across the desk and right up the nun's habit."

The last time we seen the nun today she was running down the hall screaming.

Dear John,

Earnest brings me back my clock and gives me one dollar and ten cents. He says he don't need the clock no more because most of the kids figgered out the odds. He says it chimes 8 too much.

Dear John,

The nun says everybody done bad, except for Christine Carney, on the planets so she's gonna give that one again. I figgered a good way to remember them. I just remember the sentence, Miss Veronica Eddington may join some ugly nuns pooping. Miss stands for Mars and Veronica for Venus and the beginning letter of each word helps me remember the order. I keep practicing that.

Dear John,

The nun hates it when our desks are out of order but she hates hands under the desks more than anything else.

Dear John,

It's Monday so the nun calls out the names beginning with the dumbest kids first. Every time Nicholas and Earnest are first because they're always last. Then each kid gotta sit in the next seat. Well when she calls Dennis Bowalski before me, then I know I won. Dennis Bowalski looks real surprised and almost falls into the seat in the middle row. Then he keeps listening for my name like maybe it's a mistake. I'm watching him and his face gets redder and redder. Then when the nun calls my name, he puts his head down on the desk. The nun yells at him, "Dennis Bowalski keep your hands on the desk and get your head off the desk." Dennis Bowalski wipes his eyes and then sits up.

Dear John,

I done pretty good on the test except that I got mars and mercury mixed up. I sit in the last seat, smart row. But the main thing is I sit in front of Dennis Bowalski now.

Dear John,

I told Earnest I sit in front of Dennis Bowalski now.

Earnest says, "This is very strange. You sit all the way in the back of the room and Dennis Bowalski sits in the middle of the second row. You look at the back of Dennis Bowalski's head. But you sit in front of Dennis Bowalski. A school is a very strange place."

Dear John,

Dennis Bowalski says he ain't gonna give me no dollar because I musta cheated to get to sit in front of him.

Dear John,

The nun checked our desks after school yesterday. I gotta write a hundred times "I must keep my books in the right order." My geography book was on top and the nun says it's the biggest book so it belongs on the bottom.

Dear John,

Earnest told me to come over to see the races today. When I got there his room was packed with kids. Some were shouting, "Come on Randy Buns." Some were yelling come on "Peanut Butter Lover." But Earnest was yelling for "Fred Junior." I seen the five mazes out on the bed and the roaches running. Fred Junior won. Earnest was real happy because nobody bet on Fred Junior because he only gave one to one odds on him. Most of the kids bet on Peanut Butter Lover because Earnest gave ten to one odds on him.

Dear John,

When I got home my clock is gone. I look and listen all over the place but it ain't anywhere. Maybe Earnest loaned it from me again.

Dear John,

We had another fire drill but this time Nicholas ain't the leader. When the bells rang the nun tells us to line up in alphabeticull order. This takes a long time and when we was still figgering out the alphabeticull order, the other classes are coming back into the school.

Dear John,

Earnest told me it takes about three days for cockroaches to starve to death. Earnest's mom and dad really cleaned the kitchen and got rid of all the grease and old food. Earnest hadda crawl around and clean up all the food what dropped behind the stove. Then he sprinkled lots of boric acid back there.

Dear John,

You will not believe this, John. I sit in the fifth seat, smart row. This is the order, Peter Ackerman, Patrick Garino, Franky Zacarro, Johnny Hermeski, and then me. Maybe I ain't so dumb. I don't know what happened. All I did was practice what I learned and I really practiced Thurday night and Friday morning. I got a hundred on the spelling test, 95 in arithmetic, and 85 in history. Maybe I got the system down. See I figgered I can outsmart the teacher because I'm real sneaky. I pay real good attention to stuff what she says is important. Then I practice by writing all the stuff like dates and names on cards and then the answer on the back. I carry the cards around and look at them and try to remember what's on the back. Then on Thursday I really listen when she goes over everything what we learned that week and I make sure I really know whatever she says is important. Most of the stuff what I practice is on the test on Friday. I got her figgered out. Pretty tricky, right? Like Fred Junior, it just takes practice.

Dear John,

Everybody what lives in Earnest's apartment house is mad at his mom and dad because all the cockroaches what moved out of Earnest's apartment moved into everybody else's apartments.

Dear John,

I sit in the smart row again this week. The desks in the smart row ain't screwed to the floor. The nun calls them portable desks. We need portable desks because we got 62 kids in the class and there's only 44 desks what are screwed.

Dear John,

The portable desks in the smart row ain't always straight. Everybody in the row gotta have a ruler and the nun makes us meshure one inch from the desk to the wall. If any desk is outta order the kid gotta get out the ruler, meshure and get the desk back in order.

Dear John,

Earnest's mom and dad are real happy because they don't got no more cockroaches in the apartment except for Earnest's racing cockroaches.

They ain't gonna move. The other people what live in their apartment house ain't all that happy.

Dear John,

The shades ain't always straight and the nun gets real upset. She's letchering us about neatness and she stops letchering and looks at the shades. One's up and two down and three in the middle. She puts them all in the middle and got her yard stick to make sure they is all even.

Dear John,

Tomorrow is Friday and I gotta practice what I learned this week.

Dear John,

During the history test this morning, I seen Dennis Bowalski take a little piece of paper out from under his tie. He looks at it and then puts it back. Then later he looks at it again. I think it got answers on it.

Dear John,

My mom seen a cockroach in our kitchen today. I told her, "No problem." Then she comes in and sees this white powder on the floor near the walls. She's gonna sweep it all up and she's mad. But I explain she got a choice. It's either boric acid or cockroaches. Then I tell her all about Earnest's expeerments. She says she'll give the dust a try.

Dear John,

Moving up in the world, John. I sit in the third seat smart row. I done real good on the test last Friday. Peter Ackerman is first again and naturly Patrick Garino is second. The nun keeps one eye on me when I take the tests now. I figger she thinks I cheat but I don't. I just got her figgered out is all and I'm real sneaky about it. She should be keeping her eye on Dennis Bowalski but I don't say nothing about that. I don't snitch.

Dear John,

The nun screamed when she opened her desk drawer. She shouted, "Cockroaches are in my drawer. They're disgusting."

Earnest raised his hand and the nun says, "What do you want?"

Earnest says, "Do you want me to get rid of them for you?"

The nun backs up and says, "Kill the filthy things."

So Earnest walks up and takes the wastebasket and puts his hand in the desk drawer and pulls out a wiggling cockroach. He holds it up and crushes it in his hands and dumps it in the wastebasket. The nun's face goes white. Then he grabs and crushes another one. The cockroaches start jumping out of the desk really fast but Earnest is faster and steps on some and crushes a few others between his fingers. Then he goes back to his seat and sits down like nothing happens.

Dear John,

Cockroaches are real fast but Earnest is faster. He's got cockroaches figgered out so good that he knows what way they're gonna run and he heads them off.

Dear John,

Nobody knows cockroaches better than Earnest. He thinks like one and that ain't dumb!

Dear John,

It's tuff to pay attention in the portable seats because you gotta meshure one inch from the wall every time the desk moves even a little.

Dear John,

Another fire drill. The principal nun says the whole school gotta get another fire drill because last time our class messed up and never even got outside. So we go outside again and Nicholas is first because we do row order, not alphabeticull what takes too long. So the nun sees the dog turd after Nicholas goes by and she bends down and picks it up. She screams and drops the turd. That turd ain't rubber. The last time we seen our nun today she was running into what's sposed to be a burning school. The principal was our teacher the rest of the day. She says our nun was sick.

Dear John,

Earnest laffed all the way home and kept saying that the principal is right about that nun. She is sick.

Dear John,

Tomorrow's Friday and I gotta practice so that's why I don't write much on Thursdays.

Dear John,

The nun was back today but she don't look all that good. She still looks kinda sick mainly because she got her hands dirty.

Dear John,

We was taking the test and the nun was in back of the room. Dennis Bowalski pulls out the little paper from his tie. She musta been watching him real close because she was there in a flash. But Dennis Bowalski beat her. When he heard those rosary beads coming swish, swish, he ate the paper. It don't make no difference though. She saw him. So Dennis Bowalski had to stand in the corner for the rest of the day. For homework he had to write I must not cheat five hundred times. I bet he'll never cheat again.

Dear John,

The nun says Christine Carney knows how to keep everything in order. Her desk is always in fine order and her geography is always on the bottom. The nun gives Christine Carney a very important job. She makes her the shade monitor.

Dear John,

I still can't find that clock. Earnest says he don't got it because all the kids figgered out the order even when it ain't going in the right order. Once the players figger out the order, the house starts losing money.

Dear John,

Dennis Bowalski's in the dumb row with Nicholas and Earnest. He tries to make disgusting sounds like Earnest and he tries to shoot snot like Nicholas. But he ain't good at neither. He ain't original.

Dear John,

Patrick Garino is in the first seat but it ain't one inch from the wall so the nun demotes him to the second seat and Peter Ackerman sits in the first seat again.

Dear John,

After lunch one shade's all the way up and another's all the way down. Christine Carney got them strait real fast. Earnest was the last kid outta the classroom before lunch.

Dear John,

I'm going for the number one seat. I think I can do it. Maybe Peter Ackerman and Patrick Garino will have a bad day and I can have a good day. I'm practicing real hard every night. So if I don't write, don't worry.

Dear John,

Patrick Garino ain't gonna be hard to beat. He don't got time to learn nothing. He keeps meshuring the one inch.

Dear John,

Dennis Bowalski farted under his arm pit and got caught the very first time. The nun says, "You are completely out of order. Go to the principal's office."

Then the principal sent for his mom and dad. I was sharpening my pencil by the window and I seen Dennis Bowalski walking home with his mom and dad and they was screaming at him and taking turns hitting him on the back of the head and he was crying real bad.

Dear John,

Third seat, smart row again! I just gotta practice harder.

Dear John,

After lunch the shades are all up and down again and the nun yells at Christine Carney. Earnest was the last one to go to lunch.

Dear John,

I got a real good trick. I can out smart the nun. When she teaches us something I figger it's gonna be on that test so I write it on one of my cards right away. Then when I get home I get the cards and think about what she said. It's like being a secret spy.

Dear John,

It's good sitting in the third seat, smart row. Nobody around bothers me except a coupla kids in the middle row. I can spy on the nun when she's teaching and outsmart her. Whatever she thinks is important is important for me to know and practice. Peter Ackerman and Patrick Garino don't talk much and they almost never fool around. Peter

Ackerman's too busy paying attention to the teacher and Patrick Garino is always meshuring the inch.

Dear John,

Dennis Bowalski don't get out of order no more. He just sits there in the last seat and won't do nothing. Even Nicholas sits in front of him.

Dear John,

I ask my mom if she seen my clock and she says she threw my clock away. She says it was no good because it chimed out of order. I liked that clock and it did chime in order. When it was 10, it chimed 7 when it was 11, it chimed 2. When it was 1 and 2 and 3 and 6 and 10, it chimed 8. When it was 8 it never chimed. You just hadda figger out the order.

Dear John,

Nicholas sneezed. Everybody looks worried, espeshully Christine Carney.

Dear John,

Next Friday we get the last tests. I'm gonna compete for the first seat. It's my last chance. The next teacher don't play this game of switching seat order.

Dear John,

The nun says this is the last Monday we're going to change our seats. The seats we get this Monday are going to be our seats for the rest of the year. She says it takes her all Saturday and Sunday to correct the tests and to get our grades in the right order. She says the tests are taking her away from her time to pray. She says she mostly prays that our souls will take control of our evil bodies.

Dear John,

The nun turns around and sees all the kids in the back of the room looking at Dennis Bowalski's hands what ain't on his desk. She turns real red and tells Dennis Bowalski to go to the principal's office. He gets up and goes to the principal's office but first he gotta button up the front of his pants.

Dear John,

Dennis Bowalski don't go to St. Mary's no more. He got sent back to P.S. 18. The nun told us, "Children who keep putting their hands under their desks are indecent, evil and completely out of order. Children like Dennis Bowalski belong in public schools."

Dear John,

Earnest told me his cockroaches learned the alphabet and they know that A comes before B and then C comes and all. I don't believe him so I tell him to prove it. Well, I guess that gave him an idea so he's betting everybody that he can get his cockroaches to line up in alphabeticull order.

Dear John,

We got back after the lunch and the shades look like six steps on a stairs. The nun turns real red and screams, "Christine Carney, get those shades in proper order." Christine Carney got them strait real fast. Earnest was late in getting to the lunchroom.

Dear John,

Earnest asked if I wanna bet his cockroaches can line up in alphabeticull order but I say no. When Earnest makes bets on something, he already got all the angles figgered out.

Dear John,

I went over to Earnest's apartment with lots of kids and Earnest got these five cockroaches with letters painted on their backs. He puts them all together in a shoe box maze and they line up in alphabeticull order and the A cockroach goes first and the B cockroach goes next and they all get to Randy's buns in alphabeticull order. Earnest won a buck fifty.

Dear John,

Today we got the last Friday tests. There wasn't nothing on any of the tests what I don't know. I done just great. I'm gonna get that first seat and that means I'm gonna keep the first seat for the rest of the year. This competition is fun.

Dear John,

Earnest told me that it was easy to teach the cockroaches alphabeticull order because he paints A on the fastest cockroach what got the most practice and B on the second fastest and E on the dumbest cockroach. He says he was a little worried about C and D cockroaches but they got the order right.

Dear John,

For the very last time the nun changed everybody's seat today. Just like usual she called out the names and averages starting from the bottom. I keep listening for my name and then everybody gets a seat except for me and Peter Ackerman.

Then the nun stops and says, "Bobby Anderson got the highest average of the boys in the class."

I was real happy because I practiced so hard to get that first seat. I start walking with my books to the first seat.

But the nun says, "Wait."

I stop and look at her.

"Peter Ackerman also got the highest average of the boys. Bobby Anderson and Peter Ackerman tied for first place."

Peter Ackerman and me are standing there holding all our books with the geogrpahy book on the bottom.

Then the nun says, "I have to decide in a fair way who gets the first seat."

She writes our last names on the board.

I got the second seat.

She done alphabeticul order.

Chapter 9

Hero

Sixth Grade

Dear John,

I don't sit in back of Peter Ackerman no more. The nun don't change seats every Monday no more but I got my seat changed anyways. She changed my seat back to the middle row in the back near Earnest and Nicholas. I don't sit in the first row because of all the problems what I got keeping my portable desk exactly one inch from the wall.

Dear John,

Earnest said, "It don't matter a hill of beans what order you sit in. What matters is what you get to do where you are."

Dear John,

I sit in the back of the room and I get to do what I wanna do. In the front seats you gotta be careful about everything what you do. The nun don't pay much attention to what's going on in the back of the room just so long as we don't bother what's going on in the front of the room.

Dear John,

Tests, tests, tests. I hate them, speshally the one tomorrow. It's gonna be in health. I don't know all much about health except I know one thing. It's good to get lots of sleep and sitting in the back of the room is a real good thing for my health.

Dear John,

We got that test in health today. I'm gonna flunk. I don't got no time to study. Earnest came over just when I was gonna study.

Dear John,

I was right! Just as I predickeded, I flunked. But it was a lot worser than that. See, when I'm taking the test, the nun goes out of the room and I just lean over and whisper to Donny Donello what's this word that spelled i-n-d-i-g-e-s-t-i-o-n. Now I don't ask him for no answer. I just ask him what's one crummy word and he just looks back at me. Then he turns up his eyes and puts his finger up to his mouth and shakes his head. Donny Donello ain't no help.

But the worse thing is that the nun's right outside the door and swish, swish, clink, clink, rattle, rattle. Rosary beads make lots of noise which is usually a real helpful thing because then you know where she's at. But not this time. She was hiding just outside the door, keeping real still, just listening for somebody to whisper. But she missed catching me herself which is just the thing what makes her real mad. So she stands in front of the room with her hands behind her back. She wrinkles her nose and she almost whispers, "Who was whispering?"

Nothing. Nobody says nothing. Well I ain't one to snitch, espeshully on myself. Then she says, "If no one tells me who was whispering, the whole class will stay in and write I must not whisper a thousand times." Well, that gets to me mainly because none of us don't wanna write "I must not whisper a thousand times." So if I don't snitch on myself now, it'll be a lot worser because I don't dare walk down no alleys without some kids from the class beating me up. So I'm just slowly raising my hand to turn myself in when Christine Carney's hand goes up faster than mine and she says, "It was Bobby Anderson." By that time my hand is already up but it don't count none because the nun is down at my seat, whack, whack, whack right on the top of my head and I don't even know she's got the yard stick under her habit. Nuns got big habits what hide some dangerous stuff. She laid a trap for me and she got me.

Well, she ain't gonna use that yardstick no more. The third whack cracked it over my head. It broke right in half. I got a pretty hard head what is a thing she don't figger on. After she gets done with whacking me, she takes my paper and puts a great big fat zero on the top. Donny Donello leans down and picks up the other half of the yardstick and real polite and smiling hands it to her. Disgusting! I was feeling bad for the rest of the day. My head hurt real bad. But not one tear come to my eyes, not one little tear. Not one—'til I got home, in my bed, under the covers.

Dear John,

The nun says we gotta write a report about a hero and she says we gotta stick to the facts. She says that dates and the facts what go with them are real important for understanding history.

Dear John,

The nun told Patrick Garino he can't write about no heros what are baseball players. She says real heros don't play baseball.

Then Earnest ask the nun, "Jackie Robinson, what about Jackie Robinson? He's a real hero because he broke into baseball and the Brooklyn Dodgers are all real heros cause they all let him be on the team."

The nun stops him and says, "Real heros do not play games. I do not care to discuss this further."

Dear John,

Today the nun told me to go out into the hallway. I figgered she wanted to see if her new yardstick was unbreakable. But she only wants to give me a scolding. She says she's very disappointed in me because I was doing such good work in the beginning of the year but now I'm just doing terrible work and I'm really doing terrible at remembering the facts. Then she told me to get my books out of my desk and she changed my seat again and now I sit way in the back of the room with Earnest and Nicholas. The nun thinks that will help me learn better. She's right. I will learn a lot more from Earnest and Nicholas than I'll ever learn from this nun.

Dear John,

We got this history test tomorrow all about the colonies. The nun gives us this list of dates and facts what happened. We gotta memorize stuff like this:

April 1775—Paul Revere rode to Lexington
July, 1776—Declaration of independence
August 1778—Brooklyn captured

April 19, 1775—the shot heard round the world.
February 1779—George Rogers Clark captured Vincennes
September 3, 1783—America won the revolution war

And that's just a little part of the dates and facts what we gotta memorize. I hate history and I don't do no good on history tests because I can't remember all them dates and facts. Memorizing them facts and dates makes me nutty. I ain't gonna do good on this test tomorrow but it ain't really my fault because I don't got no time to memorize all them facts and dates for the test anyways. I'm a very busy guy.

Dear John,

Today Earnest raises his hand to asks the nun a question. She's writing on the blackboard more dates and facts for us to memorize. I seen Earnest ask a nun a question a couple of times before and it never woiks out all that good. So before the nun sees his hand up, I look at Earnest and I shakes my head and whisper, "Earnest, this ain't likely a good idear." but the nun got good ears and hears me whispering. She turns around but then she looks so surprised to see Earnest with his hand up, she forgets about my whispering.

The nun points to Earnest and says, "It's too early for recess and, no, I will not give you permission to go to the lavatory."

But Earnest says, "I don't gotta go to the bathroom."

The nun says, "lavatory."

Earnest says, "I don't gotta go there neither."

Now I know Earnest knows that lavatory is a nun's word for bathroom. But he just gotta make a big thing out of it. But that don't do him no good for the question what he asks next which is, "How come we gotta memorize stuff like the dates and the facts what go with them? What good is it?"

The nun's face gets so red it looks like it's gonna explode. Well it does. She opens her mouth just in time or it woulda blown off the top of her head. She screams at Earnest, "How dare you question my authority in this classroom. The audacity of you."

I don't know how she got all the way from the front of the room to the back so fast but she is right there at Earnest's seat and she's got the new yardstick. Well that new yardstick wasn't unbreakable neither. It took only two wacks on top of Earnest's head to crack it in half.

Dear John,

Earnest says that people what sell yardsticks must love the nuns.

Dear John,

I got lots of stuff to do what's a lot better than memorizing dates and facts for a history test. The nun wants us to write that report about a hero for a history contest. I'm going to the liberry. I don't know nothing about no hero.

Dear John,

I think the nun musta been thinking about Earnest's question. She told us it was real good training for our minds to memorize all the dates and facts. She says memorizing is the best way for us to get smart. But then she says, "Boys and girls, you should never question authority. By being obedient to authority you will be like the great saints and heroes of our great country and you will get great rewards."

Dear John,

Earnest told me he ain't so sure the nun's right about saints and heros getting great rewards because the saints got burned to death and thrown to the lions and tortured and killed and all that ain't such a great reward.

But I told Earnest the nun is right. When they died, they got the great reward in heaven. I told Earnest that the heroes of our country get medals and holidays named after them and some even got their pictures in them history books.

Dear John

I met Earnest at the liberry and he was trying to find a book about rats. Now Earnest thinks rats are very interesting. We got a lot of them here in Brooklyn. They come out of the sewers and run across the street and down the sewer on the other side of the street. Sometimes they don't make it but then the pigeons get a free meal.

Earnest figgers he can learn about rats like he done with cockroaches. Earnest says he's coming over after he finds some stuff about rats. I ain't gonna pass the history test tomorrow. I ain't got no time to study espeshullly what with Earnest coming over. I took out some books about the Revolution War anyways. Maybe I can get a little time to look at the pictures.

Dear John,

Earnest came over after the liberrry and he says he seen the New York Daily Mirror is having a writing contest and the winner gets $100! The story gotta be about a famous American hero. Earnest figgers if we gotta write a story for school anyways, we can write it for the New York Daily

Mirror writing contest too and maybe something good will come of it. He says I should write it because I'm a good writer. Well, that ain't true and I hate writing. Earnest says he can do the research and help edit it. When we win $100 from the New York Daily Mirror writing contest, we can split 50-50.

Dear John,

I ain't memorized none of the facts and dates for that history test tomorrow but it's real late and I gotta go to bed now. Too bad I don't got no time to study.

Dear John,

I wake up this morning and it's real bright all over my room. It looks like bright lights are coming from the outside right through the walls. It's really cold. But I reach over to the window and open the shade and there is snow all over the place, really big snow! In the kitchen my dad puts the radio on and the man in the radio says we got a big snow storm and all the public schools in New York City are closed. Yeah! That's great! I'm terrific happy! But then I remember I don't go to no New York City Public School. I ain't so happy no more. But then the man says after the commershal he's gonna read the list of other schools what closed. Quick sit up, covers off, shiver, cold, bathrobe, where's the bathrobe? Under the bed? No. In the closet? No. Bed covers over my head, commershals almost over, run, into the kitchen, trip on covers, crash against the wall, commershals over, sh, sh, don't nobody talk, sh, sh. St. Francis School, Beth Israel School, Girls Yeshiva, Brooklyn Day School, St. James School for the Deaf, Martin Luther School for them Protestants in the Bronx, Immaculate Conseption in

Williamsburg. He keeps reading but I don't hear nothing about St. Mary's. Then I remember! The real offishal name of my school is Immaculate Consception! Yeah, yeah, yeah!!! That's me! That's my school!

Dear John,

The snow is real deep out there and it's covered the stoop and we can't open the front door to get out. My dad's gotta go to work. The Chase National Bank don't never close when it snows and the subway's still running. But my dad can't get out the door. But I know what to do. Out the kitchen window, down the fire escape, grab the shovel from the cellar, shovel, shovel, scrape, scrape, open the front door and there's my dad just waiting and smiling. My dad says, "Thanks, Bobby, you're a hero."

"Ain't nuthin to it, dad," I says.

Dear John,

Ain't nobody around to play with so I figger I'll just write you, John. The streets are all getting plowed and people are trying to get their cars started. It's a big snow storm what surprised everybody because it's almost spring. Wait, somebody's at the door.

Dear John,

It was Earnest and Nicholas at the door and I went out and at first we had a swell time. The plow came through and made a great big pile of snow right in front of the apartment house what Christine Carney lives in. It's right down the block, a few doors away. Some of the pile was slushy and some was icy but most of it was real good packing snow. We borrowed some coal shovels from the cellar and we built the greatest snow fort you ever seen by digging into the middle of the pile. Then we stocked it up with amyunition, lots and lots of snowballs. Then we seen three kids walking down the street and I know right away one is Peter Ackerman because he always wears the brightest red scarf I ever seen wrapped up around his neck and over his ears. Then we seen Patrick Garino, and Georgie Porgie. His real name is George Porgato but Porgie fits better. They ask to play in our fort what we spent all morning fixing. Nuthing doing. Go make your own fort. Well they done it but not so good as our fort because they was in a big hurry and because we make better forts than them anytime. Well, they make their fort across the street and when they get finished, they leave and go down the street. Well that's like an invitation for us to go over and knock down their fort. So we go across the street and start knocking in the wall. Wam, wam pain, three snowballs hit me in the back. Earnest and Nicholas was lucky. They was smashing down the back wall from inside so they don't get hit. Then I hear Peter Ackerman and Patrick Garino and Georgie Porgie laffing in back of me. They got our fort and they're bombarding us with the snowballs what we made and stored up. I yell, "That ain't fair" but they just laff. I jump for cover into their fort just before a million snowballs come but this time they miss. Lucky thing Earnest and Nicholas ain't knocked in the front wall of the fort first. If them other guys was real smart they wooda waited till we got their whole fort knocked down. But at least we got a crummy fort what's still got a front wall.

We hadda make snowballs fast because they can attack any time. "Best thing is iceballs," says Nicholas.

But Earnest says, "No, slushballs is better because if you hits them, they get all wet and then they gotta go home and change and then we can get our fort back."

But I says, "That ain't fair and besides they ain't throwing slushballs and they ain't throwing no iceballs. They're throwing snowballs. And if we starts fighting dirty, then maybe they'll fight dirty and then we'll all be wet from the slush balls and that ain't no fun."

So Earnest says, "It's a demockracy and we gotta vote on it."

Well I can't argue none with that so we vote and we make lots of slush balls and I hit Peter Ackerman with the very first one, direct hit on his neck and he yells, "That ain't fair. That's a slush ball."

Then I seen Peter Ackerman taking off his red scarf what's kinda wet and he's going home to change because the slush ball went down his shirt. Georgie Porgie and Patrick Garino are real good shots with slush balls but it ain't fair because they play baseball in the summer and that's real good practice for slushball fights. Well, that's how come I got to write to you about this because I hadda come home to dry out my clothes on the radiator. Shiver, shiver.

Dear John,

I went back to the snow forts after I put on other pants and a dry shirt but nobody was there and both forts are all knocked down. Then I went to Earnest's house but when he opens the door, he got a big towel around him and he says he can't come out because his pants is soaking wet and he don't got no other pants. He's trying to dry them out on the radiator.

Me and Earnest got to talking about how Peter Ackerman and his army captured our fort. I was real surprised they captured our fort because we don't even see them come down the street. Earnest says it was a traitor what musta helped them. Their army went around the block and down the alley and then they went in a back door and then they came out the front door of the apartment house. They just jumped off the stoop and they landed right there in the fort before we knowed the jig was up.

Earnest puts his hand to his chin and says, "I bet the traitor what let them through the apartment house is none other than Christine Carney."

Dear John,

I went over to Nicholas's apartment what's around the corner. When Nicholas opens the door, he got his bathrobe on and his apartment is full of smoke. He says, "I just put out a fire in the oven. I tried to dry out my clothes real fast but they all got on fire."

So Nicholas is out for the rest of the slushball season. I feel real bad for Nicholas but I go looking for Peter Ackerman and Patrick Garino and Georgie Porgie. I wanna ask them if Christine Carney helped them and was a traitor and all but I can't find nobody around so I come home to let you know what's going on. I figger everybody's at home because their clothes was all soaking wet from the slushball fight. Like what I said, slushballs ain't no fun in the long run.

Dear John,

Earnest told me what he done after I came to his house. Earnest found some old ripped pants stuffed in the bottom of his closet. They was drafty what with the wind going through and all but they was dry. So Earnest comes looking for me. First Earnest goes to the knocked down forts but he don't see me there. But he seen Peter Ackerman's bright red scarf under some snow in our fort what them guys captured. The red scarf's pretty dry so Earnest borrows it and puts the scarf around his neck.

But then Earnest seen the traitor coming down the street all by herself. For Earnest this is an opportoonity too great to miss. Christine Carney don't see Earnest because he runs into the alley. Quick he makes one snowball, one slush ball and one ice ball. Then up with that red scarf all around his face. Here she comes. Earnest steps out in the street about twenty feet in front of her, a snowball in his right hand, behind his back in his left hand a slush ball and one ice ball. When Christine Carney sees Earnest, she just keeps walking, coming closer. Earnest takes the snowball and throws it kinda slow and curving in the air. Well naturly she sees it coming and keeps her eye on it and starts to move to the right to dodge it and that's when Earnest takes the slush ball and whips it straight fast and it hits her splash right in the side of her neck. Funny thing, at exactly the same time the snowball hits Christine Carney smack right on the top of her head. She don't calculate too good except in school. Christine Carney's mad and starts coming right at Earnest but that's when he gets her. Pow right in the head with the iceball. That stops her dead in her tracks and now she's sitting on the ground. Earnest don't say nuthing. He just takes off down the street. But Earnest hears Christine Carney saying some very nasty words what he never heard Christine Carney say before and that's good because it's nice to know she got a little human in her.

Dear John,

Christine Carney wants to pay five dollars to the first person what beats up Peter Ackerman. Christine Carney calls it an open contract and anybody what does the job first gets the five bucks. I don't never hear Christine Carney talking like this before.

Dear John,

Christine Carney asks Earnest to beat up Peter Ackerman. Earnest says he's kinda busy right now but he can get around to it in a week or two.

Dear John,

The radio says we gotta go to school tomorrow. That means I'm gonna hafta take that history test. I'd study tonight and all but it's real late and I don't got no time. Too bad I don't got no time to study. Good night.

Dear John,

That history test was real tuff. We hadda write dates and stuff what happened like the date of the Boston Tea Party. I don't remember no exact year but I remember a picture in the history book and I know this is a phoney baloney tea party and these guys are dressed like Indians and don't got much clothes on so I figger it's summer time. Then I figger it don't happen in the night because then you ain't gonna see nothing in the picture, too dark, and then I figger if they calls it a tea party, it gotta be in the afternoon when real tea parties are and then I seen all these guys what are sposed be working but they ain't so I figger it's gotta be a Saturday. So I writes down the Boston Tea Party happened in the summer time on a Saturday afternoon. That's kinda like more exact and a lot more helpful than a date anyways. It's a real good anser because it showed I was thinking real good. I done that kind of good thinking for most of the questions. Maybe I'm gonna pass the test because of my good thinking and all.

Dear John,

The nun don't give no credit for good thinking, only exact answers. I got a big fat zero.

Dear John,

Earnest seen this dog make some great yellow snow this morning. Earnest went and got a shoe box and put the yellow snow in it. Earnest's woiking on a plan about hitting Christine Carney with a yellow snowball.

Dear John,

That snow storm was a big surprise because Spring is almost here and it don't snow like that in March usually. But now it's warm again and the snow is all dirty and melting.

Dear John,

I tried to tell the nun about my good thinking and why I wrote stuff like the Boston Tea Party was in the summer and on a Saturday afternoon and all. Well, now I know that they dumped that tea in December because I checked it out after the test. But if you look at that picture, it don't make no sense. Dumping the tea and making like they was Indians ain't no stupid idear because they got the English to thinking that it was the Indians and all. But these guys, not being all that stupid and all, got warm stuff to wear in the winter. But I think the guy that went and drawed that picture was maybe a good drawer but not a good thinker because he made it look like it was summer. It just don't make no sense to draw them guys dressed in summer clothes. I mean you can see how that could throw a good thinker off. But the nun says memorizing the facts is good thinking.

Dear John,

The snow is all gone and Earnest's yellow snow in the shoe box got all melted. He's gonna hafta wait til next year for a dog to make some more yellow snowball. Sometimes even the best of real good idears just don't woik out.

Dear John,

Peter Ackerman is real worried and I don't blame him. That Christine Carney got enuff money to pay somebody to torture him real slow. I kinda feel sorry for him because he don't know what it's all about. But I figger I shood just keep out of it. Earnest brought Peter Ackerman's red scarf into school in his school bag and put it on Peter Ackerman's hook in the cloak room. Peter Ackerman got his red scarf back that way without knowing what a bad thing it done to him.

Dear John,

This stuff about the Revolutionary War is really kinda interesting. This guy what's named George Rogers Clark took his soldiers and went down the Ohio River and then back tracked and got the British by surprise. They made like they was gonna attack at the front of the fort but then they sneak around and get them in the back. I bet them British guys didn't figger on George Rogers Clark coming in the back expecially in the winter with all the snow and everything. George Rogers Clark was a real hero.

Dear John,

Mostly all the time I hate to write reports and stuff for school. But if we gotta write a story about a hero, I figger right off I'm gonna do it on somebody what's interesting like George Rogers Clark. I'm going to the liberry and look up lots of stuff about this guy because there ain't all that much about him in our history book.

Dear John,

I seen Earnest on my way to the liberry and he says he ain't got nothing speshal to do so he comes along. He tells me again we can write the report together and he can research it. He says we still got time to send the story to the New York Daily Mirror writing contest and split the $100. But when I tell him about George Rogers Clark, he says the guy ain't interesting enuff for him. Earnest says he's got a real good idea for a hero because of the rats he was reading about. Earnest says rats are the first ones to leave a sinking ship and the captain gotta go down with the ship. Earnest's gonna write about a captain of a ship and he'll probably win the $100.

Dear John,

I been spending so much time at the liberry that I forget all about poor Peter Ackerman. He still don't know what's going on. Just that Christine Carney is looking to pay somebody to get him good but she don't exsplain nuthing.

Peter Ackerman keeps going up to Christine Carney and saying "What did I do? What did I do?"

She just smiles. I never seen such a devilish smile before. Maybe she got more human in her than I figgered.

Dear John,

I got lots of good facts about George Rogers Clark and I got great idears about a story. Jeremiah Hamilton is in my story and it's gonna be like he tells the story. The story's gonna be all about the facts what I learned in the books from the liberry. The history books don't say nuthing about a guy what's named Jeremiah Hamilton because I made him up. He a frictitious karacter.

Dear John,

I been thinking about the Jeremiah Hamilton story all the time except when I'm thinking about how Christine Carney's gonna get poor Peter Ackerman. But I don't say nothing what I know about the red scarf and all because it ain't right to snitch.

Dear John,

I know what it's like to have a big snowball, slushball, and iceball fight in the winter but it ain't so tuff as having a musket fight in the woods in Illinois in the winter, freezing cold winter. And them army guys didn't have no partment house with steam heat and radiators to dry out there wet clothes neither. George Rogers Clark's army even had to sleep in the water because all the rivers flooded and there was no dry ground. If Nicholas been there in Illinois he probly woulda burnt down the whole country just trying to dry his clothes. I think I'm gonna put Nicholas in my story. Nicholas can make the story a little more fun. Them soldiers need something to laff at. It's only fair that I give them Nicholas. Oh, heck, I'll give them Earnest too. That's gonna make their suffering go faster and all.

Dear John,

What with Earnest and Nicholas in the history story, the facts are gonna get even more funner.

Dear John,

I got about 5 pages done on my story about Jeremiah Hamilton and how he got into the army. Well it was the spring in 1777 and Jeremiah figgers he gotta help his new country and go jern the army even if he's only 15 years old. But his mom don't want him to go. She wants him to stay home in Kentucky and finish school because he's real good at school and gets to sit in the first seat and all. But he says it's only right that he go off because the Indians are scalping the settlers and the English general is buying the scalps and giving the Indians guns and real sharp knives for cutting off more scalps.

Well Jeremiah Hamilton's gonna join up and there's lots of teary stuff when his mom says goodbye but Jeremiah don't cry til he gets a mile down the road. Heroes don't ever let nobody see them cry. Well, he jerns up with George Rogers Clark's army what are called "Big Knives" because they think they're sharp and all. Jeremiah Hamilton gets trained in boot camp and Earnest and Nicholas get trained at the same time and they all get to be real good friends. They got about 200 soldgers in the army and they go up from Kentucky and capture a place called Kaskaskia and they don't gottta kill nobody. The people in Kaskaskia like it that they get captured so they don't put up a fight. They put up nothing but a white flag.

Then one day Earnest is in Kaskaskia and he's been having a real good time and is real tired and had just a little too much to drink like soldgers do sometimes and so he's walking down the street in Kaskakia and he meets another guy and Earnest makes like he's real sick and cons the other guy into carrying him on his back all the way back to camp. When they get to camp, Earnest jumps down and says thanks for the ride. It's only then that he sees the white collar around this guy's neck. Well the guy Earnest conned was a priest what's named Father Gibault whose a real good friend of Colonel George Rogers Clark. I left off there for a while. Maybe Jeremiah and Nicholas are gonna visit Earnest in the jail what Earnest told me is called the brig.

Dear John,

Earnest told me he's writing a report about a hero what's named Captain Edward Teach. He was a captain of a ship and he got dead in a fight with some English guy. Earnest told me Captain Edward Teach was a real good hero because the English Captain knifed him eleven times and shot him five times and Captain Edward Teach just gets up and starts fighting again. A hero ain't no quitter and when a hero dies by being a hero and all, then he gets to be remembered as a hero forever and ever.

Dear John,

When all that stuff with George Rogers Clark was going on, George Washington was having a real tuff time at Valley Forge and they had a real bad winter too. I'll hafta get something about that in my story.

Dear John,

Earnest really likes this hero what's named Captain Edward Teach. Earnest says before he died he got lots of silver and gold and treasure.

I told Earnest maybe the nun was right about heroes getting great rewards.

Dear John,

Christine Carney is still looking for somebody to beat up Peter Ackerman. Christine Carney says if no one in this neighborhood will take the contract, she's going outside the neighborhood. Earnest says, "That just ain't right. It's like my mom says we should keep it in the family. We can't let Christine Carney take this out of the neighborhood."

Dear John,

Lots of stuff was going on during the winter of 1778. Benjamin Franklin was over in France getting all kinds of help and getting them French people to be our friends. This is really an interesting fact but I can't fit it all into my story except maybe someday I can write a big book.

Dear John,

It was a real close call for Peter Ackerman last night. Christine Carney got a big kid from Flatbush to come up and beat up Peter Ackerman but it don't work out. Well lucky for Peter Ackerman, me and Earnest found out about it because Christine Carney was bragging about what was gonna happen. This guy from Flatbush is gonna be laying for Peter Ackerman in the cellar of the partment house what he lives in. So last night Peter Ackerman was coming home from the altar boys' meeting and he gotta go through the cellar of his partment house because the big front door is broke and nobody can open it for about a year. Me and Earnest get to the cellar real early with some scientific equipment what Earnest and me got together. We got this statue of a saint getting his head chopped off what we loaned from the cellar of the church and we set up some other stuff. Then we took all the bulbs out of the lights so it was real dark. And then we wait.

About 9 o'clock this big monstrous looking guy from Flatbush comes down the cellar stairs and hides behind the door. Earnest flips a switch and a little flicker of a light starts to glow right in the middle of the cellar. Real slow Earnest turns the dial on the registor box and the light grows and grows and grows and the light's growing brighter and you can see this saint with blood all over him and his eyes way up in the top of his head and then Earnest throws a moaning and groaning switch on the tape recorder. The speaker is right under the bloody saint and then Earnest turns the switch on and off on the electric magnets and a sheet what's hanging from the beams starts to shake. First this big guy comes out from behind the door just a little and looks at the light. Then his mouth opens what with the light getting bigger. Then he grabs the door when the moans and groans start and when the sheets get shaking, he's out of the cellar and running down the street. Funny he musta passed right by Peter Ackerman who comes into the cellar about a minute later. But me and Earnest are still hiding and when Peter Ackerman comes in, we try the same thing. One problem, the tape of the moans and groans runs out and the rest of the tape got a Spike Jones song with a guy singing "The Blue Danube walls, it's green not blue." It's a real swell song and all but it just wasn't all that scary. So Peter just keeps walking past the bloody saint and goes up the stairs. When Peter Ackerman gets to the top of the stairs, he yells down, "Nice try."

Dear John,

Me and Earnest almost got cort by Father McNulty when we put back the statue. Father McNulty sees us down in the church basement but he don't think much of it because we ain't no where near the bottles of wine. So I said, "Father, who is that guy and how come he got all that blood all over him?"

Father McNulty says, "That's St. John the Baptist getting his head cut off."

Dear John,

Peter Ackerman got more bravery than I figgered. St. John the Baptist looks scary even when it ain't dark. Maybe Peter Ackerman ain't such a bad kid and I think I'm gonna help him outa this problem what he got. I'm gonna think about how I'm gonna do it. But I can't snitch on Earnest. No! That ain't a good idear. It ain't right to snitch.

Dear John,

I finished my story about Colonel George Rogers Clark, Jeremiah Hamilton, Earnest and Nicholas. Earnest don't never gotta go to the brig because Jeremiah Hamilton gets this great idear about going down the Ohio River and attacking the British from the rear. They started with about a thousand soldgers what hadda travel 12 hundred miles in the freezing cold snow and I showed how tuff it was. Some cowards deserted and it was so cold some of the soldiers woke up froze to death. So by the time the army gets to this town what's called Vincennes they only had 175 soldgers in the whole army. They had no more food and all the gun powder was wet and ain't worth a darn. But the people in the town were real happy to see the army because they heard good things about the Americans from Father Girault. Now I know there's a problem here but I figger the priest said good things about the Americans but that was before he got to meet Earnest and Nicholas.

Well here's where I stretched the facts a little because I had Earnest and Nicholas go around to the front of the fort with about 10 other soldgers. That night the 12 of them soldgers made a crummy little fort in the front of the English fort. The fort looked real good from far away but it wasn't worth a darn. Then the ten soldgers go back to Colonel George Rogers Clark and tell him what they done and all.

The next morning Earnest and Nicholas run around shooting and whooping and making so much noise that the English think they was a hundred of Big Knives attacking the front of the fort. But it was only them two Little Knives. Now that ain't exactly a big stretch of the facts because Earnest and Nicholas can get so noisy it sounds like a hundred kids.

The English come out of their fort to fight but Earnest and Nicholas do the right thing. They up and run away. George Rogers Clark, Jeremiah Hamilton, and 173 soldiers just walk in the back door of the British fort what somebody forgot to lock. It was a real thrilling part when they put up the American flag and played the Stars Spangled Banner real loud on the phonograph. Then the Americans set off the hidden dynamite and blow up their own fort what the British captured. Boom! Well I made it like it was all Jeremiah Hamilton's plan and Earnest and Nicholas was real good soldgers. Only I had to make it look like a big battle so I had one of the British soldiers shoot Nicholas in the head. But that don't change Nicholas none. This all happened on a Tuesday in a freezing blizzard and on a very cold day. It was February 19, 1779.

Then the exciting part comes. The head of the English army what's named General Hamilton takes off into the woods on his horse and Jeremiah Hamilton borrows a horse and takes after him. Big chase. Bang, bang, galoop, galoop, bang. Then Jeremiah Hamilton gets knocked off his horse by a tree branch and then General Hamilton comes back to kill Jeremiah Hamilton. The general's standing over him ready to shoot and Jeremiah opens his eyes and sees General Hamilton. Jeremiah's eyes get real big, his mouth opens and he says, "Uncle Henry?" He says this because General Henry Hamilton is Jeremiah's uncle, his dad's brother. Well General Hamilton can't shoot his own nefew. So he just stands there looking kinda stoopid with his mouth open and all. Then all of a sudden a bunch of American soldiers surround General Hamilton and he gets captured. He gets put in irons in a dungeon but Jeremiah always visits General Hamilton and brings him cookies and kool aide and they get to be good friends. The story was 15 pages long.

Dear John,

Peter Ackerman almost got it last night. When he walks into his cellar, a bucket of water was supposed to fall on his head. But he was being polite and he holds the door for Mr. Bransky. Mr. Bransky got real wet and real mad.

Dear John,

I got an F for my hero story. The nun says the grade was for spelling. She counted the number of words what I spelled wrong and takes one pernt off for each. I got 122 words spelled wrong. I wooda had more only she didn't count them two times. She says my real grade was minus 22 below zero and that gets added to my average. I never heard of a minus grade getting added. Ain't that sort of a subtraction? Minus 22 below zero makes me shiver. I kinda wish she told us in the beginning she was gonna grade for spelling. Next time I write a report I'm making it real short so I don't get so many words spelt wrong.

Dear John,

I told Earnest that at least the nun ain't giving me an F because I got the facts wrong. Earnest says the nun probably never read my story. She just went right for the spelling mistakes.

Dear John,

I gotta plan to help Peter Ackerman because he ain't such a bad kid. I told Christine Carney that I'd take the contract and get Peter Ackerman. She says she got ten dollars saved up now but I don't want no money, just help in writing my hero story. She gotta write it again for me and make no mistakes in spelling or nuthing. She can do that real good. She's real surprised but says O.K.

Dear John,

It sure is funny that a kid like Christine Carney can be so good in school but in the neighborhood sometimes the same kid can be really really different. Earnest is like that too but in the opposite way. In school he can be real dumb but in the neighborhood he's smart like a jeanius.

Dear John,

It was real fun writing that hero story even if I got an F. I think it's a real good story and I think the nun wood think it's a reel good story if she ever read it.

Dear John,

I told Peter Ackerman how I'm gonna help him. He likes the idear.

Dear John,

I forgot to tell you we had a history test on the Revolution War and today we got the tests back and I passed. I got a C. I wooda got an A because I got all the facts and dates right but the nun took off for spelling.

Dear John,

Peter Ackerman came to school today on crutches with a broken arm and all bandaged up with blood coming out from under the bandages and a big scar all across his head. Christine Carney's real satisfied with my good work. Peter Ackerman says he don't know what happened. He was walking into his cellar and next thing he wakes up in the hospital.

Dear John,

Christine Carney done a great job on my hero story. She fixed the spelling and gramma but she don't change any of my idears. She even told me they was pretty good idears. I mailed it on the corner to the New York Daily Mirror writing contest.

Dear John,

I ain't gonna bother with writing no science report. It's already 5 days late so I can't get no more than a 50 and I ain't even gonna get near that because the nun's gonna find so many spelling mistakes and other stuff wrong with it. I'm gonna get a minus number again. If I don't write the report, I get zero. If I write the report, I get a minus. I get a better grade for not writing the report. Minus 22 is a lot lower than zero. I'm getting smarter at arithmetic.

Dear John,

Last week the nun was real happy because Earnest handed in his report about a hero but today she gave it back with a big fat zero. She said, "Captain Edward Teach was also called 'Blackbeard, The Pirate' and he was no hero."

Dear John,

Peter Ackerman forgot about his broken arm and all. He was playing stick ball today. Lucky thing Christine Carney ain't around to see him.

Dear John,

Earnest told me he found a book in the liberry what had some stuff about George Rogers Clark. Earnest got interested in my story because I made him and Nicholas heroes what with their whooping it up and sounding like a hundred soldiers. Earnest said that George Rogers Clark beat the English and stopped the Indians from scalping so many settlers because we put the hair buyer in jail. That's what they called General Hamilton. George Rogers Clark was a real hero. He even put up his own money to buy supplies and stuff for his Big Knives army. But after the war he asked the govament to pay him back but they never did. When George Rogers Clark died, he had no money. Nobody cared about all the good what he done. He never did get no big rewards.

Dear John,

I got a real pretty certificate from the New York Daily Mirror. It says my hero story about Colonel George Rogers Clark got honorable mention. I showed the certificate to the nun and she says, "That's nice. Now get back to your seat."

Chapter 10
Strangers

Sixth Grade

Dear John,

Every morning, right after prayers and the Pledge, we get Religion. We got this book what got questions and ansers and we gotta memorize em all, every single woird just the way it got wrote. It's the Baltimore Cattekism but Earnest calls it a Catchyakism. I don't know why but Earnest likes to change words around sometimes.

Dear John,

Earnest says the Baltimore Catchyakism got questions and ansers and he ain't never seen no other book like it. Earnest says the Baltimore Catchyakism is a real strange book.

Maybe that's because Earnest don't spend a lot of time looking at all that many books. So for Earnest all books are strange.

Dear John,

Earnest done it again. He raises his hand and asks the nun a question. That don't ever work out good. This time Earnest ask the nun about the Baltimore Catchyakism. Earnest ask, "How come the Baltimore Catchyakism ask the questions when it already knows the answers."

At first I figger the nun is going to whack him on the head with the yardstick but she don't. The nun don't even pay no attention to the way Earnest pronunciates the word. The nun jest says it's the stile of the book and it's been that way for a long time and a priest in Baltimore wrote it and that's why it's called the Baltimore Cattekism.

Then Earnest asks what stile is but the nun says "No more questions."

Dear John,

Earnest told me he wasn't all that worried because the nun broke the last yardstick and there ain't no more yardsticks in the supply closet. Earnest is getting to be real good friends with the school janitor.

Dear John,

There is this girl in my class named Delores Donovan. Something strange happened to her. All of a sudden she got real beautiful. It just happened. I never paid no attenshun to her before because she was kinda quiet most of the time. But last Friday night we had a church dance and she shows up with lipstick on and a real pretty dress what got a low front if you know what I mean, John. She looks so swell. She's real gorgeous, hubba, hubba. But the nun comes over and Delores Donovan's gotta rub off the lipstick and stuff. She hadda put on a sweater too and button it all the way up.

Ding it. She hadda do it. But I saw enuff. Delores Donovan looks real swell.

I wanted to ask Delores Donovan to dance right away. But Patrick Garino is over there in a flash and dances with her most of the night. One time I seen Delores Donovan sitting alone. No Patrick Garino around. I almost run but Patrick Garino gets there first again. He got two sodas and gives one to Delores Donovan.

But there I am on the other side of the room and I walk fast and bump into a lot of people dancing. So when I get there after rushing real fast, I don't wanna look stupid so I said, "Hi" to Delores Donovan and Patrick Garino and I ask Kathleen Kelly to dance. That's Delores Donovan's best friend. Kathleen Kelly ain't exactly bad looking but she's got lots of pimples. So we dance but I keep pretty far away. I might catch something. Later I seen Patrick Garino helping Delores Donovan put on her coat and they left the party together. Delores Donovan looked so swell, hubba, hubba!

Dear John,

I figger if a priest wrote that Cattekism, nothing can be wrong about it. Priests can't make no mistakes. The nun says the pope can't make no mistake because he's unmistakable. I guess some of that rubs off on the priests, espeshally that priest in Baltimore what wrote the Baltimore Cattekism.

Dear John,

Me and Earnest been talking about the cattekism. Earnest says, "How come that priest asks the question if he already already got the answer?"

I told Earnest that priests know all the answers to all the questions and priests are unmistakable because they get it from the pope.

But Earnest says they may be unmistakable because of the funny clothes they wear but he thinks the word I mean is infailable.

Dear John,

This is very exciting news! Patrick Garino told me that Kathleen Kelly is in love with me. Delores Donovan told him to tell me so I can ask Kathleen Kelly out. But then Kathleen Kelly got all them pimples. I don't know. Maybe I'll ask her out. I just won't look at her.

Dear John,

Earnest's done some more thinking about the Baltimore Cattekism and he says the priest what wrote the Baltimore Cattekism got the right idear after all. Earnest says some books just say all the ansers and don't never ask no questions. Then Earnest ask me, "What good are the answers if you don't got no questions?"

Dear John,

I done some thinking about what Earnest said and I ask him, "What good is a question if there ain't no way to get the answer." Earnest puts his hand up to his chin, a thing what he does when he's thinking hard, and then he says, "You jist make one up." Me and Earnest think about really strange stuff.

Dear John,

I told Earnest I'm thinking about asking Kathleen Kelly to go out with me on a date to Randy's Restaurant. Earnest says he knows all about that sort of stuff because he gots lots of girl friends. Earnest says, "The main thing about girls is they like to talk about themselves. So the main thing for a guy to do is let them talk. And if, all of a sudden, they don't got nothing to say, just ask them a question like, 'How come you got such pretty eyes?' They like questions like that one." Earnest stops and puts his hand up to his chin and then he says, "Girls gotta talk and guys gotta listen. Girls like it that way. That's the main thing to remember!"

Dear John,

It's kinda strange that Earnest knows so much about girls because I ain't never see him with a lot of girls.

Dear John,

I'm gonna ask Kathleen Kelly out. I told Earnest that I don't like Kathleen Kelly's pimples but Earnest says I gotta start somewhere to get experience just like he done. Earnest says, "Girls always got problems. If it ain't pimples it's gonna be something else."

Dear John,

I told Earnest, "The cattekism asks why God made us and then says God made us so that we can be happy with him in heaven. I guess God don't wanna be all alone. There wasn't nobody to talk to in heaven so God invented people. But we gotta do time on earth first before going to heaven. So how come God done that? Why don't God just make us already set for heaven?"

Earnest says, "If God done it that way, then we don't never hafta go to school. What would God want all the nuns to do if they don't got no schools? He done it this way to keep all them nuns out of his hair."

Dear John,

I don't know if Earnest is right but I do know he is real good at making up answers.

Dear John,

So today the nun ask, "Are there any questions about homework?"

I got no questions about homework because I don't do any. But I been thinking about religion and God and all. So I raises my hand and I ask the nun, "How come we don't just go to heaven and be happy? How come God makes us to be happy in heaven but only if we go to school and go through a lot of other trouble to get there?"

But then the nun says, "That's a silly question." Then she says, "No more questions." I don't worry so much about asking questions and getting whacked with the yardstick because Earnest helps the janitor clean the closets and Earnest made sure there ain't no more rulers anywhere in this whole school.

Dear John,

Earnest says I ask a real good question and their ain't nuthing silly about it. He thinks it's all kinda strange how God don't wanna be alone and all. He says it don't make real good sense for God to put people on earth when all He wants is to not be so lonely in heaven. Then Earnest puts his hand up to his chin and says, "I think that question you asked, got no answer."

Dear John,

I asked Kathleen Kelly to go out with me to Randy's Restaurant for lunch tomorrow.

She says, "O.K. but can Delores Donovan come?"

"Sure, of course, natcherly." I says, "Yes. That's a great idear."

So I figger it's this way. Tomorrow I go out with Delores Donovan and Kathleen Kelly can come along.

Dear John,

I seen Kathleen Kelly after school and I told her to meet me in the school yard outside the boy's gate at lunch time so we can go to Randy's Restaurant. I tell her, "Make sure Delores Donovan is there with you."

She says, "O.K."

Dear John,

At lunch time today I walk across the school yard and then I seen Delores Donovan and Kathleen Kelly. Only one problem. The problem's name is Patrick Garino. So the four of us go to the Randy's Restaurant for lunch.

Delores Donovan giggles all the time and, when she ain't giggling, she's talking about how lucky she is to have pretty hair and stuff like that. She says boys look at her all the time and even high school boys wanna take her out. Delores Donovan keeps right on showing off and bragging about how pretty she is and all.

Kathleen Kelly talks to me kinda quiet and asks me lots of questions about what I like and what I like to do and what I think are the best movies and all.

Dear John,

Patrick Garino is just a jerk. Everybody can see that, except Delores Donovan.

Dear John,

We learned today in Religion that if you're bad and commit sin, espeshally a mortal sin, that's a big one, then God condems you and you gotta go to hell when you die. From what the nun says hell ain't such a swell place at all.

But then last week the nun said God loves us and that's why he made us and He loves us even when we're bad. That's strange. If I'm gonna love somebody I don't want them to go to hell no matter what they do. How come God sends people to hell when what He really wants is company in heaven? That's really strange!

Dear John,

I ask the nun, "How come God sends people to hell if he loves them?"

She says, "God tries to save us and he died for us so we can go to heaven. God showed how much He loved us when He died on a cross for our sins. God wants all of us to be together and to be happy with him forever in heaven."

Dear John,

God done a lot of important and good stuff for us. But how come he don't figger out an easier way to save us so He don't get nailed and all. I mean like there gotta be an easier way to get us saved. I ask the nun but she just gives me a bad look and says I ask too many questions.

Dear John,

Earnest asked me how my date went with Delores Donovan. I told him about how she bragged about herself and all.

Earnest says, "She's definitly the prettyest girl in the class but the problem is that she knows it."

Dear John,

I liked Delores Donovan a whole lot better when she wasn't so pretty. She used to be quiet and nice. Now she's showing off like all the time, espeshally around Patrick Garino. She gets silly a lot and giggles. And she's always looking in a mirror.

Dear John,

Kathleen Kelly really likes to talk to me real nice. She told me she thinks my questions about religion are good questions. Kathleen Kelly is real innerested in God and stuff like religion. Her mom was gonna be a nun and her dad was gonna be a priest until they get together. They all go to church every single morning, Mass and Communion.

Dear John,

I asked Kathleen Kelly, "How come God makes people go to hell just if they commit only one mortal sin?"

She says, "God doesn't send people to hell. People have free will to do what they want." She says, "It's like the person and the devil make an agreement to be on the same side against God. So if you're on the devil's side and you die, then you gotta go and live where the devil lives in hell because you're on his side. People can choose."

Dear John,

The devil tricks people because when you're in hell, you don't get to be with nobody else not even the devil talks to you. Kathleen Kelly says hell is a real lonely place. I figger a place that's crowded can still be a lonely place.

Dear John,

Kathleen Kelly gives me good answers to my questions. She's smarter than the nun.

Dear John,

I like talking to Kathleen Kelly. She's real smart and talks real good. She talks a lot like a teacher. She don't say stuff like, "I ain't." She says, "I am not." Another thing. She's almost as smart as Christine Carney but she don't show none of that. Maybe Kathleen Kelly just don't wanna show off. I figger she let's Christine Carney get better grades on purpose. O.K. I know Kathleen Kelly got pimples but they ain't bad looking pimples. I seen worser pimples in my life.

Dear John,

We gotta memorize questions and answers from the cattekism every night and then every morning the nun calls on a coupla kids. She asks the questions and we gotta answer exactly the same way that the priest wrote it. I try to memorize all them woirds but it's hard. I'm glad the nun ain't called on me yet but any day now my number's gonna be up.

Dear John,

I think I know why Earnest calls it catchyakism.

Dear John,

Kathleen Kelly says that first I gotta understand what the question and answer mean and then it's easier to remember. She says she's gonna help me understand them first and then I can memorize them better.

Dear John,

I walked into the classroom and I seen Kathleen Kelly. Surprise! No pimples. I keep looking at her and she smiles at me and her face gets just a little pink. She looks really pretty. Hubba, hubba. Then I look closer. I walk right down her row and look right at her about an inch away from her nose. Well the pimples are still there but they're under something else. At lunch we got a date at Randy's Restaurant and she tells me she went to a doctor and she got medsin to put on the pimples. It covers them up and helps them dry up too. She gotta put the medsin on and wash her face real good and she can't eat no more butter and candy and stuff. No more Randy's greasy hamburgers. Kathleen Kelly had a apple for lunch. The doctor says all her pimples are gonna go away pretty soon.

Dear John,

I'm sittin in class real low in my seat today but the nun calls on me for a cattekism answer anyways.

She holds the book up and reads, "Why did Jesus die on the cross?"

"Well," I says, "He got court and nailed so that the gates can get open to heaven. They been closed since Adam and

311

Eve ate the apple and God was so mad that he just shut them gates. See the sin was so bad because they got into like a partnership with the devil and went against God. But then God don't like being alone and maybe Him and the angels don't got nothing new and exciting to talk about. So God hadda fix this whole mess what Adam and Eve made. So God figgers the best way to handle this is to send his son, named Jesus, down here and to die because no person could be important enuff to die for such a big sin. So God hadda become man to be important enuff to atone (I remember that word from the book) for our sins."

I was gonna keep going but the nun cuts me off right there and says that's not the answer word for word from the catechism. Now I gotta write the catechism answer 20 times.

Dear John,

Now I really know why Earnest calls it a catchyakism.

Dear John,

Kathleen Kelly says that my answer was really good because it showed that I understand but I also need to memorize the right words.

Well I know that my answer was O.K. in meaning because Kathleen Kelly explained it all to me last night but I don't have no time to memorize the exact words. I figger it's more important to know what your talking about and just say it in your own words. If you say it in your own words, then you really know what it means. But that don't do it for the nun.

Dear John,

Patrick Garino got called on for a cattekism question. The nun ask him a question about purgatory and he got all the words eggsactly right. At lunch time I ask Patrick Garino what it means when the cattekism says purgatory is the place where we atone for our sins. Patrick Garino says, "I don't know." Patrick Garino just memorizes the answers but he don't know what it means. He got a hundred in religion and I got a big fat zero.

Dear John,

Me and Kathleen Kelly kissed last night. I was over at her house watching the Ed Sullivan Show. Her mom was watching with us but she don't like Polish tight rope walkers. Mrs. Kelly gets up and leaves when the Polish tight rope walkers come on. She says, "I hate Polish tight rope walkers." And she goes into the kitchen. I'm sitting on the couch next to Kathleen Kelly and I watch her mom leave. Then I hear the water running and the dishes getting washed. Then I reach over and grab Kathleen Kelly's hand. She turns slowly and I put one right on her lips. She smiles.

Dear John,

I was going to the store on Grand and I met Kathleen Kelly. We got to talking and Kathleen Kelly takes out a pepermint life saver and ask me to take one. I say "No thanks, I ain't hungry." She says, "Take it. It'll be good for you." I don't want it but I take it. Then Kathleen Kelly's gotta go home but first she gives me little kiss smack right on my lips.

Dear John,

Earnest seen me talking to Kathleen Kelly. I told him about the life saver what Kathleen Kelly really wanted me to take. Earnest told me, "When a girl asks you to take a life saver, you gotta take it because it ain't about being hungry." Then Earnest asks me if I had garlic for lunch. I don't eat no garlic for lunch. I had a hamburger with a roar onion.

Dear John,

I got lucky today. The nun calls on me for a catechism answer what I memorized. Maybe Kathleen Kelly's right but sometimes it's real hard to understand what you gotta memorize. So I done what Patrick Garino says. I memorized it real quick because it's short. The nun ask, "What is the sixth commandment?"

I says, "Thou shout not commit adultairy."

Dear John,

I ask Earnest if he knows what adultairy means. He says he knows all about it. He's gonna splain it to me but then Kathleen Kelly's coming and Earnest says, "It ain't right to talk about it when girls are around because adultairy is one of them fighting words."

Dear John,

Earnest splains to me that adultairy is what older people do when they fool around. He says his mom and dad fight about it all the time. He says his mom don't want his dad fooling around no more. She says he gotta stop doing adultairy.

Dear John,

Earnest says we don't gotta worry about committing adultairy because it's only for older people and that's why it's got adult in its name.

Dear John,

I figger it's O.K. for people like Kathleen Kelly to be real religious, what with going to church every day and all. I go to church almost every Sunday. That's enuff for me.

Dear John,

Father McNulty come to our class yesterday and says he needs more altar boys. Peter Ackerman and Patrick Garino are already getting to be altar boys. Then Father McNulty reads a list of boys names what the nun gives him. I'm listening for my name, "John Volare, Anthony Gucci, Ralph Bramski, and Johnny Paizano." Then he says these guys should study the Latin and take lessons from him and then they can be altar boys.

I raise my hand and ask, "How come my name ain't on the list?"

The priest looks at the nun and the nun smiles and says, "It would behoove you to learn English before venturing forth into Latin."

Dear John,

I talked to Kathleen Kelly about what the nun says. She splains that the nun means I gotta learn English real good.

I tell Kathleen Kelly, "Maybe I don't know English like a lot of people but I know American real good. Everybody I know understands what I say and I understand what everybody says except maybe the nun sometimes. That nun talks real strange."

Kathleen Kelly smiles and says that she can help me improve my English if I want.

Dear John,

They been trying to teach me to talk and write good in school for years and it ain't never woiked. I mean I memorize all them parts of speech and the defnitions, diagram sentences, and I done my homework in the Amsco Review Book some of the time. But I don't talk or write any different. When I take the spelling tests, I can do pretty good but then I don't remember to spell them woirds write on letters and stories and stuff. I hate writing. Kathleen Kelly says she can help me with English like she done with religion.

Dear John,

I ask the nun about the adult part of adultairy but she says "No more questions." Then she says Father Smott will be in next week to splain what adultairy means. I guess he's coming back because what he told us last time don't take.

Dear John,

Earnest says he's been thinking lots about that sixth commandment. He says you gotta get married before you can do adultairy.

Dear John,

An acrobat team from Peru was on the Ed Sullivan Show last night. Kathleen Kelly's mom gets up and goes into the kitchen. She says, "I hate acrobat teams from Peru." So I got to kiss Kathleen Kelley when her mom leaves the room. That medsin sure is good for Kathleen Kelly's face. She got almost no more pimples.

Dear John,

Kathleen Kelly can't eat nothing sweet or greasy. So when we go out on a date at Randy's Restaurant, she just drinks water with her sanwich. I used to get two straws and we use to share a chocolate malted. That was real romantic. Kathleen Kelly says, "It's a choice between sweets and pimples." I figger she's right because every day she keeps getting prettyer and prettyer.

Dear John,

After school today me and Kathleen Kelly go to Randy's Restaurant for a soda but Kathleen Kelly says she just wants a glass of water. So I figure it can still be romantic if we both drink the same water. So I ask Randy for two straws with the glass of water. Randy shakes his head and says, "You get one straw and only one straw with a glass of water." Me and Kathleen Kelly had a two cents plain with two straws.

Dear John,

Kathleen Kelly told me that she gets real scared when she thinks about going to hell if she dies with a mortal sin on her soul.

Dear John,

When I go out with Kathleen Kelly, we talk a lot and I try to talk good like she does. I don't say "I ain't" no more. I say, "I am not."

Dear John,

Kathleen Kelly and me both got invited to a party at Peter Ackerman's house on Friday night. Delores Donovan and Patrick Garino are going. And Peter invited guess who? Christine Carney. Swell. Peachy keen. Christine Carney gonna be a party pooper.

Dear John,

Peter Ackerman says anybody can do adultairy.

Earnest asked him, "Can you do adultairy?"

Perter Ackerman says, "Of course."

Earnest asks "How long you been married?"

Dear John,

We played spin the bottle at Peter Ackerman's party. I got to kiss Delores Donovan. It wasn't so great. Then I hadda kiss Frances Magatarino. Boy does she give wet ones. But when I hadda kiss Christine Carney, I almost throwed up. I didn't get to kiss Kathleen Kelly with spin the bottle but then we played post office. That's a swell game espeshally with all the lights out. It wasn't no little peck on the cheek. I guess one kiss took ten minutes. Then we all wanted to play it again except for Jimmy Veepy who got Christine Carney. Franky Bazaaro was all set to play it again right after he washed off his face. He had Frances Magatarino. Then I danced with Kathleen Kelly almost all night. I like the slow dances some times because I get to hold her real tight. I like Rock Around the Clock too. It's like a fast Lindy. We played it about 10 times. I walked Kathleen Kelly home and I kissed her on her front stoop. Then all of a sudden the light above her door goes on and her father opens the door. I said, "Goodnight." Me and Kathleen Kelly shake hands.

Dear John,

I'm gonna invite Kathleen Kelly out on a real date to a movie. Elizabeth Taylor, hubba hubba, is in a movie and I seen that movie is on the Legion of Decency Bad List. But we can go because when we hadda stand up in church and pledge not to go to bad movies, I don't say nothing. I moved my lips but not one word comes out and besides I had my fingers crossed. It's O.K. for Kathleen Kelly because she don't know it's on the bad list. So it ain't no sin for her.

Dear John,

I took Kathleen Kelly to the movies last night. She wore lipstick and stuff and looked real good. Hubba, hubba. The picture wasn't so good. It was called "A Place in the Sin." That Elizabeth Taylor is real pretty except she talks kinda funny. But we sat in the back row and hugged and kissed a lot. I put my arm around Kathleen Kelly and we sat real close.

Dear John,

In our Amsco book we have to fill in sentences with the words "good" and "well." Good is an adjective and well is an adverb. But I don't got no idear what that means. I always thought well meant you weren't sick. I ask Kathleen Kelly and she splains it. It ain't easy but now I understand it real good.

Dear John,

We had a test in English on adjectives and adverbs. I didn't do so good. But Kathleen Kelly says it's real important that I know both English and American. She says I can't go to college if I don't write English good. No. She don't say it

319

that way. She says, "I can not go to college if I don't write English well." I never figgered on going to college before. But Kathleen Kelly says I got enough brains. I don't know.

Dear John,

Butch Bronson from upstairs in my house goes to Brooklyn College and my dad says his mom and dad are just showing off. My dad says, "The Bronsons think they're better than everybody else because Butch Bronson goes to Brooklyn College." My dad says people what go to college are pushy and college is a waste of time. My dad never even finished high school and he got to be a clerk in the Chase National Bank.

Dear John,

I told Kathleen Kelly to kick me every time I make a mistake in English. She says no but she will kick me only when I say good when I should say well. She said that if she kicks me at every mistake I won't be able to walk any more.

Dear John,

Peter Ackerman says that if you go steady with one girl and kiss another girl, that's adultairy. So he says sometimes you don't gotta be an adult. You just gotta act like an adult to commit adultairy.

Dear John,

Earnest says he checked it out and he thinks Peter Ackerman's wrong about adultairy. He says if you get married and kiss another woman, that's adultairy. He knows because he seen his dad doing adultairy just last week with Mrs. Glendetski who lives upstairs from him. He knows that was adultairy because Earnest's mom saw his dad and Mrs. Glendetsky kissing and when she was screaming at him, she said adultairy over and over for days.

Dear John,

We gotta write a research report about some animal and I ask Kathleen Kelly to help me but she gotta go with her family to Hoboken, New Jersey, for the weekend. So I gotta write it myself. I'm going to the liberry and find out about dinosaurs.

Dear John,

I don't make it to the liberry. I seen Earnest and then we went to Randy's Restaurant and I had a two cents plain. Randy asks us if we want two straws and one soda. Me and Earnest don't think that's funny.

I told Earnest I'm writing my report about dinosaurs. Earnest's report is about rats.

Dear John,

I never got time to look up stuff about dinosaurs but I wrote the report anyways. I think it's pretty good. I used big words and it's like original. I even ask a question like the stile what that priest used in the Baltimore Cattekism. I don't copy none of it from the ensyclopedia like what I use to do. Here's what I done.

Research Report

I done my research report on flying dinosaurs and I figgered why they got extinguished. If you got a real emeny, then you got a predator. Well, the flying dinosaurs had predators named Neanderthals. So Neanderthals went after the flying dinosaurs. Why?

Well you ever walk under a building what got pigeons on the ledges? After you wipes crap out of your hair, don't you feel like killin every pigeon? Well when Neanderthals got crapped on by big flying dinosaurs, they went and extinguished every singel flying dinosaur. I'm glad too because it isn't too safe to walk in the street now anyways.

Dear John,

It's real strange this weekend because I wanna go see Kathleen Kelly but she's gone to Hoboken.

Dear John,

I let Kathleen Kelly read my report on Monday morning. I showed her how I knowed enuff not to write "ain't." I even used "well" three times too. I think she liked it and was proud that I ain't using ain't no more and that I used well three times because when she reads it, she's smiling. She says she's real sorry she had to go to Hoboken and she promised to help me write the next report.

Dear John,

Earnest says his dad and mom was fighting about adultairy again. His mom told his dad he gotta stop fooling around.

Dear John,

The nun gives me a big fat zero for my report on dinosaurs. On top of the page it says, Poor grammar, poor spelling, poor research. Then she marked up the paper so you can't see nothing but red ink. I hate writing. I just ain't no good at it and I hate it and I don't wanna go to college anyways. Kathleen Kelly got 95 and, of course, Christine Carney showed her 100 all around the class.

Dear John,

My dad's right about college. It's pushy and ain't for me.

Dear John,

My leg is all black and blue from Kathleen Kelly kicking me.

Dear John,

Sometimes she's all ready to kick but I say "well" instead of "good." Now we're gonna work on something else what I kinda remember learning about a long time ago. She splained why it ~~ain't~~ isn't ~~good~~ well to use two nos or nots in a sentence. She says that two negatives, that's a no or a not, don't mean ~~nuthing~~ anything. One knocks out the other. So I said I get it. Double or nuthing. Kathleen Kelly splains stuff better than the nun any day. So now Kathleen Kelly's gonna help me with double or nuthin negatives. I told her to punch my left arm for that one. My leg still hurts bad.

Dear John,

When I'm with Kathleen Kelly, I have to talk well but when I'm with my dad, it works better for me to talk good.

Dear John,

~~Me and Kathleen Kelly~~ Kathleen Kelly and I went to the church bazaar last night. It was really fun but I spent a

323

lot of money, $5. It takes me about a year to save that much. But it was worth it because Kathleen Kelly and me had such a swell time. She's fun to be with. The best thing was the ride on the Big Wheel. Kathleen and— me —I got stuck on the top for about 15 minutes. That was O.K. because we sat real close and kissed when her dad wasn't looking up at us. Her dad and mom drove us all home, me, Patrick Garino and Delores Donovan, Peter Ackerman, Franky Zacarro, Ralph Bramski, and of course their own daughter Kathleen Kelly. It was so crowded in the back of their Ford that Kathleen Kelly had to sit on my lap. I liked that real— good —well. Except her dad kept looking at me in the mirror.

Dear John,

Peter Ackerman and Patrick Garino got to be altar boys for the first time last week. They were on at the 9 o'clock Mass Sunday. I heard them saying the Latin. Sounded pretty well. Now I found out that tomorrow they get to be altar boys at a funeral during school. They get out of religion class and they don't have to worry about memorizing the catechism that day. Being an altar boy is a real well thing to be.

Dear John,

Kathleen Kelly only had to kick me three times so far this week for saying good instead of well. My leg feels well but my left arm don't feel all that good.

Dear John,

I forgot today was first Friday and I didn't go to Mass. See on First Friday we gotta go to school early at 8 and then we all line up in the school yard but we don't go to school.

We go to Mass. I got there at 8:30. Nobody's in the school yard so I figgers out what happened. So I waited around behind the church and then when my class came out, I just cut in the line like I was there all the time. The nun looked surprised when she turned around but she don't say ~~nothing~~ anything.

Dear John,

   It was real bad that I missed going to church on First Friday on account that it was the ninth one. I went to eight in a row and if I made it to just that last one, then I'd get a guarantee that I can go to heaven when I die. See the nun says that with nine First Fridays in a row, you get saved no matter what. She says that she ~~knowed~~ knew a man and he was real bad all his life and did adultairy and don't go to church and did bad stuff. Well, when he was drunk and got hit by a car, he asks for a priest and there a priest was there right away. The priest gives him extra munkshion. Then this guy dies but he got saved. The nun says that God sent the priest to save the drunk because he made the nine First Fridays when he was a kid. It was real helpful that the man what was driving the car what hit him was the priest.

Dear John,

   Earnest's dad don't live with him and his mom ~~no more~~ any more. He moved out and lives with a strange lady in Flatbush.

Dear John,

   I like being with Kathleen Kelly real well and talking to her. She helps me write and talk well and I like kissing her and hugging her because she feels well.

Dear John,

My dad says that when I talk to Kathleen Kelly, I sound real pushy and uppity. He says if I keep talking like that, people will think that I ain't from Brooklyn. He says I sound like a stranger. My dad says ain't a lot but I do not say anything about that to him.

Dear John,

~~Kathleen Kelly and _me_~~ Kathleen Kelly and I like watching the Ed Sullivan Show every Sunday night. Last night Ed Sullivan says that the act up next is Jugglers from New Jersey. But Mrs. Kelly gets excited and she don't get up. She says, "I love jugglers from New Jersey."

Dear John,

Kathleen Kelly says maybe we shouldn't kiss and all because of the sixth commandment. But I splained to her that the sixth commandment got nothing to do with kids. It's only for adults what fool around and ain't serius. She says she's not so sure. But then I kiss her and she smiles.

Dear John,

Kathleen Kelly says that dying isn't the worst thing to happen. She says the worst thing is going to hell and being alone forever. Sometimes Kathleen Kelly gets real serius.

Dear John,

Now I find out that altar boys get big bucks for funerals and weddings too. Patrick Garino and Peter Ackerman are really in the chips. Last week two funerals during school and one wedding on Saturday morning. In a well month I make maybe a buck delivering groceries on my bike but Patrick

Garino and Peter Ackerman get about two bucks for every funeral and wedding. If I made that much money, I could take Kathleen Kelly to swell places like the movies and when the church has the bazaar, we could go up on the Big Wheel all the time and maybe it'd break again.

~~I'm gonna~~ I am going to ask Father McNulty if I can be an altar boy. I'm getting better in English. Maybe I can be ready for Latin soon.

Dear John,

That sixth commandment is real inneresting but it's kinda strange that the nun never answers ~~no~~ any questions about it.

Dear John,

My dad heard me talking to Kathleen Kelly and says, "You're getting uppity talking like that. You sound stranger and stranger every day."

Dear John,

Patrick Garino gives Delores Donovan a friendship ring and he says they are going steady now. ~~Well ain't that swell!~~ Isn't that swell! I think that's the most stupidest idear I ever heard of. Just because he got enuff money from altar boying he thinks he can go steady. I think going steady is the stupidest idear ever. I think friendship rings are stupid too.

Dear John,

Earnest thinks going steady is the stupidest thing he ever heard. ~~Earnest says he ain't never going to~~ He says he won't ever go steady and get trapped by a girl. Earnest says

327

he likes to play the field. I told him I ~~ain't never~~ won't ever get trapped. I think friendship rings are stupid!

Dear John,

I gave Kathleen Kelly a friendship ring. I loaned some money from Earnest. That means Kathleen Kelly and I are going steady.

This is what happened. We had this date on Saturday to go the movies. I picked the movie real careful so that it is romantic. An American in Paris. That's like where all the romance started. It was sad and Kathleen Kelly cried and then I had to kiss her to make her feel well again.

Then we went to Randy's Restaurant and sat all alone in a booth and then I wips out the friendship ring. Kathleen Kelly was real surprised. When I ask her to go steady, she got tears in her eyes. I had to kiss her again to make her feel well. She says she has to think about going steady because this is a very serious thing to do. So she sits and thinks about a minute and then right away she says, "Yes." So Kathleen Kelly and I are going steady. What do you think about that, John?

Dear John,

Kathleen Kelly told me I shouldn't axe people because that would hurt them. She says the word is ask. I learned how to spell it the right way a long time ago but when I talk, I pronunciate it like axe. I have to work at that one because it's real hard to say ask and it's real easy to say axe.

Dear John,

I'm talking to Kathleen Kelly and my dad is there and he's listening to the way I'm trying to talk well and not axe ~~nobody~~ anybody and not saying ~~no~~ any double negatives and all. He walks away but he says, "Hi, Ho, The Lone Stranger rides again."

Dear John,

Father Smott came to our class today and talked to us about the sixth commandment. He says boys and girls can't touch except maybe shake hands and we definitely can't kiss, not even a quick smacker on the cheek, and we can't go steady and girls can't sit on boy's laps and we can't do ~~nothin~~ anything that leads to temptations to sin. He says all that is adultairy and we'll go to hell forever if we commit adultairy. I looked at Kathleen Kelly's and her face is real red when he's talking to us.

Dear John,

Kathleen Kelly won't kiss me no more. She don't wear my ring anymore.

Dear John,

Patrick Garino and Delores Donovan ain't going steady anymore neither.

Dear John,

I tried to kiss Kathleen Kelly but she yelled at me for the first time ever! She ~~ain't gonna~~ won't kiss me or nothing anymore. She says she went to confeshion and told the priest that we committed adultairy and he was real mad and she gotta say the rosary every night for a week for her penance.

Dear John,

Earnest says he committed adultairy lots of times. But he ain't gonna confess it to the priest because you gotta tell him how many times. He says he got too many times to count.

Dear John,

Earnest went to stay for a week in Flatbush with his dad who is living with Mrs. Glendetski who is Mr. Glendetski's strange wife.

Dear John,

I got nobody to talk to. I'm all alone. It's like being in hell.

Dear John,

I'm sitting all alone in Randy's Restaurant drinking a glass of water out of a straw and Kathleen Kelly walks in. She walks over like she's going to talk to me but she don't say nothing. She takes my hand and puts her ring in it. I put my arms out but she turns and walks out real fast.

Dear John,

I seen Kathleen Kelly in school and I try to talk to her. I just wanna talk to her but it don't do—no—any good. She acts like she don't know me anymore. It's just like we're strangers. Nothing ain't going well no more.

Chapter 11

Consequences

Sixth Grade

Dear John,

Peter Ackerman and Patrick Garino get to go to Rye Beach for a whole day because they're altar boys. They get to go during a school day and they even get $5 from the church and get to spend it all on the rides. They get to go up the East River on a big boat and I been thinking about becoming an altar boy.

Dear John,

I asked Father McNulty if I can be an altar boy and if I get to be an altar boy before June, can I go on the boat ride to Rye Beach and get the $5 and all. He says that I shouldn't want be an altar boy because of worldly things but I should have spiritual reasons deep in my heart for serving on the altar of God.

"Oh, yeah," I says, "That's the main thing. I really got spiritual reasons down at the bottom of my heart but at the top I just figger I can get done with all the Latin faster if I can get to go to Rye Beach and all."

Dear John,

My mom and dad and I went to the beach way out on Long Island. It's a place called Beau Rivage and it's in a little town called Freeport. It was still too cold to go swimming but we rented a row boat and my dad and I took turns rowing. Then we dropped the anchor and my dad took some pieces of chicken and stabbed them with a piece of wire. Then he showed me how to tie some string to it and we dropped the chicken into the water. I sat holding the piece of string with the chicken down on the bottom of the water. All of a sudden something starts tugging on my string. I pull it in real slow and there's a crab hanging on. My dad picks up a net and puts it down in the water under the crab and pulls it up and the crab is in the net. We got about 20 big crabs. They're called blue claws.

On the way home, first we got a flat tire on Sunrise Highway. I helped my dad change the tire and put the spare on. Then we got going and the motor overheated and we had to stop again on the Belt Parkway. My dad had to walk to a house and ask for some water for the motor. My mom was real thankful to God for the flat and the overheating. She says that God was stopping us because probably we would be in an accident or something worse if God didn't help us by giving us a flat tire and overheating our motor.

Dear John,

I told Earnest I wanna get to be an altar boy and he asked me why I wanna do a stupid thing like that. I told Earnest about the boat ride to Rye Beach and all but I said, "It's not really for the boat ride to Rye Beach. It's the spiritual reasons."

Earnest listens and says, "Whenever anybody tells you it ain't for the boat ride and it's for the spiritual reasons, it's for the boat ride."

Dear John,

Those crabs were really good. We berled them in hot water and then cracked open the shells and dipped them in butter. Pretty messy but really good.

Dear John,

I'm really glad I wasn't born to be a crab. I mean the crabs go around all the time picking up stuff what they eat and everything's O.K. But then one day they pick up jist by chance a piece of chicken and they wind up in a pot of berling water. I'm kinda sorry for the crabs what we cort and berld and ate.

Dear John,

My mom thinks that God watches over everything we do and she says that the old model A Ford we got is blessed because God protects us from worse things than flat tires and overheating.

My dad says, "It's time to buy another car."

Dear John,

The church is too small. So we're going to have a bazaar to get money to build a new and really big church. The church got a brand new beautiful Dodge for the big raffle and all us kids get to sell chances and whoever sells the most chances in each class gets a statue of Jesus getting crowned with thorns and with a lot of blood dripping from his head and back. It's real beautiful and makes you feel real sad and spiritual.

Dear John,

Dennis Densky and Freddy Miller showed me how to play poker last night. Freddy Miller is Dennis Densky's best friend and they just transferred from PS 18 to St. Mary's. I'm not too friendly with Dennis Densky but at least he don't go round beating up on kids any more which is a thing he used to do when I was back in PS 18. So we played poker and I lost 25 cents. When Freddy Miller deals, he always makes deuces wild and that means twos can count for any card you want it to count for. Freddy Miller's real lucky because he always winds up with two deuces in his hand whenever he deals and he always wins. He gets really lucky when he deals.

Dear John,

Kathleen Kelly's dad got a new job in Hoboken. She's going to move to New Jersey right away. I'm going to miss her. But she says that she's going to be coming back to visit the old neighborhood all the time.

Dear John,

Earnest said, "Whenever anybody says they're moving but they'll come back and visit the old neighborhood all the time, you ain't never gonna see them again."

Dear John,

My dad says the car needs to go to the gas station. It has big problems that will cost a lot of money. It needs a tune up and change of earl. The car is boining lots of earl and that's not good for the motor. But we don't got a budge it for that so we can't get the car fixed. My dad told my mom, "Getting that car fixed is throwing good money after bad."

My mom says, "We just need to put the car in God's hands and He'll always get us home safely. We don't need to get the car fixed. We just need to pray."

My dad says, "Right! We just need to pray for a new car."

Dear John,

Hoboken, New Jersey is really far away from Brooklyn. You got to get there by going over a bridge or under a tunnel or you got to take a ferry and go to Staten Island first. I'm going to miss Kathleen Kelly real bad even if we don't kiss anymore because of Father Smott and the sixth commandment and all. Ding it, dang it, darn!

Dear John,

Mrs. K is a real nice old lady who lives down the block and across the street in an apartment house. She likes to look out the window and she watches everybody and she always knows what's going on in the neighborhood. My mom told me Mrs. K use to run a beauty parlor in a store on the corner and that was a good place to get her hair cut but it was the best place to find out all the news of the neighborhood.

Mrs. K was coming home from the A & P and she had two big bags and it looked real hard for her to be carrying them. I asked her if I can help her and right away she gives me both bags. They were really heavy. My arms were getting real tired just after three blocks. But when we got upstairs to her apartment, Mrs. K gave me a piece of chocolate cake and a big glass of milk. Then she told me she heard that my love affair with Kathleen Kelly was over. She told me it made her happy to see us walking together holding hands. It reminded her of when she was young and Mr. K and her were in love. I couldn't finish eating all the cake because I got this lump in my throat. Her story was real beautiful but it made me kinda sad.

Dear John,

Mrs. K told me that our car sounds real bad and it makes very black smoke when it goes down the street and that means the car has a big problem with the motor. She told me I should tell my dad either to get it fixed or get another car.

Dear John,

I lost 50 cents to Freddy Miller and Dennis Densky last night. Freddy Miller got 3 deuces most of the time when he was dealing. He was real lucky again.

Dear John,

My mom and dad went for a ride today in the old car. It's a 1929 Model A Ford. It looks like a big box. They was supposed to be home at about 5 but it's now 8 o'clock. I'm getting worried about them.

Dear John,

It's O.K. My mom and dad got home but the car didn't make it. The motor blew up and somebody felt sorry for them and drove them home. Now we don't got any car. My mom said, "A new car is not in the budgit." That means we don't have enough money to buy another car. I hope my mom or dad win one of the chances for the new car at the bazaar.

Dear John,

Father McNulty gives me the altar boy card with all the Latin on it. Patrick Garino said that he'll help me say the words right. The card got the Latin on the top line and then it got the way to say the words on the bottom line. Like the first word in Latin is "Introibo . . ." but the way to say it is In-tro-ee-bo. But the card don't say nothing about what Introibo means.

Dear John,

My mom's real thankful to God for letting the motor of the Ford blow up because God was protecting us. She says chances are that God stopped us from being in a terrible accident.

Dear John,

I've been all around the neighborhood trying to sell chances to win that beautiful Dodge. But almost everybody bought some raffle chances already and nobody wants to buy any from me. Lots of other kids got to them first. I figgered Mrs. K would buy some from me because she likes me and all but I didn't ask her. I know she doesn't have a lot of money and she doesn't need a new car. I only sold two books.

Dear John,

Christine Carney sold 20 books. Mrs. Carney bought 18.

Dear John,

Earnest hears me saying some of the Latin what I been practicing and then he asks me what it means. I don't know what it means. Earnest says I shouldn't say any words if I don't know what they mean even if they are in Latin. He says you got to be careful about them getting you to say something that later on you're going to regret.

Dear John,

Today was Kathleen Kelly's last day at St. Marys. She's moving tomorrow morning. I walked her home and carried her books and hugged her real tight and then she started to walk up the stoop but then she turned around, walked down and kissed me on my lips. She ~~done~~ did that right in front of her mom. Kathleen was crying. I said goodbye but I didn't cry. Not at all, not one little tear, 'til I got home, in bed under some covers.

Dear John,

Earnest says, "I ain't never going to be no altar boy because that it ain't right to say stuff when you don't know what you're saying." Earnest doesn't trust anybody.

Dear John,

I will try real hard to say things the way Kathleen Kelly helped me with English grammar. This way I will always remember her.

Dear John,

Mrs. K called out the window to me and asked me to come up. She said I was looking very sad and she wanted to know if she could help make things better. I told her about

Kathleen Kelly moving and I'm going to miss her. Mrs. K just took my hand and held it real tight. Her hand was shaking. We didn't say any more.

Dear John,

I asked Father McNulty about the Latin and if it's OK to say stuff when you don't know what it means. Father McNulty says it pleases God to hear prayers no matter what language they're in. But then Father McNulty gets out a book what is called a Roman Missile and he shows me what the Latin means in English. Introibo means I will go. I don't see any harm in saying that.

Dear John,

I told Earnest that it's O.K. to trust priests and Introibo just means "I will go . . ."

Earnest said, "Maybe you can trust priests but there's no chance of my ever trusting nuns."

Dear John,

I guess God don't care that altar boys don't know what they're saying. He don't care so much if you don't know what you are saying but it's real important that you say it the right way and be real sincere and spiritual when you say it.

Dear John,

When I told Earnest about what the priest told me about Latin, Earnest said, "There's got to be some good reason for the priests saying prayers in Latin. Maybe God understands Latin better than English."

Dear John,

My mom bought one chance book and my dad bought another one. That's all they can afford. I sold four books and nobody wants to buy anymore. I guess I won't win that statue. Anyways I hope we win that Dodge. It's really beautiful with dark blue on the bottom and light blue on the top. It's a streamlined car and it even got fluid drive. That means you don't have to shift the gears so much. We really need a new car. I'm going to pray my mom or dad win it.

Dear John,

When I become an altar boy, I'm going to have to get a cassock and a surplus. The cassock is the black thing what looks ~~kinda~~ like a dress and the surplus is the white thing what you put on top. I wouldn't wear anything like that under ordinary conditions like out in the street but church ~~ain't no~~ is no ordinary condition. Patrick Garino says he paid ten dollars for his cassock and surplus. He got it used. That's a lot of money but I'll worry about that after I learn my Latin stuff. I miss Kathleen Kelly. I'm trying to write English real well.

Dear John,

Earnest said he can see how a cassock might cost a lot of money but the surplus got to be cheap because they got more than they need and that's why they call it a surplus. He smiles a lot after he says stuff like that.

Dear John,

Sometimes I don't understand what Earnest is talking about.

Dear John,

I learned some of the Latin stuff all by myself but it took a long time. The longest parts get said right in the beginning of the Mass. First the priest says something and then the altar boy says something. They go back and forth like that for an awful lot of Latin.

Dear John,

I spent hours and hours learning the Latin and then I was showing off to Patrick Garino. But then he tells me that I learned the wrong part. I learned the priest's part. Now I got to go back and learn the altar boys part. I miss Kathleen Kelly.

Dear John,

It's real tuff learning the Latin and getting anything else done like homework.

Dear John,

I was talking to Father McNulty about learning Latin and all and I asked him how long he had to go to school to be a priest. He says he had to go to college for 4 years and then 4 more years after that. "Wow, that's a long time but I guess it takes that long to learn what you're talking about in Latin." He says he had to learn a lot more than Latin.

Dear John,

This nun, what I got for a teacher, is young and probably pretty under all that habit and stuff but she's meanest nastiest nun I ever seen saw and she's strict too. Her name is Sister Celestine and she gives lots of homework and then checks to make shore it's all done.

Dear John,

I got lots of homework piling up real fast. Well, the homework isn't really piling up because it's not getting done. It's what I owe, that what's piling up and that don't make such a big pile because there's nothing there.

Dear John,

My sister, Maggie, works in New York City and gets home late every night but she says she'll help me with some of my homework next Saturday if I promise to rub her back whenever she asks. I agreed mostly because Maggie's not home all that much. And when Maggie is home, she and my mom spend most of the time fighting and then Maggie goes flying into the bedroom with the door slamming behind her.

Dear John,

Chances are real good I'll be all caught up with the homework what I owe by Monday morning. My hands are getting really tired. Maggie and my mom called a truce.

Dear John,

The nun made Freddy Miller stand in the corner with his face looking at the wall for two hours today. He got into trouble because he was sleeping. He had his head on the desk and the nun probably wouldn't catch him except he was snoring so loud.

Dear John,

I don't know why this nun is so mean. She's young and kinda pretty in a nunny sort of way. But it's real hard to tell what nuns are really like what with their habits and all. I wonder what color hair she got. Sometimes you can tell if they don't put their head habit on just right. But I ~~ain't seen no~~ have not seen any hair on this nun. Maybe she's bald. Maybe that's why she's a nun. Maybe that's why she's mean and nasty. Bald headed nuns got to be the meanest nuns of all.

Dear John,

Christine Carney and Patrick Garino are tied for first place in selling chance books.

Dear John,

I think learning all this Latin is too tuff for me. I got other things what I got to do. I don't got ~~no~~ enuff money for the cassock and surplus.

Dear John,

The only problem with my sister Maggie doing my homework for me is that Maggie's handwriting is a lot better than mine. Yesterday we had to write a short story in class. Usually I stall and then get to do it for homework but this time we all had to hand it in no matter how much we got done. So when the nun looks at my story she asks me what happens to my beautiful handwriting because this is all sloppy. So I tell her that I slipped and probably broke my hand coming to school. She says that's too bad but what about the spelling. She says that my homework papers are always spelled better than this. So I says that when I fell I bumped my head real bad and mest up the spelling part of my brain. She just looks at me, shakes her head, and says chances are that I'll never amount to anything. Then she says that I'll never be able to learn the Latin to become an altar boy. She shakes her head and screws up her upper lip and says real low, "Not a snowball's chance in hell."

Dear John,

Well who told the nun about me becoming an altar boy? I never did. So who done it? I mean. Who did it? What big mouth is talking about me to the nun?

Dear John,

They're putting up all the booths for the Bazaar. The nun says we're not allowed to go to the Bazaar at night because of the rowdy people who go to those things.

Dear John,

I told Father McNulty about Latin being too tuff for me. But he says I can learn it. He tells me to sit down on the steps outside of the church and he opens up his book what he calls his Roman Missile. Then he sits down next to me, only it takes him a real long time and his teeth are tight together and his face is crunched up. I think he's got something broke in his sit down.

But then he's OK and he reads "Introibo ad altare Die" and he says that first word means "I will go" and the next two say "to the altar" and the last one is "of God." Well that makes sense to me because that's where the priest is going. Then he tells me to go into the rectory with him and he lets me borrow a book what gots has Latin on the top line and then the English right below telling you what it all means.

Dear John,

Dennis Densky fell asleep in school today and he had to stand in the corner for two hours.

Dear John,

That does it. If the nun says I ~~ain't gonna~~ can not do it, well I'm gonna do it! I know I can. At least it's a chance I ~~gotta~~ have to take.

Dear John,

I saw Earnest sleeping in school today but the nun don't catch him. Earnest doesn't snore.

Dear John,

I'm really learning that Latin now but I got real trouble learning the one that goes like this: Suscipiat Dominus scrificium demanibus tuis ad laudem, et gloriam nomimis sui, ad utilitatem quoque nostram, totiusque Ecclesiae suae sanctae. I copied that from the card because I figgered it would help me learn it but that didn't help.

Dear John,

I showed Earnest the Roman Missile what Father McNulty loaned me. Earnest says it's OK now because I ain't saying nothing what will get me in trouble later on. He says you should never promise what you can't keep. You can't tell no big lies because you got to pay for the consequences. Earnest says he does some things what ~~ain't~~ aren't good but he always tries to tell the truth. But then he stops and puts his hand up to his chin. He says sometimes you just can't tell the truth because the consequences would be worser. So then you just got to figure out what to do. He says it's all a matter of Truth and Consequences.

Dear John,

Earnest just learned the word "consequences." Whenever Earnest learns a new word he uses it a lot.

Dear John,

Earnest told me that we should go to the bazaar at night to see what rowdy people do. I told Earnest if he wants to see a rowdy person, he should look in the mirror.

Dear John,

So Dennis Densky and Freddy Miller are both standing in two different corners because the nun catches them sleeping. Then she sees Earnest and Tony Fanzini are talking and they got to stand in the other two corners and then the nun sees me looking at the altar boy card when I'm suppose to be doing the workbook page. She's all set to send me to a corner but she looks around. Then she takes my altar boy card away and tells me to get back to work. She ran out of corners.

Dear John,

Me and Earnest and Nicholas went to the Bazaar last night and nobody knows it because we wore disguises. Earnest put on my coat and I put on Nicholas's coat and Nicholas put on Earnest's coat. Then Earnest burned some cork from his dad's wine bottle and we rubbed it on our faces so it looked like we had beards and mustaches. That was a real good disguise. I saw some people looking at us like we were strange but they don't know who we are and that's the main thing.

The Bazaar was kind of boring mainly because we don't got any money and we didn't see ~~no~~ any rowdy people at all. The biggest disguise of all was that Earnest acted like a normal person so nobody can tell it's him.

Dear John,

I asked the nun for my altar boy card back today. The nun says she won't give me back the altar boy card because it's a waste of time for me to try to be an altar boy. She said only the best boys can be altar boys and she'll never permit anything but the best boys to be on the altar of God. She looks at me and says, "You, an altar boy? Not a chance."

Dear John,

I don't need ~~no~~ the Latin card. I got a Roman Missile what I loaned from Father McNulty.

Dear John,

No problem. I learned that Latin what begins with suscipiat in no time flat. All I done was to make it sound like American. Like where it says in Latin, "Suscipiat Dominus scrificium demanibus," I says, "Suspicious that Dominic sacrificed them many buses. Where it says, "Ecclesiae suae sanctae," I says, "Eggclaires Sue ate. Sank tea." I say that real fast and nobody's gonna know the difference. It sounds like real good Latin. But it's really not so good American.

Dear John,

I got all the Latin learned in no time and I even know what it says. Anything I got trouble with I just made into

American and zapped it cold. Tomorrow Father McNulty's gonna test me.

Dear John,

A really big family, the Rileys, with ten kids moved into Kathleen Kelly's apartment. Jean Riley is in my class and she's really pretty. Her sister is Maria and she's pretty too. Franky and Willy Riley are their two brothers but they're a little older than me. I said hello to Jean Riley and she smiled back and asked me my name. She's got long blond hair and a nice smile.

Dear John,

But I still really really miss Kathleen Kelly.

Dear John,

Christine Carney won the statue today. Mr. Carney bought 10 more chance books.

Dear John,

Father McNulty can't test me because he's gone to Lourdes. It's in France and he's a pilgrim and he's gonna take a bath to cure his back ache and all when he sits down. He won't be back for about a week. So Father Smott's gonna give me a chance to pass the Latin test.

Dear John,

We can't get a car because my mom and dad don't have enough money and they can't budgit it. My dad tried to sell the old Ford but nobody wants to buy a car what got a burned up motor. We can't go crabbing again. That's a good thing for the crabs. Maybe God is helping them crabs out.

Dear John,

I passed the Latin test! Father Smott said that I learned the Latin really great and that he never heard anybody say it so good and so fast. I asked him "Do you understand what the Latin says?" He says, "Oh, of course! Priests have to know Latin and what it means." Then he says that my pronouncing is so good that he's able to understand the whole thing in Latin. I guess he knows Latin real well.

Dear John,

They're going to raffle off that beautiful Dodge tomorrow night. I'm really praying so my mom and dad win.

Dear John,

Father McNulty's back from Lourdes and he gives a little bottle of special holy water to all the altar boys. Patrick Garino and Peter Ackerman and Ralph Bramski were showing their bottles to everyone.

Dear John,

I hope Father McNulty saved me a bottle of that holy water from Our Lady of Lourdes for when I get to be an altar boy.

Dear John,

Father McNulty gave the sermon at the nine o'clock children's Mass today and he said that his back feels a lot better. He got cured by dipping his sit down in the Holy Water.

Dear John,

I got a real close look at that Dodge. It's not that great. It's really the ugliest Dodge what was ever made. I hate blue cars anyways. Christine Carney's mom won the crummy Dodge.

Dear John,

Father McNulty was real surprised when I told him that I know almost all the priest's part in the beginning of the Mass. He asked me how come I learned the priest's part. I said, "It was for the spiritual reasons way down deep in my heart." Then I showed off more by saying both the priests and the altar boy parts in Latin. Then I smiled like with real sincerity and then Father McNulty patted me on the top of my head. I didn't say nothing about Rye Beach but I figger I got it in the bag. At least I got a real good chance of going. Father McNulty said that after I learn the regular Mass, then I can get to learn the Solemn High Mass and maybe work my way up to being a master altar boy. Master altar boys get to work most of the funerals and weddings. Big bucks! Now I got to learn what to do on the altar during the regular Mass. But I still got a problem getting the money to buy the cassock and the surplus.

Dear John,

Freddy Miller and Dennis Densky asked me over to their gambling room in Freddy Miller's cellar. That's where they play poker. They start playing at 7 tomorrow night. But I said I got cleaned out the other night but Dennis Densky says they ain't playing for money, just for fun. Dennis Densky says it ain't no ordinary poker game and I seen him wink at Freddy Miller. I don't know about them two guys but I says I'll be over after supper probably about 8.

Dear John,

Earnest says that he seen they got army and navy surplus stores where you can buy stuff real cheap. Maybe they got a altar boy surplus store.

Dear John,

I walk into the gambling room in Freddy Miller's cellar at 8 tonight and there is Freddy Miller and Dennis Densky playing poker with Maria and Jean Riley but their dresses are on the floor and they are sitting there wearing just their underwear. Freddy Miller says, "Come on. We don't play for money. We play for clothes." I say, "Not me. Not a chance!" I turn around and run up the cellar stairs. I got out of there real fast.

Dear John,

I been thinking a lot about last night. I don't like that stuff and I know it's real sinful and no altar boy oughta do that stuff. Besides I ain't good at poker and I don't wanna take my clothes off for nobody.

Dear John,

Dennis Densky was real mad at me today for not staying for the poker game. I don't want to tell him about not being right for altar boys to do that stuff. So I tell him, "I ain't going to take my clothes off for nobody." He laughs and says, "You don't ever got to worry about that. I don't never take my clothes off because I don't never lose." I asked him, "How come you don't never lose?" He says, "Freddy Miller showed me how to deal myself a good hand and I know how to get a better hand when I ain't even dealing." I says, "I'm interested in learning." But Dennis Densky won't show me how if I don't play strip poker.

Dear John,

The Bazaar is over. They counted all the money and now they got enough to start building the new church. But they only got enough to build the bottom part. First they got to hire an architext to make the blue drawings.

Dear John,

I asked Earnest if he knows how to deal cards so he gets deuces all the time. He says sure, so I asked him to teach me. So Earnest teaches me how to control two deuces or whatever cards I want when I shuffle the deck. The first shuffle you slip the deuces to the bottom. Then you keep them on the bottom of the deck until you do the last shuffle. Then you bring them up real careful so they fall in where you need them. I practice that and then he shows me anudder way you deal from the bottom real fast so that I get the cards I want. Then he shows me what he calls is the false cut and a Hindu shuffle. You shuffle and somebody cuts the deck. It looks like the cards get mixed but everything really stays the same. Then he shows me how to hold onto all the deuces after you deal. I practiced a little but I got to practice more because I'm real slow and this stuff only works when you do it fast. Earnest says, "Your hands gotta be quicker than their eyes."

Dear John,

Dennis Densky asked me to play and he'll teach me how to control the cards. He says, "See, you don't got to worry about taking your clothes off. There's another game tonight with Maria and Jean Reily and they got a friend for you." But I says, "No thanks." I need a lot more practice.

Dear John,

I've been practicing controlling the deuces and the false cut and the Hindu shuffle. I'm getting faster at them all. I remember what Earnest says about my hands gotta be faster than my ears.

Dear John,

I asked Earnest about cheating at cards. It ~~don't~~ does not seem right.

Earnest says, "It is a thing like big lies and white lies. The big lies got big consequences but the white lies hardly have ~~do not got none~~ any at all. And sometimes the lies work out better than what is true. What good comes out if you point your finger at somebody what's really ugly and you say, "You are ugly." Maybe it is the truth but it is better to say, "You got a nice hat." Earnest says, "That's why when Ralph Edwards says 'Truth or Consequences' on the television show, the word truth is always with a big "T." Earnest says there's big Lies and little lies and there's big Truth and little truth. And sometimes neither of them do ~~not do nobody no~~ any good. Then he puts his hand up to his chin and stops. Then he says, "The main thing is this. It's all about the consequences. Don't get caught."

Dear John,

What are the chances I might get caught?

Dear John,

Maybe sinceerity works with Father McNulty but Sister Celestine don't go for it. Father McNulty wants me to be an altar boy but the nun told me she won't permit it. She says that being an altar boy is O.K. for boys like Peter Ackerman, Patrick Garino and Ralph Bramski because they're smart and well behaved.

Dear John,

Peter Ackerman and Patrick Garino are not so smart. They don't even know the Hindu shuffle. I asked them and Peter Derman starts telling me about some Hindu god that dances all around fire.

Dear John,

I changed the nun's name. I call her Sister Cellar Stink. Nicholas and Earnest say her new name fits her just right. But Patrick Garino and Peter Ackerman say it's ear reverend and it's sack religious.

Dear John,

I asked Earnest again about cheating at cards. I told him I still think that it is not right and I shouldn't do it even if I know how. Then Earnest asked me what I was going to use the winnings for. So I told him I need ten dollars for the cassock and surplus. Earnest says he don't know if it's right. Maybe I shouldn't cheat. Then he asks me who's going to get cheated. I told him about Freddy Miller and Dennis

Denski. Earnest says he'll think about it and figger it out so it comes out the right way.

Dear John,

I'm getting real fast with shuffling the cards and controlling two deuces. I keep practicing because there's a real good chance Earnest is gonna figger it O.K. to cheat after he thinks about it. Earnest is real good at figgering out why it's O.K. to do something when it's not O.K.

Dear John,

Earnest's been thinking about it and he's figgered it out. Earnest says it's OK to cheat at cards under certain circumstances. There are two reasons why it's OK for me to cheat. Earnest says one good reason is if you do something good with the winnings and buying a cassock and surplus is definitely a good use. But even more better is that it is definitely O.K. to cheat a cheater because Freddy Miller cheated first. But Earnest says I can only cheat Freddy Miller and nobody else. It's fair and it even helps Freddy Miller learn about the consequences when he cheats. So in my case cheating does good for both the one who cheats and the one who gets cheated.

Dear John,

I been practicing controlling the cards and I'm getting real smooth at the Hindu shuffle and the false cut. I play with a mirror looking at me and when I deal I can't even see the switch. My hands are quicker than my own eyes and ears. I'm getting so I can control all the deuces when I deal and when I don't deal, the deck got no deuces.

Dear John,

Sister Cellar Stink says that it's a rule that you got to have a B+ average to be an altar boy and my average for the midterm was 73 and that's a C-. I never heard that rule before. I think she just made it up. But I figger I'm going to have to work real hard to get my grades up. Maybe she can do an average just before I get to be an altar boy.

Dear John,

Dennis Densky and Freddy Miller both fell asleep during arithmetic and had to stand in the corners again. Maybe they shouldn't snore. Maybe they shouldn't stay up all night playing poker.

Deat John,

Freddy Miller asks if I wanna play poker tonight. I tell him I will play for money but not for clothes.

Freddy Miller says that's OK because Maria and Jean Riley won't be there. Their mom is real upset about their dresses what with the dirt from the cellar floor all over them. Maria and Jean Riley are getting punished. They can't go out after school for a week.

Dear John,

I played poker with Dennis Densky and Freddy Miller last night and won 50 cents. They were real surprised. Freddy Miller couldn't get any deuces even when he deals. I had a real lucky night.

Dear John,

Earnest told me his dad came home last night but he ain't going to stay. He just stayed over last night because his car didn't start up. A wire in the motor got cut. But he got somebody to fix it this morning and he went back to Flatbush.

Dear John,

I was talking to Father McNulty in the school yard and telling him about my problem with the rule about needing a B+ average. So he walks over to Sister Celestine and asks her to make an exception for me because I got sinceerity and all but she shakes her head and says it's not right to make an exception to the rule. Then Father McNulty asks her to do my average again in about a month when I'm ready to be an altar boy. She says O.K. But she does not think I have a chance.

Dear John,

The nun told us we have to do a science report on a bird that lives around Brooklyn. I never do good in report writing. When I use the ensyclopedia, the nun always says I copied. When I don't copy, the nun says I don't keep to the facts.

Dear John,

Earnest asked the nun how do you write a report. The nun says, "You should have learned that last year."

Dear John,

Earnest told me every year he asks a teacher how to write a report and every time the teacher says, "You should have learned that last year."

Dear John,

Me and Earnest figgered out how to write a report. First we check what ensyclopedias they got in school and then we go to the librerry and get one what they don't got in school. Then we found stuff about birds and copied every other sentence and changed some of the words just a little. We both ~~done~~ wrote it that way. Earnest did his report on eagles and I did mine on blue jays. I told Earnest there ~~ain't~~ are no eagles in Brooklyn but he says he does not care. Earnest likes eagles and he figgers there has to be one around, probably in the garden what's botanical in Prospect Park.

I like blue jays because they got spunk. You get too close to their nest and they come right at you no matter how big you are.

Dear John,

Earnest asks me what's the difference between the nun and bald eagles. I don't know. Earnest says, "Bald eagles ain't bald."

Dear John,

Jean Riley fell asleep in school today. She don't snore but everybody knows she fell asleep when her head hits the desk. Klunk.

Dear John,

Earnest got an A+ on his eagles report and I got a D—for the blue jays.

Dear John,

I played poker with Freddy and Dennis Densky again last night. I won 75 cents. Another lucky night. No problem getting money for my cassock and surplus.

Dear John,

Sister Cellar Stink gave me a 50 on my arithmetic test when I really got a 100. I got every single answer right but she says that my writing is sloppy and that's why she took off points.

Dear John,

I been wondering why this nun is so mean. I never done anything bad to her. Never. But she got this idea that she got to give me a real ruff time.

Dear John,

Today the nun gives me a big fat zero on my spelling test. I really got a 90, two wrong out of 20 and I done it real neat but she says I got the looseleaf paper holes on the right side and the two holes must be on the left side. "If you don't have the looseleaf holes on the left side, you deserve a zero," the nun said.

Dear John,

I ~~ain't~~ will not give up. I am not going to give up. I really want to be an altar boy so I can serve on the altar of God and go to Rye Beach next month. Father McNulty got Patrick Garino to teach me all the altar boy moves when introibo ad altare Dei.

Dear John,

Father Smott was in the sacristy when Patrick Garino is teaching me the altar boy moves. The sacristy is the place where the priest puts on his chasubell and cincture and stuff. The sanctuary is the place where the altar is. It's real important for an altar boy to know the names of these places and lots of other stuff.

Well anyways, Father Smott walks over to us when I am making the moves on the altar and he said my Latin is really good and he can understand every word. Then he says, "You know, boys, Introibo and the rest of that means, 'In troubled times such as these days we need to pray."

In my books it says Introibo and the rest of that means "I will go into the altar of God." Maybe the book is wrong or maybe Father Smott is wrong. They can't be both right.

Dear John,

Earnest whispered to me in school, "You're right about picking garbage. I keep finding great stuff."

I whispered back, "What you think is great stuff is not the same as what I think is great stuff. I remember what you found about a year ago."

Earnest said, "I remember too. You won't believe this but I found stuff what's even better and even more useful than a dead cat.

Dear John,

Father McNulty gave me another altar boy card. This one got the meaning in American and I checked out Introibo. The card says almost the same thing as the Roman Missile. The card says 'I will go to the altar,' and my book says, 'I will go into the altar.' but it don't say nothing about trouble or praying in times of trouble. Maybe a priest can get it wrong sometimes.

Dear John,

Teachers can get you whenever they wanna. You can't fight them because they control the deck. The nun got her own Hindu shuffle.

Dear John,

Earnest told me, "You gotta get some leverage."

I asked Earnest, "What's leverage mean?"

Earnest shows me a science book what he got in the librerry and he shows me this picture of a thing what looks like a see-saw. A guy's lifting the whole world with a long pole.

Earnest told me, "You can get a lot of things changed if you got some leverage. And I think the leverage in your case is in the garbage. I am getting to know a lot about people what live in this neighborhood." Earnest makes a big smile and says, "Amazing what you can find out about people from their garbage."

Dear John,

Earnest told me that Tuesday morning is garbage collection day and Monday night the garbage is out there for anybody to just take. The school got garbage and the convent got another garbage pile. It just got dark and I gotta go meet Earnest at the church. I'll let you know what we find.

Dear John,

Mostly stinky stuff, that's what you find in the garbage. First we tried to check out the school's garbage but too many Knights of Columbus around. So we checked out the convent's garbage. That was the stinkiest stuff. They had fish last Friday. But Earnest stuffed lots of papers into two big bags and he says we got more than stinky fish. We took the bags to Earnest's room and started to look through them. But it got late so I had to come home. Earnest's bedroom smells real stinky and it's not just dead socks.

Dear John,

Earnest said he went back after the Knights of Columbus went home. He got into the school garbage and he found all our reports about flowers what grow in Brooklyn. We never got them back. Sister Celestine never even read them.

Dear John,

I went up to see Mrs. K today. She knows everything what's going on in the neighborhood. She knows me and Earnest are real good friends and all and she says, "Earnest is a very smart boy. He's always doing something interesting."

Then she asks me about Earnest's mom. Mrs. K thinks Earnest's mom isn't feeling well. I told her I don't know much about that except Earnest told me she throws up a lot in the bathroom. Maybe she is sick or something.

Dear John,

~~Me and Earnest~~ Earnest and I was looking at the pile of garbage what we dumped on the floor in his room. We seen the word Celestine on one piece of ripped up paper and then we looked for the rest of that paper and that's the one we put together. It's a letter from St. James University. It's all ripped but all the pieces are there and like a jigsaw puzzle it all goes back together real neat. The letter is from the Dean of the College of Education and it says that Sister Celestine McDonnel (I did no know her name was McDonnel) is failing three courses at midterm because she did not hand in three reports and that she is on probation and if she does not improve, they are going terminate her, what means they are going to throw her out. There was also a card all ripped up but we put most all the pieces together. Last December she got one D and three F's on her report card. All the time we are putting the pieces together Earnest keeps saying "Leverage, leverage, this is real good leverage."

Dear John,

I told Earnest that maybe I can tell Sister Cellar Stink that she can rub another nun's back who's better at getting the home work done. Earnest says he's got a better idear.

Dear John,

Earnest keeps finding more great stuff what we got from the convent garbage. Sister Carmalita's dad is a real famous guy named Carmine De Gilvio. His name is in the newspaper all the time because he's being investigated for murdering an Assistant District Attorney. The newspapers say he's a big crime boss.

Dear John,

Sister Mary Frances got a doctor's bill for curing her hemorhoids. Lots of interesting stuff. Earnest says we are going to go back for more leverage tomorrow night. It don't does not hurt to get more information when your dealing with somebody who stacks the deck. Leverage makes it fair.

363

Dear John,

Earnest found something else about Sister Cellar Stink. Before she got to be a nun she had a boy friend named Paul McFarley and he wrote to her and says that he wants to marry her but she has to leave all that nun stuff behind. He says he was wrong to take up with Veronica but she shouldn't join the convent just because of that. I had to help Earnest piece it together because it was ripped up in tiny pieces. Earnest says this nun ain't is not very smart. Stuff like this got to be burned.

Dear John,

In the school yard I saw Earnest walk over to Sister Cellar Stink. He starts talking to her but then it looked like she wasn't exactly enjoying the conversation. When Earnest walked away, the nun sat down on the school yard bench. I've never seen a nun sit down on a school yard bench before. I got to talk to Earnest.

Dear John,

I ask Earnest about his conversating with the nun in the school yard today and this is what Earnest tells me, "I said to the nun, 'Sister, Paul McFarley sends his regards.' The nun just stands there with her mouth open. Then I says, 'You know Paul don't like Veronica any more.' The nun's mouth opens bigger and she leans against the school yard fence. Then I says, 'See ya later, Sister.' Then I walks off. I looked back and she is sitting on the school yard bench."

Then Earnest stops and thinks. His eyes look up at the sky and he says, "You know, that's the first time I ever seen a nun sit down on a school yard bench."

Dear John,

Sister Cellar Stink was real cranky all day today. She screamed at Christine Carney for blowing her nose. Christine Carney sniffled all afternoon. Christine Carney ain't used to being screamed at.

Dear John,

Sister Cellar Stink is not a happy nun.

Dear John,

Earnest told me he saw Sister Cellar Stink looking curious at him this morning so he figgers maybe she wants to talk some more.

Dear John,

I'm watching Earnest talk to the nun in the school yard again and I see she has to sit down on the school yard bench after he walks away. That's the second time I ever saw a nun sit down on a school yard bench. I got to talk to Earnest.

Dear John,

I asked Earnest about his conversating with the nun in the school yard today and this is what Earnest tells me. He said to the nun, "Father Burkely at St. James University hopes you're going to do all your homework for now on. It's nice of them to give you a chance to do better in your grades." Then Earnest walks away and the nun sits down on the school yard bench.

Dear John,

Earnest told me he was going to do more conversating with the nun in the school yard today but before he even gets one word out, she tells him, "Drop dead and go to hell." Earnest never heard words like that coming from a nun before. He says, "I was shocked, shocked to hear such words from a nun."

Dear John,

Even Patrick Garino and Peter Ackerman called her Sister Cellar Stink today. She was in a real bad mood.

Dear John,

Earnest says his mom went to Freedman's candy store and called his dad in Flatbush. Earnest says his mom's real happy about something but she won't say ~~nothing~~ anything to him about what it is.

Dear John,

This morning Earnest told me, "I saw Father Smott hand a note to Christine Carney in the hall. Christine Carney goes right to Sister Cellar Stink and gives her the note. Sister Cellar Stink reads the note. Then she puts it in her pocket and gives us some work to do. Well I keep one eye on her and she takes out the note again and reads it and then she rips it up into little pieces and throws it in the garbage pale."

Earnest was watching her too and he whispers to me, "Leverage."

Dear John,

Earnest is acting real strange today, I mean even weirder than usual. He is not doing his work, but that is not strange at all. But this is strange because about every five minutes he gets up to sharpen his pencil and along the way he keeps picking up papers and garbage from the floor and he brings them back to his desk and puts them into his school bag. On his last trip to the pencil sharpener, he dropped a rag on Christine Carney's head. The rag was full of snot what Earnest borrowed from Nicholas. Well that done it. The nun says he has to stay after school for a punishment. Christine Carney got excused from school for the rest of the day. Earnest is up to something.

Dear John,

I saw Earnest walking home from school real late like 4 o'clock and I asked him what he was up to today in school. He says after school he was real polite and worked real hard and was writing his punishment real good. But Sister Cellar Stink doesn't wanna be with him in the room and he figgers on that. So she goes down the hall to talk to Sister Mary Frances.

Right away Earnest is up to the front of the room with a paper bag and his school bag's filled with paper. He turns over the basket and everything goes into the paper bag. Then he dumps the garbage out of his school bag and into the waste paper basket. Back to his seat just in time! Sister Mary Francis comes in and says, "What was all that noise in here? It sounded like a fight." He looks around real innocent like. Then he smiles and says, "Nobody else here. I guess it was my guardian angel fighting off the devil." She don't go for it, nobody would. She just shakes her head and tells him to get busy with the punishment. Sister Cellar Stink never came back. Sister Mary Francis checked that he wrote "I must behave at all times and show respect" two hundred times. Then Sister Mary Francis told Earnest to go home.

Then Earnest tells me, "Meet me in the cellar at your apartment house in a half hour."

It's been half an hour so I got to get downstairs. Earnest is up to something.

Dear John,

Earnest was in the cellar when I got downstairs and little pieces of paper are all over the floor. His school bag and a paper bag are in the corner empty. Then we do the jigsaw puzzle. Piece of paper fitted right up to pieces of paper and first I seen the word night, then tonight, then 9:30 tonight, then—school basement—nursing office.

Earnest says, "This is gonna be big time leverage!"

Well it's ten after nine. See ya later, John.

Dear John,

This is what happened. My mom and dad are watching Jackie Gleason on the TV. I make like I'm going to bed and fix up the covers like I'm in the bed, a thing what I learned from my sister, Maggie. Then into the kitchen, out the window, down the fire scape where Earnest is waiting for me. And awaaay we go! The doors to the school basement are not locked because the Knights of Columbus have their meetings in the church basement on Thursday nights. Nobody sees us. They're too busy drinking beer and talking about the commies and how Senator McCarthy is doing great things about all the commies. So— me —Earnest and I just walk in, open a closet and wait in there till it gets real quiet. We just wait and try not to breathe. It's real crowded with the two of us in the closet what with a ladder and smelly wet mops. I do not want to breathe much anyways because Earnest is smelly too. So I open the door just a crack, real dark, clock near the exit light says 9:25. Earnest taps me and we close the door. Then we hear all the Knights of Columbus go home. In a couple of minutes we hear click, click. I open the door just a crack.

Footsteps click click click.

Close closet door, quiet.

Click click click click.

Peak through crack.

Key in lock. Click click click click. A door squeaks open. Door closes.

Wait, quiet.

Different footsteps clop clop clop. Door squeaks. Clop Clop, door closes.

Squeak.

We peak out through the crack. Earnest points to the nurse's office.

Light shines, two shadows together on white painted glass door. The ceiling light shines through the small window on top of the door. We slide our shoes off, open the closet door fast, no squeaking, hugging along wall to the nursing office, peak in key hole. Nothing. I look under door, nothing, yes, a ladder, back to closet, ladder, quiet, back along wall, open ladder, quiet. Earnest goes one step up, two steps up, three, four, looking through the little window on top of the door. Then Earnest gets down and points for me to go up. Step, step, step. I'm looking through the window. On the nurse's couch! Sister Cellar Stink and Father Smott! She got blond hair. He got hairy legs. Giggle. Ladder shakes, squeak, squeak, squeak. Sister Cellar Stink looks at the door. Worried faces. Fast down the ladder, run, run, across basement floor. Crash, smash, nurse's door against ladder. Glass tinkling. We run back out onto the street and hide in an alley. We watch as Father Smott comes out onto the steps and looks around. Buckling his belt. We hug the wall real tight in a dark corner. Father Smott walks back into the church basement. We run down the street as fast as we can. Earnest says "We'll talk tomorrow!" Up the fire scape, through the kitchen window. My mom and dad are still watching television in the living room. I hear Jackie Gleason say, "How sweet it is." I smile and quietly shake my head!

Dear John,

This morning I'm looking all over my room for my shoes. Lucky thing I found my sneakers. My shoes are still in the church closet.

Dear John,

What Father Smott says and what he does don't match. I wish Kathleen Kelly did not move to Hoboken. Maybe she would go steady with me again if I told her about Father Smott and the nun.

Dear John,

Earnest told me his mom's going to have a baby. That surprised me. I figgered there was no chance God wanted another kid like Earnest to get born.

Dear John,

We had gym class today in the church basement. My shoes are still there and nobody sees me get them.

Dear John,

A couple of days ago we had an arithmetic test, a spelling test, a geography test and a history test and today we got back our tests. I got one hundred on every test and the nun says that zero what I got does not count. I got a B+ now for everything since the midterm. I'm going to be an altar boy. How did that happen?

Dear John,

Earnest asked me what I got on the tests and I told him I got all one hundreds. Earnest looks at me and smiles and tells me he got all one hundreds too. Earnest says he got something real important to tell me but not in school. I'm going over to his apartment. I'll let you know.

Dear John,

Earnest told me about what he did yesterday. He says, "Remember when we were lining up in the church basement because it was raining?

"I remember."

Earnest continues, "I thought it would be a good time for me to conversate with Sister Cellar Stink. So I walk up to Sister Cellar Stink and points to the Nurses Office with the board covering up where the window used to be and I ask real slow, 'Sister, whatever happened to the window in the Nurse's Office? Was you there when it broke, Sister?' Then I smiled just a little, like a little devilish, and before she can say anything I say, 'Bobby Anderson wants to be an altar boy real bad. Maybe his grades will get better.' Then I walk away before she says anything. I looked back and she was leaning against the wall. She couldn't find a bench."

Dear John,

We got a new teacher. The principal comes in this morning and says Sister Celestine got a scholarship to study at St. James University because she got such good grades. So she's going to have to study and go to school all the time and she won't be back so we got Mr. Craig for our substitute teacher for the rest of the year. I never had a man teacher before. I wonder what that will be like.

Dear John,

I've been practicing all the parts to the Mass and Father McNulty gave me my first job this Saturday morning. It's just a regular Mass and no bucks like for a funeral but that's O.K. Good practice for them paying jobs what come later. I bought a cassock and surplus for 10 dollars from Ralph Bramski who can't be an altar boy no more because he got caught drinking the church wine. We all knew he's been hitting the bottle for a long time but everybody noticed it last Sunday when he fell off the altar during Mass. No problem getting money. I just play poker a couple times a week and I get real lucky what with the deuces wild and all.

Dear John,

I been practicing so hard on the Mass that I don't always got time to do all my homework. So today Mr. Craig comes around to check homework and I got only half of mine so he says for me to get into the cloak room closet. So I get up and go in and he comes in after me and POW he slaps me in the side of the head and then another in the other side. I'm dizzy and then he ponches me in the stomach. Sick. I'm doubled over.

He screams, "Stand up, look at me."

Sick. I stand up, look at him and throw up all over him. I got sent home for being sick. Mr. Craig had to go home for being smelly.

Dear John,

Mr. Craig was back today and he's out to get me. Earnest says we got a big problem because we don't got nothing on him. Bad mess, no leverage. But at least I got my first funeral tomorrow and that means I'll be out of the classroom most of the morning.

Dear John,

The funeral was real good and sorrowful and all and I even got a dollar for being an altar boy and the best part was that I got out of class for most of the morning.

Dear John,

Mrs. K asked me to go to the A & P to buy her some milk and bread. She fell and hurt her leg and she can't walk none too good. The stairs are real tough for her. We sat and talked. I listened because most of the time my mouth was full of apple pie. Mrs. K likes to talk about the good old days when she was young and all. She loved all the parties when she was a young girl during the Gay Nineties. I like to listen to her. She told lots of stuff, like how the Brooklyn Dodgers got to be called Dodgers. It was because people in Brooklyn were always dodging between trolley cars to get across the street. Then she started telling me about Germany where she grew up before coming to America. But then she stops and tells me I better go home because it is getting late.

Dear John,

Earnest says his mom's real happy because his dad told her he's breaking up with that strange lady in Flatbush and he's going to be moving back home and all. Earnest's mom told Earnest a baby's going to give them a better chance to stay together.

Dear John,

Earnest says his mom knows about leverage and consequences.

Dear John,

I'm going to be an altar boy at the 11 o'clock Mass every Sunday till the end of June. That's good because then I don't have to go to the kids Mass at 9 every Sunday. The best part is I don't have to look at Mr. Craig on Sundays.

Dear John,

I didn't go to school today. I hate school. I told my mom that I had a real bad stomach ache and that I felt like throwing up. My mom took my temperture but it was normal. She says I can stay home just for today. If I don't got a temperture tomorrow, I have to go to school.

Dear John,

Earnest came over my house this afternoon and he told me about wearing blotters in the bottom of my shoes. He says that blotters pull the cold air down to your feet and then it gets real hot in your mouth and you get a temperture and can stay home. He says he did that lots of times and it's been scientifically proven to work.

Dear John,

I been wearing blotters in my shoes but I did not get a temperture. So I had to go to school two days in a row. Mr.

Craig keeps looking at me and trying to catch me doing something bad. I've been real good. But I hate it.

Dear John,

I have to go to school tomorrow because I have to be an altar boy at a funeral. Maybe I can get sick after the funeral. Maybe those blotters will start working by then.

Dear John,

I made like I was real sick to my stomach after the funeral and I went down to the nurse's office. That window in the door is still broke. I got so many blotters I can't hardly get my foot in my shoes but I still do not have a temperture. I had to go back to class. Mr. Craig calls me vomit face all the time. I just take it. What can I do? I got nothing on him. No leverage.

Dear John,

Earnest says the main problem is that we don't know where Mr. Craig lives and he ain't telling nobody. Not even a hint!

Dear John,

I asked Father McNulty if his back still hurts and he said it's a lot better since he went to Lourdes and some other place in Cairo. I told him I didn't even know he went to Egypt.

Father McNulty looked at me and said, "I didn't go to Egypt."

I told him, "Cairo is in Egypt and I know that because we just learned about that in geography."

Father McNulty said, "I went to a Cairo Practor."

"Oh, Cairo Practor ain't in Egypt. That's a different place."

Dear John,

Earnest was telling Nicholas about his mom having a baby and all. Then Earnest got an idear from Nicholas but an idear from Nicholas? That's never a good idear.

Dear John,

This is disgusting what I'm going to tell you.

Earnest was holding a bag and he told me he went into New York City and bought something really special. He told me to close my eyes and I did. Then I hear him making disgusting noises and I open my eyes and there this disgusting vomit on the table. Then Earnest starts laughing and he picks it up. He bought fake vomit.

Then Earnest tells me, "We can use the fake vomit on Mr. Craig. It's only fair because he calls you vomit face all the time."

So we made a plan. The only thing is that I have to go fifty-fifty on the cost of the fake vomit because Earnest figures we ain't likely to get the fake vomit back. Vomit costs three dollars.

Dear John,

Kathleen Kelly came back to the old neighborhood for a visit because her dad had some business to do here. Kathleen Kelly told me about Hoboken and her new friends and her school and stuff. I told her about Father Smott and what happened to the nun and about Mr. Craig but she's not real interested in that stuff. It's different, like Kathleen Kelly's a stranger. I know she's never coming here again. Everything changed since she's gone.

Kathleen Kelly shook my hand and said, "See you again real soon."

I said, "Goodbye."

Dear John,

Earnest's dad drove up in his Ford filled with his suitcases and stuff. He moved back home.

Dear John,

Earnest's mom told him that this is a miracle baby and that God wanted them to have this miracle baby so they can all stay together. She says she prayed to have the baby and now they all gotta pray every night. She says, "A family what prays together stays together."

Dear John,

Christine Carney heard me and Earnest talking about the fake vomit and Earnest figures she's going to tell Mr. Craig about it. He's trying to come up with another plan. A buck fifty down the drain!

Dear John,

I was an altar boy at the 11:00 o'clock Mass today and after everybody left, Father McNulty walks with me out to the front door and he asks me to sit down on the steps. So he sits down and he didn't have to tighten his teeth. Going to Lourdes and Cairo Practor helped him a lot.

Then Father McNulty says I'm a real good altar boy and I say the Latin well and know what to do and all. Then he reaches in his pocket and gives me a little bottle of Holy Water what he got in Lourdes. That was a real swell thing.

Dear John,

If I can just hold out for a couple of weeks, then school will be over for the summer. The main thing is that I get to go to Rye Beach in only two weeks.

Dear John,

I had to stay home today because I got a temperture. The best way to get a tempature is to wait till your mom leaves the room and then put the thermometer up to the light bulb. But you have to shake it down. The first time I had a 107 temperture and that's too high. But I shook it down to about 101. That's a good temperture.

Dear John,

Mrs. K asked me how I was feeling. She didn't see me go to school yesterday and she was worried. I told her I'm O.K. but maybe I should stay home from school a few more days to get really well. She's a real nice old lady and she doesn't miss a trick.

Dear John,

Earnest shows me the Daily Mirror and there's a picture of Sister Celestine only her name is Mary McDonnel and it says she's getting married to Paul McFarley.

Dear John,

They got an archetect's drawing of what the new church is going to look like. It's mostly square and modern and I think it's the ugliest church I ever seen. It don't look like St.

Patrick's Cathedral. Now that's a real swell church. The new church looks like a factory.

Dear John,

Earnest came over after school. He said that Freddy Miller and Dennis Densky both got black eyes. Willy Riley and Franky Riley beat them up for playing strip poker with their sisters. Earnest just shakes his head and says, "See it's all about consequences. Freddy Miller and Dennis Densky did not think about the consequences."

Dear John,

Earnest and I were in the school yard today and Earnest told me he's going to do the vomit trick on Mr Craig anyways. So he tells the nun on yard duty he's gotta go to the boy's room real bad. Earnest goes in the school.

After lunch we are all in the classroom and Mr. Craig pulls out his chair and looks down at it. Then he says, "I've been waiting for this to show up." Then he pulls the chair out all the way and shows the class the vomit on the seat. Some of the kids started gagging. But Mr. Craig says, "Don't be upset. Watch this." Then he sits down right on top of the vomit. Then he jumps up real fast. His pants are covered with real vomit. He went home.

Dear John,

Earnest gave me back the dollar-fifty because he says he didn't lose the fake vomit and the real vomit did not cost him even a penny. He borrowed the mustard, lots of salt, vinegar and other stuff what he used to make a drink.

Dear John,

I did not write to you for a long time because I been in the hospital. See I was complaining a lot about my stomach hurting because I don't wanna go to school. My mom called Doctor Weinstein and he comes to our apartment and touches my stomach and asks, "Does that hurt?"

I says, "Yeah, real bad." What else am I going to say?

Then he does it again. I says, "It hurts real bad."

Wam! In no time I'm in the hospital. Next day I'm going to get an operatshion. I try to tell them it does not hurt any more. I'm all better. The pain's all gone. But they don't believe me. I even confessed to only fooling but they don't believe me. Then a real sneaky nurse gives me a needle with some medicine in my rear end to keep me quiet. Next thing I know they're wheeling me down to a big room and a nurse is putting a mask over my face. Then I wake up and my stomach really hurts. No fooling this time. They took my appendix out.

Dear John,

I got this great big scar up and down my stomach. One thing good is that the summer vacation is here and I don't have to go back to school and get called "vomit face" by Mr. Craig. But there is one really bad thing. When I was still in the hospital, all the altar boys went to Rye Beach.

Chapter 12

So Mature

Seventh Grade

Dear John,

We've got a new kid in the neighborhood. His name is Franky Bazaaro. He moved in above a store on Grand Street. He's in my class.

Dear John,

Earnest met Franky Bazaaro and Bazaaro put out his hand to shake. Earnest did his usual thing. He farted. That's the latest thing about Earnest. He always farts hello to new kids. But Bazaaro said, "That's disgusting." Earnest will drive Bazaaro nutty.

Dear John,

Earnest says, "Bazaaro, what a dumb name. Biggest creep I ever seen."

Dear John,

I just saw a girl I never saw before. She was walking down the street and I almost bumped into her. She smiled at me and said, "Excuse me."

I smiled and said, "Oh, you, you, it's, it's, don't. O.K. It's O.K. Excuse me too." Then I turned and walked right into a telephone pole. Beautiful girls drive me nutty.

Dear John,

It is funny how sometimes two people meet and they hit it right off from the very beginning. Other times two people meet and right from the start they hate each other. I don't know why.

Dear John,

Bazaaro is always saying how disgusting Earnest is and that makes Earnest act even more disgustingly. Earnest says Bazaaro must be retarded and got bad family blood because he doesn't know how to play stoop ball or even to pitch pennies or nothing.

Dear John,

Earnest said that when God was giving out brains, Bazaaro was standing behind the door and didn't get much of anything.

Dear John,

Mrs. K. sits upstairs looking out the window most of the day. She's getting real old but she likes to watch us play, especially stoop ball, slap ball, and stick ball. I wave to her and she waves back.

Dear John,

I saw that beautiful girl again and this time I don't say anything stupid because I don't say anything. I just sort of stand there with my mouth open. I just do not know what to say to a beautiful girl.

Dear John,

I was with Earnest this time when I saw that girl. She was wearing a red sweater. I pretended I didn't see her because I don't want Earnest falling in love with her too. But Earnest saw her.

Earnest says, "That girl in that red sweater is very pretty and you can see from her sweater that she's very mature."

But then I stopped in front of a grocery store window and said, "Look, Earnest, there's a really big mushroom."

Well that got Earnest distracted and he starts telling me what he knows about mushrooms and how they are fun guys. It was a good thing for me to change the subject when Earnest was looking at the beautiful girl. I probably saved his life.

Dear John,

I wanna be friendly to Bazarro but Earnest says, "Life's too short to worry about being friendly to everybody you see."

Dear John,

Earnest and I were watching Bazaaro walk down the street. Earnest says, "That kid doesn't even know how to walk right. He limps or something. He's a gimp!"

Earnest is right about Bazaaro not doing much right. But Bazarro is right about Earnest. Sometimes Earnest does disgusting stuff.

Earnest says Bazarro is immature and that means he isn't growing and maturing like a normal kid. But Earnest heard that Bazaaro's going to be in our class at St. Mary's and Earnest figgers that's good because then there's gonna be one more kid what's dummer than Nicholas.

Dear John,

The Dodgers won the pennant and they're gonna be in the World Series.

Dear John,

Earnest told me the Dodgers are real good players what with Peewey Reese and Gil Hodges and Jackie Robinson and all. He says they never win the World Series before because they just got to be a mature team and this year they are going to win the World Series.

Dear John,

Bazaaro showed up in school today at St. Mary's. The nun asks Bazaaro to read and Christine Carney gets all set to beat Peter Ackerman to the correcting. But when Bazaaro reads, he does not make any mistakes, not one. Everybody was real mad. Bazaaro's no fun.

Dear John,

That beautiful girl was talking to Bazaaro today and they both walked into the apartment house where Bazaaro lives. I'm going to ask Bazaaro if he knows her name.

I just heard an ambulance coming and it just stopped across the street. I looked out the window and two guys with white jackets went into the apartment house across the street. I'll be right back.

Dear John,

Mrs. K fell down the stairs. She went to get the mail. She did not want to go to the hospital or anything. The ambulance guys helped her back to her apartment and then they drove away.

Dear John,

I told Bazaaro I saw him talking to the most beautiful girl what I ever seen yesterday and I asked him, "What's her name?"

Bazaaro looks at me like I got two heads and says he does not know any girl like that. He does not know the name of any beautiful girl.

Dear John,

I asked Earnest why he isn't friendly to more people.

Earnest exsplained, "I don't have no time to be nice to lots of people. I got too much to do and life's too short to be nice to everybody." But then he stops and puts his hand up to his chin. He smiles and says, "Some people are worth my time. And you, Bobby, are worth lots."

That made me smile. Then Earnest asked me what I thought about the Brooklyn Dodgers game. I told him the Dodgers are going to beat the pants off the Yankees and the Dodgers are gonna win the World Series.

Earnest and I think the Dodgers are the greatest.— Me and —Earnest and I are getting to be real good friends.

Dear John,

Bazaaro's more trouble to the smart kids than he is to kids like Nicholas and Earnest. Bazaaro got five hundreds on five tests. Christine Carney said he must be cheating. She got four hundreds and one ninety-five. She's going to watch him really close. Maybe Bazaaro's smarter than Christine Carney.

Dear John,

Bazaaro can't be too smart if he doesn't know that girl's name and he can't even remember talking to her.

Dear John,

The nun put Bazaaro in the top reading group. Earnest says, "Bazaaro's good at reading O.K. but he's real bad at running and everything else."

At lunch in the school yard Earnest tells Bazaaro he'll race him. Bazaaro backed right down and says he can't run very well.

Earnest told him "You're right about that!" Earnest says it's O.K. to read good but what good is it if you can't run or even walk right? Earnest thinks maybe Bazaaro's family got some retarded stuff going on.

Dear John,

Bazaaro wants to play stick ball with us but Earnest says "You gotta learn to walk before you can learn to run and you gotta learn to run before you can play stick ball." Earnest is always making up stuff like that.

Dear John,

Mrs. K. opened her window and was watching us play stick ball. Then she calls down to us and she's pointing at Earnest, "That kid, you, Earnest, the Polish kid, come up here. I want to talk to you."

Earnest doesn't want to go but his team was up and he shrugs his shoulders like he's figgered he got nothing to lose so he goes up. Then our team takes the field but Earnest is still up in Mrs. K.'s apartment. So I yell, "Earnest, come on we're taking the field."

Earnest comes to the window and waves. He doesn't say a word. He just waves like we should go on playing without him. Well, we can't because we're one man short. But then I see Bazaaro sitting on the stoop watching and I ask if he wants to play. He smiles and runs limpy-like out to the street. He takes the outfield. Bazaaro didn't catch one ball when he had to run after them but he caught three what came right to him. He's real good at catching as long as he doesn't have to run.

We finished the game and everybody had to go home for supper but Earnest is still up in Mrs. K.'s apartment.

Dear John,

That beautiful girl was in Freedman's Candy Store and she was buying the New York Daily News and Mr. Freedman gives her change and says to her, "Thanks, June."

Her name is June. I'm in love.

Dear John,

Earnest wasn't in school today and I have not seen him since he was up in Mrs. K.'s apartment.

Dear John,

I think maybe June likes me. Maybe, sort of. I saw her look in my direction yesterday. She smiled. Golly Jee, I hope she was smiling at me. My face always gets real red when I jist like a girl a little. I think my face was like on fire when she looked at me. I don't know on account I turned around real fast and almost walked into a telephone pole.

Dear John,

I can't think about anything else. I think about June all the time. When I fall in love, I don't fall off chairs like Earnest. He's always joking around but this is the real thing for me. June is the most beautiful girl I ever saw in the whole world.

Dear John,

I saw Earnest talking to Bazaaro on the corner of Maujer and Grand. I don't know what they were talking about because I was about two blocks away. Then I saw Earnest put out his hand and then Bazaaro put out his hand and they shake hands.

Dear John,

Big news. After I went shopping, I was eating a piece of chocolate cake and talking to Mrs. K and I asked her about this new girl who just moved into the neighborhood and if she knows anything about her. Mrs. K says, "Yes. Her name is June Bazaaro. June is Franky Bazaaro's sister."

That is Big News. Mrs. K knows everything what's going on in this neighborhood and she sees it all from her window.

Dear John,

Franky Bazaaro ain't such a bad kid. He's got a real nice sister.

Dear John,

I asked Franky Bazaaro how come he didn't tell me his sister's name and he said, "You were talking about the most beautiful girl in the world. June's my sister. I never thought she was all that pretty."

Dear John,

Franky Bazaaro doesn't walk all that well but his sister walks like an angel on a cloud.

Dear John,

I was talking to Earnest about Franky and his sister and all. Earnest said, "When God gave out the stuff in the walking department, He gave it all to June and Franky just got the left overs." But then Earnest says we gotta be nicer to Bazaaro because it hurts people's feeling real bad when we are not nice to them. He said, "I've been a kind of bully to Franky and that's just not right."

Dear John,

We're playing stick ball again and Mrs. K.'s up in her window watching us. When we're choosing sides, Earnest picks Bazaaro to be on our team. Then I ~~seen~~ saw Earnest look up. So I look up. Mrs. K is up in her window and she is smiling at Earnest.

Dear John,

I want Franky Bazaaro to introduce me to June. How do I do that without letting on that I love her? I'm not telling Franky I love June or anything like that. Last week I just said she's real pretty.

Dear John,

Franky said, "June's O.K. but she's not that pretty. Besides, June is seventeen and she's too old for you."

Dear John,

Well, so what if I like older women. June's seventeen but when I'm twenty, she'll be in her twenties too. Now that does not sound as bad as seventeen and twelve what I'm going to be in two months. I wonder when she's going to be eighteen. I love older women.

Dear John,

I asked Earnest how come he treats Bazaaro so nice now and if Mrs. K. told him to or what. Earnest told me that Mrs. K. told him about when she was a little kid and she came from Germany and none of the kids were nice to her and how bad she felt and all.

Dear John,

I'm real good friends with Franky now. I go over to his house like every day. Sometimes twice. Sometimes Earnest comes over.

Dear John,

June, June, June! I really love that woman.

Dear John,

When Earnest meets Franky Bazaaro now, he says, "Hello." That's a lot better than his usual hello farts. I'm really glad Earnest stopped being mean to Franky Bazaaro. Earnest doesn't even make fart sounds under his arm. I told

Earnest, "Don't ever make fart sounds when June is home if you want to keep your armpit."

Dear John,

Yesterday we were visiting Franky in his apartment.—Me and—Franky, Earnest and I were talking and June came right into the living room. She even looked at me and said, "Hi." She is gorgeous, hubba, hubba. She was wearing that red sweater. She looks so grown up in that red sweater.

Dear John,

I asked Franky how come lots of boys don't never hang around June. "Don't she got no a boy friend?"

He said, "She's not interested in any other guys."

I figured maybe that's because she's gonna going to wait for me to grow a little more.

But then Franky says, "She's going steady. Her boyfriend's name is Ryan and he's in the army in Korea."

I figured it was something like that. She can't really pay me any attention because she's going steady. I thought it had to be something like that. But I am not worried. Lots of people get unengaged and even divorced. And maybe it's not nice to think about it but the army in Korea isn't exactly the safest place in the world. If he doesn't come back, then she'll probably think about me.

Dear John,

I am walking down Maujer and Mrs. K. calls down from her window and points to me. She says, "Bobby Anderson, please come up here."

So I go into the apartment house and the front door is already buzzing before I put my finger on the bell. So I push open the door and run up to the third floor. Mrs. K is standing on the landing at the top of the stairs. When I get up there out of breath, she opens her apartment door and I go in. Mrs. K doesn't look good. She's looking really really old and her hands shake and she's got a cane to help her get around because she fell down the stairs.

I figure I'm in trouble for something because I know Earnest got a good talking to about Bazaaro so I ask, "Are you going to yell at me or something?"

But Mrs. K. says, "No, you are not in any trouble. I like watching you play ball and you play fair and I think you are a very good boy."

Then Mrs. K. goes over to a shelf. There are two old fashioned ships with sails and flags and all. They look like the Santa Maria and Pinto or Nino or something. They're beautiful. She takes one down and hands it to me and says, "My husband carved this when he was your age. Now I want you to have this. I think you'll like having it."

I thanked her and took it home real careful. It is a very beautiful ship.

Dear John,

I'm in Bazaaro's living room and June comes in and she's like real surprised to see me mainly because she got a bathing suit on. I guess she was up on tar beach and she did not figure on anybody being there when she comes down from the roof.

But June puts a towel around her and smiles. She asks me, "Well, what's your name?"

"Bobby Anderson. What's yours?" (As if I didn't know!)

She says, "I'm June and it's a pleasure to meet you, Bobby Anderson."

Gosh! I'll never forget those words. Never. Never!

Dear John,

I was so lucky to see June in a bathing suit. She is the most beautiful woman I ever saw. Hubba, hubba!

Dear John,

I told Earnest how I met June and she was wearing a bathing suit and I was trying to tell him more about how great she looked in that bathing suit.

Earnest looks at me and says, "I understand. June is really, really mature."

Dear John,

That ship what Mrs. K. gave me is a real work of art. It's not a toy. My mom says I can keep it in my room but it's not for playing. It's for looking. It's got sails made from leather and the wood is carved real well. It's real old but it's a beautiful ship.

Dear John,

June's going away for two weeks. She's going to California and then Hawaii to see her boyfriend. He got a leave for a week. Her mom's going too so the two of them, June and Ryan, should not be alone too much. I know all about that. They might kiss.

Dear John,

I never heard Earnest sing before but today he looks at me, smiles and sings sings, "June is bustin out all over."

Dear John,

I told Franky I can't go over to his house for a couple of weeks on account that I got to study more. It's true. June ain't the kind to look twice at a guy who doesn't know a lot. She's real smart and so mature.

Dear John,

The nun says we got to learn algebras. In arithmetic you got to find the answer but you know the question. In algebras you know the answer but you don't know the question. So you put down the number for the answer but for the question you put X and Y and Z and stuff like that.

Dear John,

I really miss going over to Franky's house but I got a 90 on my algebras test and that's the first time I even past an algebras test in seventh grade. I still don't know what good it is. I never saw anybody ever do any algebras except in school.

Dear John,

I got to write a composition for school about winter. I hate writing because I get crummy grades most of the time. But this time the nun said she won't grade for anything except creativity and vocabulary. We have to use a new word that we learned this week. I'm going to write about harbinger.

Winter

Winter is a beautiful time of the year when the snow is covering the ground. It is a quiet time but something is missing. No boids chirping and singing. Winter looks beautiful but it sounds lonely. It is too quiet without the songs of boids. Quiet is a lonesome sound.

But then just yesterday I heard and then seen two robin red breasts and I felt glad because robins are harbingers of spring. The robins were building a nest in the tree outside my window. The beautiful winter is quietly leaving and noisy chirping songs of boids was flying on spring into Brooklyn.

I was happy but then nature played a dirty trick. It got real cold last nite. This morning I look out and I seen these two robins on the ground. I run outside and pick them up. Stiff as cardboard. They frozed to death. They just harbingered too soon.

Dear John,

I put here that composition what I wrote about winter so you can see it's really creative just like the nun said. I gave you the draft because the handwriting is sloppy. I wrote it again for the nun. I handed in the neat one. I think this time I'll get a good grade because I used creative ideas and I wrote harbinger two times. Do you like the one about the birds flying on spring into Brooklyn? I think it's real creative. I even looked up some of the words so I spelled real ~~good~~ well.

Dear John,

Earnest passes me this note during algebra today and it says, "The nun keeps talking about X but I don't know Y."

Dear John,

I hope June is coming home soon. She's so mature.

Dear John,

The nun lied. I got a D for that composition. When I got the paper back, it was full of red pencil marks. So many I couldn't read it all. Something about spelling and grammar and stuff. I threw it away. I hate writing. The nun says she gonna grade for creativity but then grades for spelling and grammar and stuff. It ain't fair. I really hate writing and I'm never going to write again.

Dear John,

Earnest says I should not have wrote about the robins harbingering. That was wrong because harbinger means four runner and birds only got two legs to run on and they mostly don't run. They fly except for a dodo bird what got clobberd and extinguished when they don't fly away. Earnest knows a lot of interesting stuff.

Dear John,

I askd Franky Bazaaro when is June going to be home. He said, "This Friday."

I told him we got to get together this Saturday over his house and make plans for the club we're starting. It's really a gang but we call it a club so old people don't get upset. That gang from Bushwick is big trouble so we gotta defend Williamsburg.

I hope June wears her red sweater. She looks so mature in it.

Dear John,

~~Me and Earnest~~ Earnest and I was over Franky's house today. We planned the gang. We talked real quiet so nobody knows our plans. We all shut up when June walks in. She just smiles at us, especially at me. She was wearing her red sweater. I did not say almost anything for the rest of the meeting. June is really mature.

Dear John,

We had another meeting of our club today. We are meeting in Franky's apartment and June walks past the living room and goes out. But before she closes the door she turns and smiles. She was wearing a blue sweater. She looks so mature in that blue sweater.

Earnest walked with me back to my apartment house and he was singing, "June is busting out all over."

I don't think Earnest knows the rest of the song.

Dear John,

Mrs. K gave the other ship to Franky Bazaaro. I seen it in their living room. It's on a shelf. I asked Franky about it and he told me that Mrs. K. walked all the way down the stairs and gave it to him. She told him he was a very nice boy.

Dear John,

My mom told me that Mrs. K.'s been giving everything away to people she likes because she's getting ready to die. I felt real bad but my mom says that she's had a real good life. She's in her eighties and getting ready for her next life after death. I think she knows she can't take nothing with her.

Dear John,

The Dodgers lost the World Series. The darn Yankees won it three times in a row. When are the Dodgers ever ~~gonna~~ going to win? No wonder they are called the Brooklyn Bums!

Dear John,

I was over at Franky Bazaaro's house today and I'm sitting on the couch waiting for Franky to come back from the bathroom when all a sudden June walks in and sits right down on the couch next to me. My heart's thumping and my face burns tomato red.

June says, "I'm very happy that you and Franky are friends. He never had many friends before."

I'm trying to stop my heart from thumping because I know everbody can hear it. I say, "Oh yes, Franky is a good friend."

Then June moves closer.

I can't hardly stand it. The walls are gonna shatter, the windows are gonna smash from the thumping.

Then June gets real close and whispers, "Franky does not want people to know but he has trouble walking because he had polio." Then she smiles and says, "Thank you."

I was hoping she was gonna give me a little kiss, just a peck on my cheek, but she didn't. Maybe next time.

Dear John,

Mrs. K. just sits in her window looking at us and she's smiling. She really looks happy. I never seen her look so happy.

I just heard an ambulance stop on the next corner. I looked out the window and a lot of people are standing around. I think there was an accident. I'll be right back.

John,

June got hit by a car. She's dead. I can't write no more.

Dear John,
    I can't.

Dear John,
    I went to the funeral parlor with the gang today. I was cool and stay in the back of the room. After we all left I told the guys I had to do some other important business. I walk around the block and then I go back into the funeral parlor. Nobody's there. Just June. I walk up to the casket. There's June like sleeping. I never cry. I'm cool. But I want her to be alive so bad. Why are you dead? It ain't fair. I know I can't ask her but there's God on the cross on top of the casket. Why, God, why did you let June die? I don't cry. She's so beautiful. I want her to open her eyes. I want her to say, "Hi, Bobby. How are you doing?"
    "Hi, June," I whisper. I look around. Nobody. All alone, "I love you, June." I bend over the casket and kiss her cheek. Cold. Dead. "Your boy friend's in the army in Korea and you're dead in Brooklyn. It ain't fair. God, it's not fair." I don't cry. Not one tear. I don't cry at all until I get home, on my bed under the covers.

Dear John,
    I'll never forget what she said, "I'm June and it's a pleasure to meet you, Bobby Anderson." The last thing she said was "Thank you."

Dear John,
    I don't think I told you how it happened. Mostly I don't want to talk about it much. See June wrote this letter to her boyfriend and she went and mailed it. The mail box is on the other side of Grand Street. After she put the letter

in the box she turns around and steps into the street. This blue Chevrolet is turning the corner going real fast, brakes screeching leaving rubber, and hits her. June was thrown onto the other side of the street. The driver puts on the gas and gets away before anybody knows what is happening. Hit and run. Nobody knows who done it. People said it was a blue Chevrolet and that's all. He got away with killing June.

Dear John,

It ain't fair. June was only seventeen. It just ain't fair. She was so beautiful and so young.

Chapter 13

Perfection

Seventh Grade

Dear John,

I got ashes all over the front of my head. So does everybody at St. Mary's. It's the beginning of Lent and today's Ash Wednesday. The priest says in Latin that we should always remember that we are dust and when we die, we will return to dust. The ashes are to remind us about death. I don't need no reminder about death. I think about June all the time.

Dear John,

The ambulance was back at Mrs. K's apartment. This time they carried her out on a stretcher and took her to a hospital.

Dear John,

Every time I hear an ambulance my stomach drops and my heart hurts.

Dear John,

The nun gives us a lesson on Lent and how we have to be perfect as is our Father in Heaven. She says perfection is more than just keeping the commandments. To be perfect you must do more than avoid sin. You have to give up something you like like candy. Like like candy? That's funny. Sometimes language is funny.

Dear John,

The nun tells us about the devil taking Jesus up to a mountain and how the devil tempted Jesus.

The devil says "I will give you power and glory if you tell me what a great guy I am."

But Jesus says, "No deal."

I don't remember the exact words what the nun said but it went something like that. But the main thing is that Jesus showed that He could resist temptation and gave us an example by letting the devil tempt Him. The nun said that the devil will be ready to tempt us during Lent. He will try to get us to break our promises.

The nun said, "You must learn to resist the temptations of the devil now because if you don't, the devil will return with even bigger temptations."

Dear John,

We had to think about what we're giving up for Lent and tell the whole class. The nun called everybody's name and we had tell everybody what we're giving up.

Peter Ackerman was first to get called on and he said, "I'm giving up dessert."

Patrick Garino said, "I will give up my time by watching Bishop Sheen's television show every week. It's called 'Life is Worth Living'."

Christine Carney's up next and you can tell she's been thinking about this real hard. She says, "I have no need to give up anything because I already refrain from the pleasures of this world. I will be going to Mass and Communion every day. In addition, I will study even harder. I also intend to make every possible effort to be even kinder to everyone I know."

Christine Carney thinks she's just swell.

Dear John,

Mrs. K. died last night. She was in the hospital when she died. I wish she did not die but she did and I wish she could have died in her own bed. I think that's better.

Dear John,

The nun told us what she's giving up for Lent, "I will control my anger and I will not yell at any of you."

She's giving up getting mad at us. This Lent might be O.K.

Dear John,

Earnest often takes what a nun says as a challenge. He told me, "We gotta help the nun out because it won't help her none if we're good all the time and she's got no reason to yell at us. We have to take the nun up to the mountain and offer her a temptation. Just like Jesus, the nun's got nothing to gain without a little temptation."

Dear John,

Earnest read Mrs. K's obituary and then Earnest gave it to me. Mrs. K was born in Germany in 1863 but she came to the United States when she was ten years old. Before she married Mr. Kresselmyer her name was Hilga Fromm. She went to a teacher training college and then she taught German and French in high school. But then just before the First World War she and Mr. K went back to Germany and she taught in a gymnasium and they both spied on the Kaiser and his friends. They were almost captured but they escaped to Switzerland. After the war she came back here and she got medals for bravery. Mr. K died in 1947. They were heroes.

Earnest said, "I wish I spent more time talking to Mrs. K."

I think that one time they talked was real good for Earnest.

Dear John,

Mrs. K. died but the main thing is she really lived!

Dear John,

Today the rest of the class had to tell what they were doing for Lent. It was a lot more fun today because yesterday the nun called on the good kids and they aren't doing anything exciting for Lent. Kids like Earnest and Nicholas and me are different. Nicholas says, "I am giving up spinach. Earnest says, "I would like to give up going to school but that would not work because going school is not a thing what I enjoy. So giving up something you don't like will not do the trick. So for Lent I will give up playing hooky." Me? I'm giving up taking baths.

The nun keeps getting madder and madder.

Earnest raises his hand again and says, "I'm gonna be twice as good as Christine Carney and every day I am going to Mass and Communion two times."

Well, that does it. The nun is really mad because you can't go to Communion two times in one day except if maybe you're a priest. So she yells, "You blast feemer!" and comes down the aisle whips out a yard stick and hits Earnest. While she's at it she hits Nicholas and me too.

Dear John,

We were playing stick ball and I looked up at Mrs. K.'s window. I miss seeing her there.

Dear John,

Franky Bazaaro's moving away. His mom and dad don't want to stay around here any more. Every time they cross Grand St. they all start crying. Me too.

Dear John,

Earnest says, "We gotta be more helpful for the nun because it is far too easy for her to keep her Lent promise if she does not get a temptation now and then. Like the devil says he will return with bigger temptations.

Dear John,

The nun's trying something different on account some of us kids won't give up anything good for Lent. She says Christine Carney gave her an idea. We have to work on being the very best we can be. That's more than just giving up something. The nun says during Lent we must be perfect.

Dear John,

Earnest says he ain't for it. He says, "I am not now and I will never be for being perfect. I am just going to be me and that sure ain't perfect. But I do not say a thing such as that to the nun on account we already know she broke her Lent promise."

Dear John,

Me and Earnest went over to Franky Bazaaro's place today. We said goodbye. I couldn't go inside the apartment. Earnest and I just stood outside and shook Franky's hand and all. They loaned a truck from a friend and his dad and some big guys were loading the furniture. I left when I seen the furniture what used to be in June's room. Bye, Franky. Goodbye, June.

Dear John,

Earnest and Peter Ackerman were arguing about perfection. Earnest is not kidding about perfection. He is against it.

Peter Ackerman says, "Everybody has to try real hard to be perfect. It's when you're perfect that you can be happy and you can't be happy till you get to be perfect. And if you fail to be perfect, you can't go to heaven and that's the main thing!"

Earnest says, "Oh, yeah? If you try to be perfect, you are gonna go crazy and then you can be happy all the time—in the Happy Farm." And then Earnest stops and puts his hand up to his chin. He says, "Anyways I ain't planning on going to no heaven. I'd rather be with my friends."

Peter Ackerman gets real red in the face, but he walks away so he does not show he's mad. That kid is really trying to be perfect. Sometimes Earnest gets some pretty good idears, but this time he's dead wrong.

Dear John,

Earnest says, "Maybe it's O.K. for other people to try to be perfect but it is not for me. The timing is just not right for me."

Dear John,

Earnest's been thinking about this perfection stuff and says, "The perfect people what I know are perfectly boring. If everybody is gonna be perfect, then everybody will be just like everybody else. Nobody would be different and that wouldn't be no fun. It is the stuff we do when we mess up that makes life fun. Perfection is boring."

Dear John,

June was perfect and she wasn't boring. But I didn't say anything about that to Earnest.

Dear John,

We're learning all about perfection and the nun says she wants perfection for the whole of Lent. The nun tells us that the Bible says that we gotta be perfect as our Father in Heaven is perfect.

Dear John,

I asked Earnest about what the Bible says. I think I got to Earnest with that one because he says, "I will take a remark such as you have stated and think about it."

Dear John,

The nun says we must try really hard to be perfect all the time. Now she tells us we gotta do a project for science and it must be perfect. You should have seen Earnest's face. He was up sharpening his pencil, which he does about ten times an hour, and just when she says that, he turns around and crosses his eyes, sticks out his tongue, and wiggles his ears. Most of the class almost died from trying to stop laughing. His timing was perfect.

Dear John,

Earnest isn't perfect at most things but he is at some. Different people got different stuff to be perfect at. Earnest sure is working at making perfectly funny faces and now he's even learned to wiggle his ears and that takes real concentration. But nobody's as perfect as Earnest at making disgusting noises. This nun doesn't know he got that talent yet. Whenever he lets one go under his arm pit, she gets red and talks louder. She thinks it's the real thing. Sometimes it is. I hate it when that happens.

Dear John,

I'm going to try to be perfect for Lent. I'm going to write perfect and I'm going to read perfectly and I'm going to do arithmetic perfect. Wait, that's going to be too tough. Arithmetic is not exactly my perfect best thing. O.K., I'll give it a try just for Lent.

Dear John,

Earnest says that Christine Carney tries to be perfect and she's the most boring person he knows.

Dear John,

Now we got a great big Perfection Chart hanging in our classroom. It's got everybody's name. Everytime we get a hundred, or do something the nun thinks is perfect, we get a star next to our names. Christine Carney already got three stars and Peter Ackerman got two and Patrick Garino got one and that's all anybody got so far.

Dear John,

Earnest and I are going to confession tomorrow. Earnest don't really want to go, but it's real important. See, John, maybe you are not a Catholic and don't know that if you die with a big sin, like a mortal sin, on your soul, then you go to hell for ever and ever what's also called eternity. Hell is a real bad place, with fire and brimstones falling on you all the time, and eternity's a long time to be in such a bad place. But confession's real good because after you tell the priest everything what you did wrong, then you got a clean soul. If you get killed right after going to confession, then you can go to heaven. That's the very best time to die. But first you have to say the prayers what the priest tells you to say. The prayers are a penance. Most of the time I have to say three Hail Marys and three Our Fathers and three Glory Bees. You got to tell everything bad to the priest, because if you forget something on purpose, then you commit another sin. That's a sin of oh mission.

Dear John,

Well nothing good ever comes out of it when Earnest raises his hand and asks a question but this time it really wasn't good. This is what happened.

The nun was telling us about original sin and how Jesus and Mary were the only ones born with no original sin on their souls. That's why they got to be perfect because that's the way they started out. Earnest asks, "Did we all get born with sin on our souls?"

The nuns says, "Yes."

Then Earnest says, "Nobody can be perfect if God got us started wrong and sinful."

The nun did not say anything but just looked at Earnest real long and hard.

But Earnest keeps going and says, "Nobody should try to be perfect when God made us unperfect." Then Earnest says something that really gets the nun mad. He says, "If God expects us to be perfect when he makes us unperfect with original sin and all, then God ain't playing fair."

The nun's face gets red and redder and she screams, "Blast feemy." She comes down the aisle swinging a ruler, but Earnest figures what's happening and this time he doesn't wait around. Earnest gets up and runs right out of the classroom. Nobody saw Earnest for the rest of the day.

Dear John,

Earnest was back in school today. He looks like he got a bad beating from his dad because the nun got his dad to come to school and she yelled at Earnest's dad. But Earnest doesn't want to talk about it. I bet he thinks it over a couple of time before he asks any nun another question.

Dear John,

We had a spelling test today and I think I got a perfect score. I hope I start getting some stars. I can see Christine Carney is real happy about being the most perfect kid in the class. She got ten stars and Peter Ackerman got seven and Patrick Garino got four. Nobody else got any, yet. Maybe I'll get one for my spelling test.

Dear John,

The nun says we're going to take a big I.Q. test in a couple of weeks. She says it's a stranded eyes test. I don't know what that means but the nun says, "This is a very important test. It will go on your permanent record cards. That means for the rest of your lives everyone's going to see it and know how smart you are and how smart some of you are not."

I'm going to try real hard for that test. The nun's going to give us practice stuff for it. I don't think I'm going to do perfect because I heard that stranded eyes tests are really tough.

Dear John,

We got our spelling papers back and I got one word wrong. I spelled *neighbor* wrong. I spelled it nieghbor because I remember that i comes before e except after c, but then I forget about the rest of the rule that says or when sounded like "a" in neighbor and way. I didn't get a star.

But Christine Carney got another star! Maybe she's perfect but nobody likes her, except maybe the nun but that doesn't count for much in this neighborhood.

Dear John,

The nun explained about an I.Q. Test what's stranded eyes. She said that it's not like a regular test because you can get more than one-hundred. If you get between 90 and 110, you are normal. If you get about one-hundred and twenty, then you are really smart like a genius. But if you get less than eighty you are kind of retarded. All the time she's telling this Christine Carney's smiling and she really smiled when the nun says the word *genius*. Christine Carney just thinks she's swell.

Dear John,

I told Earnest he's wrong about being against perfection because all the kids what got stars are real happy because they got perfect papers. So it's just like Peter Ackerman says, "When you're perfect, you're happy." I am not perfect and I am not happy about it. But Earnest said, "I'm perfectly happy about not being perfect."

Dear John,

Tomorrow I'm going to try do everything just perfect.

Dear John,

I didn't do it. I'm definitely not perfect yet. It's going to take a little longer. I made about twenty million mistakes today. First, I was counting them, but I gave up. Too many. Like, I made some mistakes in reading. See, I was reading and I got to some reel tuff words and I said the wrong ones and Christine Carney kept correcting every mistake what I made. And in spelling I got five wrong. There were 20 words on the test and I got one crummy little letter wrong in just five of them. I'm getting real good at making mistakes. It's discouraging. That's a new word we learned today and the nun says it comes from Latin roots what got something to do with your heart. So I guess I got a bad heart.

Dear John,

We got another spelling test tomorrow. I'm going to try real hard to get it perfect. One problem is that we don't spell words the right way. We should spell words like "idea" with an "r" at the end because that's the way you say it. Then there are other words that should have an "i" in the middle but they got an "r" instead. Like "word," everybody pronounces it like "woid" but you can't spell it that way. Then there's "New York" and it's got that "r" in it but you don't hear any "r" when you say it. It sounds more like "New Yuck." Then there's "fort" and "fought" which sound exactly the same because they are what's called "homonyms." Potato should be spelled potater. It's all mixed up. No wonder I have spelling problems! It's tuff! Well that's wrong too because it's *tough*!

Dear John,

We had to write a story today in class and I thought I was real smart to use that new word what we learned yesterday. Discourage means dishearten. So I used it in a sentence. I wrote, "The martyr what got eaten by the lion got discouraged." Only the nun says I used it wrong, but it makes sense that the saint got no heart when the lion eats him all up. I spelled it wrong too and the nun was real mad at all our spelling mistakes and she says we have to try real hard to be perfect in spelling. But I figure I'm never going to use new words any more. I'll just stick to the short ones what I already know and then I won't make so many mistakes. If you're going to be perfect, you got to be real careful. You can't take ~~no~~ chances.

Dear John,

Earnest got a hundred in spelling today and everybody's real surprised. I asked him how come he got a hundred.

Earnest said, "I do not memorize the words and how to spell them. I try to figure out the rules. For example, one rule is that if the word has an "r" in it when you say it, leave out the "r' when you spell it. If the word does not have an "r" in it when you say it, try to stick one in some place.

Dear John,

I am thinking about what Earnest said yesterday about spelling rules and all. So today I asked Earnest what about exceptions and I give him a word like "talk." I asked, "How do you remember how to spell a word like that?" Earnest says, "It is indeed a puzzle the way the English language is spelled for it is not the same as it is pronunciated, at least not in the neighborhood in which we reside. The trick is to think about a word what you already know how to spell that sounds mostly like the one you're trying to spell. You tap out the part of that word what sounds like the word you are trying to spell and pour it into the new word. Complicated as that sounds it works like a charm everytime. I will provide an example using the very word you offered up to the sacrificial language gods. Everybody knows it rhymes with fork." Then Earnest spells it for me, "t-o-r-k.'"

Dear John,

Earnest is acting weird lately. I know he is always kind of weird in the way he acts but now he's weird in the way he torks. When I write what he says, I try to write the way he is saying it.

Dear John,

I have not seen Earnest since yesterday so I go looking for him and find him sitting on the stoop in front of the apartment house where he lives. One thing that surprises me is that Earnest is sitting very still and this is a most unusual thing for Earnest to be doing. But the thing that surprises me most is that Earnest is sitting on the stoop with a book open and he's looking at it as if he is actually reading the book. So I sit down on the stoop next to Earnest and I ask him, "What are you doing? I mean this is a most unusual thing you are doing, sitting on the stoop with a book. Are you just looking at the pictures in a funny book."

Earnest looks at me and then holds the book up so I can see the pages. Earnest asks me, "Do you see any funny pictures in this book which I am holding?"

"Not one picture. Just lots of words. So are you trying to read these words," I ask.

"I am not trying to read. It is a matter of fact that I am indeed and actually reading a book."

"Earnest, this is a surprise because I did not think you know how to read."

"So let this be our secret for it would not be in my favor for the nun to know this about me."

Dear John,

Everybody in our class must do a science project. But the nun says we must do it in committees. We must elect a kid in the group to be the boss. The nun's going to tell us who's in the group, but then the group can say what we're going to make. Then we're going to get a grade for how perfect our project is. Whatever science thing we make, if it don't work perfect, then everybody in that group fails.

Dear John,

The nun put us in groups and the nun says we must call them "committees" but there's a problem with my group. Nicholas and Earnest are in my committee. Tomorrow we get to vote for the boss of the committee and then we got two days to say what we're going to make. I don't see how this science project is going to be perfect.

Dear John,

It's a lot worse than I figured. Our group met again and we elected the boss. We had a lot of fun doing it and we laughed a lot. We elected Earnest for boss. At the time I thought it was a perfectly good idea because it is a very funny thing to do but now I think we're all going to flunk.

Dear John,

Our committee met and talked about the science thing what we are going to make and everybody got mad because we all want to make something different. Tony Pugnisi wants to make a car what really drives and Nicholas wants to do a biology thing and make a model of a body. He wants to make a woman's body. We all thought about that but we voted against it because the nun's not going to like it even if it is perfect.

Finally Earnest said, "Since you elected me the boss of this committee, I am hereby taking responsibility and I am going to do this democratically. I am going to think about it and then we can talk about that which I am thinking and then I will tell you what we are going to make."

Tony Pugnisi said, "That's not democratic if you tell us what we're going to make."

Then Earnest said, "I am going to let you talk about it and that is the democratic part. You can talk and keep passing the buck but I'm the boss and the buck stops here. Besides that's the way great presidents like Teddy Roosevelt and Harry Truman do things and they are democrats."

Well, we can't argue against that. So Earnest is going to be democratic and let us talk about it and then he'll stop the buck and tell us what to do.

Dear John,

We got a new kid in our class today. His name is Steven Stinger and he comes from South Carolina and he talks real funny. The nun says he's going to be in our group. I guess she already figured out he was dumb, probably because he talks so funny.

Dear John,

Earnest figured out what we're going to make, but he says we gotta keep it a big secret. It's such a big secret Earnest doesn't want anybody to know about it. That's why he's not even telling us what we're making. But Stinky knows about it. That's Steven Stinger's nick mane. He says everybody calls him Stinky in South Carolina.

Dear John,

I can see Earnest talking to Stinky in the school yard. Earnest is waving his arms and is otherwise very excited about what they are conversating. Stinky is standing there smiling and looking as proud of himself as anyone can be.

I walk over to Earnest and Stinky and ask, "What are you guys talking about?"

Earnest says, "We are addressing the concerns of the science project committee and you and all the other committee members are sure to find the results of our conversating to be of great value."

So I ask, "So what is this what you are conversating about?"

Earnest turns around and as he walks away, he looks back and says, "That is a secret."

Dear John,

Tony Pugnisi got mad and asked Earnest, "How can we make something when we don't even know what it is? And how come Stinky knows when nobody else knows? Earnest says Stinky's a consultant. Earnest and Stinky are going to tell us what we need to get and what we gotta do and we're going to be real happy when we find out what we made. I told Earnest that ain't democratic. Earnest says, "Right. It is not. That part is republican."

Dear John,

I know why they call him Stinky in South Carolina. He's stinky in Brooklyn too. I went over to Stinky's house today and his mom was cooking cabbage. Stinky says they have cabbage every night. That's why Stinky smells like stinky cabbage all the time.

Dear John,

We got to go find all we can for our expeerment in the garbage. I like that. First thing we have to find are big tin cans. Earnest won't even tell the nun what we're going to make. He says it's a surprise. The committee wants to know but Earnest is not about telling us. But then he says, "OK. I'll tell you this much. It's a chemistry expeerment."

Dear John,

Christine Carney's the boss of the smart girls' group. They're going to make a printing press just like the one made by that Guttingburg guy. The nun thinks it's a swell idear. Peter Ackerman's the boss of the smart boys' group. They're going to make a flying dinosaur. Patrick Garino is boss of another group and they're going to make a volcano. Mary Marino is boss of the girls' dumb group. They still don't know what they're going to make. Nicholas says, "They should make a magic potion so they ain't ugly. Mary Marino's group takes ugly pills."

Dear John,

The nun gives us a practice test for the stranded eyes what we are going to take for real next week. That practice for the stranded eyes test is real easy. I keep getting most of the stuff right on the practice tests. Maybe I'll get a perfect score on it.

Dear John,

Me and Tony Pugnisi are walking all over the neighborhood looking for big tin cans. Yesterday I found one in back of the gas station on Gates and Greene but it was real smelly from gasoline and Earnest said it was way too small. But today we saw a really big can in front of the Grand Chemical Factory. It was real heavy. So we couldn't budge it. We tried but then some big guy comes out of the factory and saw us and yells, "Hey, you kids, get away from that stuff." We ran. Then I went and got Stinky and showed it to him. We was about a block away but he could see it and he says it's perfect. And it's just going to be thrown away.

Dear John,

Tonight after the Grand Chemical Factory closes, me and Stinky and Earnest and Nicholas go over there and we see that the big can is still outside. Stinky has this old wagon made from carriage wheels. We were going to put the can on it and take it to Stinky's back yard. The can's just there with a lot of other garbage just waiting for somebody to come along and take it. Stinky checks it over. He says it's a 55 gallon drum and that's just perfect. First we try lifting it onto the wagon but it was way too heavy. There's something still in it. So Stinky finds a plug near the bottom. He got a hammer and screwdriver what he keeps in his wagon for such emergencies. He hits the plug a few times and some of the stuff starts coming out. It's like red water. But then we can move the drum a little. So we get the wagon right up next to the drum and push it over. Perfect! At first. It lands right on the wagon. But then the boards creek and the wagon cracks right in half. We left everything because the noise woke up the night watchman and he was yelling, "Get out of here, you brats."

Dear John,

It rained today and you should see red stuff pouring down Grand St. The can must have been filled with red dye or something. I don't know what we want the can for but Earnest says it was just as good we did not get it. I guess it wasn't so perfect.

Dear John,

My stomach was real upset all night and I had a headache and I didn't want to go to school but my mom says I gotta go because she figures I was just trying to get out of taking the stranded eyes test but I wasn't. You know I don't ever, hardly ever, lie. And I don't never lie to you, John, I was really sick and I even throwed up in the boys room as soon as I got to school. I told the nun about being sick and throwing up and everything but she don't believe me. But I figured that she won't believe me. That's why I didn't flush after I throwed up. That way she can see the evidence. But the nun didn't want to look. She tells Peter Ackerman to go and look. But some other kids got there first and flushed it just before we got there. All the evidence flushed. So I had to take that stranded eyes test anyways. My head and stomach was really hurting. And there was lots of stuff on the test what I don't know. That made me even sicker. I had to leave the room because I felt sick again. So the nun sends Peter Ackerman with me to watch me throw up. But I only got the dry heaves. Then Peter Ackerman keeps watching me with the dry heaves and he turns a little green and he throws up on the floor. The nun sent him home. He had the evidence.

Dear John,

I feel bad about not knowing much on the test but you should have seen Christine Carney. There was stuff on it she don't even know. She was so mad about not knowing some of the stuff on the test, she was crying. She says it— ain't —is unfair to have a test when you don't know everything on it. She's never had such a bad experience. Poor Christine Carney!

421

Dear John,

Nicholas said, "I don't know what Christine Carney's complaining about. That happens to me all the time."

Dear John,

I'm giving up on trying to be perfect. Perfection is just too tuff.

Dear John,

We got the two cans for the science project. Stinky's dad drives a truck and he got them for us at a warehouse. He talks real funny, same as Stinky. He says stuff like, "you all" and "sho nuff" an "fixin to." He don't talk like the men what come from Brooklyn. And he smells like cabbage same as Stinky. But the 55 gallon drums are real good and clean and Earnest and Stinky say they're perfect. Now we got to find a smaller drum and some pipes and marbles to make the chemistry expeerment. I don't know what we're making but I hope it's going to be better than Mary Marino's committee because they still don't know what they're making. Nicholas told Mary Marino what they should make, some medsin so they all aren't so ugly. Mary Marino got mad and took a swing at Earnest. He ducked but she got him on the side of his head. But Earnest says it don't hurt much. Nicholas says Mary Marino is ugly and a weakling. I told Earnest it's just not right to tell girls they're ugly even when they are.

Dear John,

Earnest had to stay after school for a punshment and he told me what happened. Earnest hears the nun whispering to another nun out in the hall. So Earnest goes up near the door like to sharpen his pencil because it's always a good idea to hear what nuns got to say to one another. Our nun's talking to the eighth grade nun. The nun said that our science projects are an expeerment for her college. She's doing an expeerment about perfection and creativity in smart kids and dumb kids. She says the way she decides the smart and dumb ones is how the children read. So she put all the smart kids in the same group and figures they're going to be more original and perfect than the kids like Earnest, Nicholas and me. The nun says that smart children are going to be more perfect at doing science expeerments because they're more careful at reading. And she says that more careful readers are more creative.

Dear John,

I think Earnest can read real well when he wants to. He just can't read school books because he doesn't want to.

Dear John,

I was doing my favorite thing the other day, you know John, investigating the garbage in the neighborhood and I seen this box in Christine Carney's garbage. It's empty but it has a picture on it for making some kind of a kit. It's a real good box and you never know when you're going to need a real good box. So I take the box home and put it under my bed.

Dear John,

Earnest is talking really weird like all of a sudden he's sort of uppity. I think it's something to do with the book what he's reading.

Dear John,

Our committee had a meeting and Earnest told Nicholas and Stinky what the nun said about smart kids being more creative and perfect than dumb ones like us. Earnest says Christine Carney and Peter Ackerman got nothing original about them. Earnest says, "Now it is our chance to demonstrate our special talents. What we have here is a real big challenge. We have to make a better expeerment than the smart kids. We got to do this on behalf of all the dumb kids in the whole world."

Dear John,

Earnest gives me the job of getting the marbles because I'm the best marble shooter in the neighborhood. I got a lot of marbles already, a big bag full. But Stinky says, "You all gotta get fixin to get lots more marbles. Sho nuff you don't got nuff, you all."

At least I think that's what he said. I can't hardly understand him. He talks funny but in a way what's different from Earnest's funny talk.

Dear John,

We got the scores on that I.Q. test today. Christine Carney was real happy. She's better than perfect. She got 120 and Peter Ackerman got 115 but I don't know what nobody else got. They were the only ones bragging about the scores. Me? You probly want to know what I got. I flunked. The test says I got a 55 I.Q.

Dear John,

My mom got three phone calls from other kids parents to tell her how smart their kids are. Most of them got like in the eighties and nineties. She didn't tell anybody what I got. I guess I was born with some brain parts missing or something.

Dear John,

The nun said there was something wrong with Earnest's I.Q. Test. She says there's a mistake in the correcting so she won't tell Earnest what he got until they check it again.

Dear John,

That's it! I ain't perfect and I ain't going to ever be and it ain't my fault because I got a dumb I.Q. and brain parts missing. So there!!!!

Dear John,

The nun says she knows there's a mistake with Earnest's I.Q. Test but they can't find what the problem is. The score what they got for Earnest is 140.

Dear John,

I asked Earnest about how he got 140 on his I.Q. Test and he told me he cheated. How did he cheat? He says, "I read the questions and then picked the best answers."

Dear John,

I'm winning lots of marbles. See I got this little lucky killer marble and I can shoot it straight and it hits the other guys' marbles every time. Maybe I'm not so smart at taking I.Q. Tests but I'm good at some things and marble shooting is definitely one of them. But then I'm bad at somethings and writing is definitely one of them.

Dear John,

I got enuff marbles and the other guys got everything for the expeerment. We put everything in Stinky's back yard. We got nuts and bolts and pipes and a top of an electric stove and a thermometer and clamps and a rubber gasket and lots of other stuff. And now I figured out what we're making. It's a fruit juice machine. I know that because I saw Stinky got lots of rotten fruit from the markets. He got it sitting in a barrel with water and he poured something from a bottle what says "Malted". Maybe it's a malted fruit soda. I guess it'll taste O.K. but I don't think it's such a great science project. I guess we're going to make something like apple juice.

Dear John,

Earnest told me it's not exactly fruit juice but it's something like fruit juice. What we're making is called *Kickapoo* and the idea came from some little guy named Abner who lives in Dogpatch.

Dear John,

We started putting the kickapoo stuff together and I had to put the marbles down a long pipe. I guess that's to help crush the fruit into juice. But some stuff didn't fit right so we asked Stinky's father to help. But Stinky's dad says he'll help us with problems but he says we got to learn to do it on our own or it won't be fair. He says he hates people what don't be fair like the McCormicks in South Carolina. He told us a story about what he called "feudin" but I understand almost nothing else what he says. Only thing I could figure was that the Stinger family was emenys with the McCormick family but the McCormicks don't fight fair. I think he says the Stingers stop shooting and the McCormicks kept shooting

426

at them still. He said something like that. I think he said, "The Stinger family moved to Brooklyn to get away from all that feudin, fussin and fightin."

Dear John,

We got our kickapoo chemistry project done and it really does work perfect and it's a lot more perfect than I figured it'd be. We made a whole lot of kickapoo. It's like juice what tastes terrible at first but then it tastes better and better. We felt real good and we were laughing at the craziest stuff. Stinky says it's called "kickapoo joy juice." Tomorrow Christine Carney's group goes. We go the next day. I feel dizzy.

Dear John,

I woke up with my head hurting this morning. Today Christine Carney's committee is going to show off their expeerment. Tomorrow our group goes.

Dear John,

Earnest told us we need to get a box to carry some of the parts to our expeerment so they don't fall all over the place. I told Earnest I got a real good strong box what I found in the garbage. I got to remember to get it out from under my bed.

Dear John,

Earnest came over and I got the box out from under my bed. Earnest asked me where I got it and I told him about finding it in the garbage where Christine Carney lives. Earnest told me, "This is a real good strong box and it is real important that I bring it to school tomorrow. That is a great box and it is going to help us a lot."

Dear John,

Well, the first group to show off their expeerment was Christine Carney's and they got out this little wooden and iron machine and some paper and they printed some page all about how God is perfect but nobody can read it because it's in Latin. The nun thinks it's a swell expeerment and she says it's perfect and real original and creative and that's when Earnest ups his hand and says, "Sister, that expeerment ain't exactly original." The nun looks real surprised but Earnest says, "This box was in Christine Carney's garbage." Earnest reaches under my desk and pulls out that box. Earnest points to a picture on the box. It's the same exact printing press what the smart kids committee just showed off. Christine Carney's face is real mad and she says she never saw that before but then Earnest brings the box up and there right on the outside of the box is Christine Carney's name and address. The nun is real surprised and gives Christine Carney a I'll-talk-to-you-later look. But the nun says it's a real perfect expeerment anyways and it works perfect. So everybody in Christine Carney's group gets a A+.

Dear John,

The nun is still using that chart for perfection and Christine Carney and Peter Ackerman, and Patrick Garino got their lines all full up with stars. Earnest and Nicholas and I don't have even one star for all three of us.

Dear John,

Tomorrow it's our turn to show off our expeerment. The nun wants to know what kind of expeerment it is. So Earnest says, "It's a chemistry expeerment."

Dear John,

It is raining today and we had to stay in our classroom for lunch. It was as smelly as ever but at least it is not a Friday. It was more like a baloney smelly classroom. Earnest asked, "Tell me. Who are the most boring people in this class?" At the same time Nicholas, Earnest and me point to the chart, the names what got the stars. We laff. Then after school we went to Stinky's house to test our expeerment.

Dear John,

We tried that kickapoo joy juice again and it's real swell.

Dear John,

My head hurts a little, but I had to get up real early this morning anyways because we had to set up the Chemistry expeerment before anybody else gets to school. All the kids in my group had to carry lots of stuff to school and set up the chemistry expeerment and that wasn't so easy because we all got headaches. We started out real early and got most of the stuff set up in the school yard and Earnest got the fire going under the 50 gallon drum even before the nuns went over to church. We even had some juice dripping outa the tube. I'm home for breakfast and an aspirin. Got to get back to school now.

Dear John,

It was our turn next to show off our expeerment. The whole class had to go down to the school yard. That's where we had it all set up. The juice was really dripping outa that tube and the bucket was almost full. Earnest tastes it and puts just a little more sugar in the bucket and says the best way to show how good the expeerment works is to try some of the juice. The nun's suspishus so she checks in the gallon and sees the fruit. She asked, "What is this?" Earnest says, "Cooked fruit juice." So he pours out some into a little cup and gives it to the nun. She sips it and coughs a little. Then some of the kids say they'll try some. Stinky gives Christine Carney a big glass and she chokes a little but drinks it. Well, then the nun says it's a pretty messy expeerment and it's most certainly not perfect because it doesn't do anything special. She says "There's nothing creative about cooking fruit juice." Earnest says it's better with more sugar in it. So he pours some out into a big glass and puts more sugar in it and hands it to her. The nun says, "That's very sweet of you." Then she giggles.

Next Peter Ackerman's group is up and they got this real funny looking thing what they call a flying dinosuar made with a lot of paper-machier. So Peter Ackerman puts it on the ground and spins the dinosaur's propeller. Whoever heard of a dinosuar with a propeller? He finally gets it started and that flying dinosuar sounds just like a model gasoline airplane. But then it doesn't do anything but run real slow along the ground. It's probly too heavy to get off the ground. But the nun says, "It's a real good experiment and perfect because it looks just like a flying dinosaur." And the nun hiccups and continues, "They probly didn't fly too good and that's why they all got distinguished." But then she changes her mind and says, "Extinguished. They got extinct." Then the nun laffs a little. Earnest told Peter Ackerman that he should try flying it off the roof of the school. The nun heard him and says, "That's a great idea." She was real happy about it.

So the whole class walks up to the roof. The nun takes little sips and the glass is empty when we get to the roof. Then the nun says, "I wants to try to fry the thing." Then she hiccups and laffs and says, "I wants to fly the fling." So Peter

Ackerman gets the flying dinosaur started and the nun holds it over her head. She's wobbly and then she throws it into the air. It flies but then it takes a dive and heads down real fast. Right for the rectory. You ever notice how sometimes things go in slow motion, speshally when you can see what's going to happen isn't all that good? Well, that dinosaur plane was just like in slow motion even though it was flying down real fast. Then crashing, glass smashing, tinkle tinkle. The stained glass window in the priest's house don't look good what with the big whole in it and the rear end of a dinosaur hanging out of it. The nun was laffing so hard she couldn't stop. She's like wobbly and heading right for the railing around the roof. She hits it and wobbles back and forth with her hands stretching to hold onto something. She steps back almost catches her balance but she don't. Her habits going back and forth like clothesline wash on a windy day. She wobbles right for the edge again. I know what's going to happen, slow motion again. So I'm already running to grab her before she starts to topple. Earnest gets there at the same time and we pull her back and straighten her up. But then she sits down on the ground and hiccups and giggles and then laffs real loud. But not for long. Next she sobs and cries. She says "My expeeriment didn't work and now I won't get my degree." We all stand around and I feel bad for her. Most of the kids ask each other, "What she say?"

Then the principal and the pastor are up on the roof and they help her down the stairs. We all follow real quiet. We can hear her crying even with the principal's door shut. When we get to our classroom, we're real quiet, except for Christine Carney who is walking wobbly all arown the room and hicupping. For the first time Chrisine Carney ain't boring. It's perfect.

Dear John,

Today we got a sub. The principal says, "No more experiments." Mary Marino's group does not gotta do any experiment which is lucky for them because they still can't think of any. I hope the nun is O.K. because I kind of liked her when she was sitting on the roof crying. Sometimes nun's ~~ain't~~ are not all that spiritual and perfect. Sometimes a nun can be a normal person.

Dear John,

Earnest sits me down and gives me a real serius talk about perfection not being all that great. He says, "Take the nun, for example, we can respect her and all when she was like acting real perfect, and maybe we kind of think Christine Carney's really smart and all, but it is only when they're making mistakes and not being all that perfect that we like them. Perfect people are just not that likeable."

"Now," Earnest says, "take you and me, Bobby. We are not perfect, far from it. We make mistakes all the time and we are just about the best liked kids in Brooklyn. People like people what make mistakes. All the time we're messing up but that's because we're trying to figure new things out. People don't like people what don't make no mistakes. They can admire perfect-like people but people like us, they love. You just can't love people what are perfect. You can have other feeling about them but it ain't love."

Dear John,

I'm thinking about what Earnest says and I figure maybe he's got something. I never met nobody I liked what was trying to be perfect all the time. I think maybe I ain't going to try to be perfect no more. I'm going to try just to be me and that's far from perfect!

Dear John,

God's perfect. How come we love Him? Do perfect people make perfect things? If God is perfect, how come he made us to start right out not perfect with original sin and all? Maybe Earnest knows.

Dear John,

The nun's O.K. today. But we had to take the kickapoo machine apart because that juice was real powerful. Stinky's father said, "I'll take care of getting rid of it for you." He says he'll take care of the left over juice too. That was real nice of him.

Dear John,

I asked Earnest about God being perfect and us loving Him and all.

Earnest thinks for a long time and says, "Maybe it's O.K. for God to be perfect because that's who He is and what He's real good at doing that and all. It's when people try to be perfect it's like they're being somebody who they ain't and then it's real hard to like them." Then Earnest thinks some more and says, "Maybe God's doing just what comes natural. When people are perfect, they ain't doing what comes natural."

Dear John,

The Bible says we gotta be perfect like our Father what art in Heaven but maybe Earnest and the Bible are both right. God's perfect because he don't pretend to be nobody else. People can be perfect if they stop pretending to be perfect.

Dear John,

I had to read and I didn't make so many mistakes, mainly because Christine Carney's sick and she didn't correct every little mistake. Maybe it's also because I don't care all that much about being perfect.

Dear John,

The less I try to be perfect the closer I get to feeling pretty good.

Dear John,

Stinky's dad got lots of people coming out of his house with jugs under their arms.

Dear John,

The best thing about this Sunday is Easter and Lent is going to be over soon.

Dear John,

The nun stopped talking about perfection and that is just perfect.

Chapter 14

The Sign

Eighth Grade

Dear John,

Next week is vocation week and we have to think about what we're going to be when we are all grown up.

Dear John,

The nun says all the boys should think about being priests and all the girls should think about being nuns because maybe God is calling us. But if you don't listen real carefully for the calling, and if you miss it, you can be in big trouble.

I don't want to be in big trouble with God. But I don't know what I want to be. Peter Ackerman's really sure he's going to be a priest and, of course, Christine Carney's absolutely certain she's going to be a nun. But me, I don't know. Maybe God will whisper in my ear. I'll try to listen real hard.

Dear John

The nun does not talk about being anything except priests and nuns. They say they are the highest vocations and everything else is below them.

Priests can't get married but I don't see that as a big problem. Most men I see who are married do not seem all that happy about it.

Dear John,

I asked Earnest what he's going to be when he grows up. He says he wants to be guy knee colygist. He really likes girls and this way he can get to be in and around them. Then Earnest winks at me like he does when he just made a joke. I don't get it but I winked back anyways.

Dear John,

Of course, I like girls. Well, some I don't and Christine Carney's at the top of that list. But I like most of them and some even like me.

But maybe I'm going to be a priest. I don't know. Maybe I will. Maybe I won't. I don't know.

Dear John,

This morning I go looking for Earnest and I see him sitting on the stoop in front of his apartment house. He's doing that thing what is a very strange thing for Earnest to be doing. He's reading a book.

I walk up a few steps and sit down on the stoop. Then I tell Earnest, "I've been thinking about becoming a priest."

Earnest looks at me and shakes his head and says, "Personally such a thought is one that indeed upsets yours truly for it is well known to one and all that nuns are recruiting people to their persuasion and it seems to me that you are indeed falling for the nun's persuasion.

Before I carry forward our conversation, I ask Earnest, "Why are you talking like the way you just talked? I am trying to follow what you say but your way of talking is getting more weirder and more weirder every day.

Earnest holds up the book and says, "I am influenced by the language of books such as this one. The author is a New York newspaper reporter and writes this book which I am holding for your enlightenment."

Earnest holds up a book with yellowing pages and a ripped cover. The title is *The Damon Runyon Omnibus.*

Dear John,

Earnest and I did not complete our conversation this morning because my mom was calling out the window like this, "Bobby Anderson! Bobby Anderson!" I try not to hear her calling because I want to carry forward my conversation with Earnest but then I hear my mom yell at the top of her voice, "Robert Steven Anderson!" That means no more playing deaf so I have got to run home. She wants me to run to Teitelbaum's deli for eggs. She is baking a lemon merang pie and needs eggs in a big hurry. I don't mind at all running to Teitelbaum's if a piece of lemon merang pie is in the works.

Dear John,

This morning I found Earnest sitting on his stoop again and we continue our conversation when Earnest puts down Damon Runyon and asks, "Why do you want to do a thing like that? Personally I do not think there is any good coming from such a way of thinking, I mean about becoming a priest."

I told Earnest, "I've just been thinking about what I'm going to become and neither one of us is getting any younger and it's time to think about stuff like that."

Earnest puts his hand up to his chin and says, "Hmm. Well, I have no intention of offending you but let's face it. You have never been lucky in love. In fact you have been extraordinarily unsuccessful when it comes to the females here and about. Maybe you should become a priest."

I told Earnest, "It's got nothing to do with not being lucky in love. It's got nothing to do with girls."

Earnest says, "Whenever a guy says it got nothing to do with girls, it's got everything to do with girls."

Dear John,

The priests got together enough money to buy the property for the new church. They're going to build the new church right across the street from where I live. Do you remember what's there? Right. They're going to tear down the Victorian Mansion.

Dear John,

I told Peter Ackerman that I don't know what I want to be. But he says it's not important to know what you want to be. What counts is finding out what God wants you to be.

Dear John,

I asked my mom if she thinks maybe God wants me to be a priest.

"That's great, that's wonderful, my prayers are answered. My son's going to be a priest. I'm going to be the mother

Peanut Butter Fridays

of a priest." That's what she said and then she kisses my forehead.

I said, "Mom, stop talking like that. Are you practicing to be Italian or something?"

After I said that, she didn't say much more. But she's real happy that I'm going to be a priest. Am I?

Dear John,

My mom's been thinking about my becoming a priest and she told me, "Bobby, God will give you a sign. I don't know what the sign will be but you just have to look and listen for one."

Dear John,

The bulldozer came and in no time the Victorian Mansion was down. Earnest and I sat on the stoop and just shook our heads and then we smiled a little.

Dear John,

Earnest says, "It is important to be what God wants you to be but it works out best when what God wants and what you want are the same thing."

Dear John,

I was looking at the new church that's getting built and I saw Father McNulty looking at it too.

He asked, "What do you think about it?"

I told him I liked the old wooden one better because it always gives me a warm feeling like I'm really in God's little house. I love the old wood beams on the ceiling and the carvings on the confessionals and all.

He says, "I know what you mean."

Then I tell him, "I wish they wouldn't wreck the old church."

He says, "I wish they didn't have to."

Then I asked him, "Father, do you think I should be a priest?"

He says, "Maybe. You should at least think about it because you're a real good altar boy and because you love the old church."

Maybe that's the sign.

Dear John,

I really got to think hard about what I'm going to be because I'm in the eighth grade now and I got to think about high school for next year. The nun says we should all try real hard to go to a Catholic high school like Bishop Loughlin or Bishop McDonald where the girls go.

Dear John,

Earnest says he wants to go to Bishop McDonald.

Dear John,

I told my dad I want to sign up for the tests that you have to pass to get into a Catholic high school. I told him the nun says Bishop Loughlin is a very good school and anybody who gets accepted would be fortunate and blessed by God. My dad said he heard Bishop Loughlin's not what it's cracked up to be. He says he knows a guy who works at the bank where my dad works and this guy makes lots of mistakes and he went to Bishop Loughlin. This guy didn't like Bishop Loughlin so he quit school and went to work at the bank.

I ask, "How old is this guy?"

"He's about 45 years old."

Dear John,

I am going to take tests for the Catholic high schools and one public one, Brooklyn Tech. The nun's going to help us get ready for the tests. In two weeks I'm going to take the test for St. John's Prep and the next week for Brooklyn Tech. The nun says the best one to get into though is Bishop Loughlin.

Dear John,

My dad says I should go to Eastern District High School. He says he got a real good education the year he went to high school.

Dear John,

The nun says that Bishop Loughlin is a really good school. And then she says that if you get accepted, it's free because it's paid for by the Diocese of Brooklyn.

Dear John,

I told my dad that Bishop Loughlin is a real good school and if I pass the test and get accepted the Brooklyn Diocese pays and it's free for me.

Dear John,

My dad says I should study to pass the test for Bishop Loughlin. He says it's a very good high school.

Dear John,

The nun said, "Not everybody needs to worry about taking the tests to get into high school. Most of you are going to Eastern District. Only the smart ones will take the tests."

I figured that would get me off the hook but then she says, "I'll read the names of those students who should prepare and take the tests." Then she reads about ten names and mine's on the list. I am surprised. I never figured I was one of the smart kids. She didn't call out Earnest's or Nicholas' names.

Dear John,

I met this real nice priest. He comes from St. John's and his name is Father Lawler. He says Mass here at St. Mary's almost every Sunday and he's the vocation director for the Vincentian priests. He was talking to me about becoming a priest and he says, "Bobby, you got to pray real hard and then God will show you a sign if He wants you. But I think you are just the kind of young man God wants."

Maybe that's the sign.

Dear John,

My mom and dad are going to have a party tonight.

My mom told me, "Earnest is not invited."

Dear John,

We had a party in our apartment last night and my mom sang, "Tora Lora Lora That's an Irish Lullaby." My mom tells everybody she's Irish. I think I will call her Mom McAnderson.

Dear John,

At the party last night after a few beers my dad tells everybody, "Bobby is going to Bishrop Lafflin lockin and it's a very good hight school. Can you magin dis? It's a Catholic school what is fee, free. Can you magin dat?"

My dad forgot that I have to take a test first and my chances of getting in are not all that great.

Then after a few beers my mom tells everybody, "Bobby is going to be a peas. I will be the modder of a peast.

I think mom and dad drank a little too much beer.

Dear John,

I'm praying real hard at church today after school. I was just asking for a sign and I feel a tap on the shoulder. I turned around but nobody's there. Maybe that's the sign.

Dear John,

I told Earnest about the tap I felt on my shoulder. Earnest says, "The old church got cockroaches. It was probably a cockroach crawling up your shoulder."

Dear John,

Wow! It's Sunday and I didn't have to be an altar boy at any Mass so I went to the nine o'clock children's Mass. That was the scariest sermon I ever heard. The priest's the vocation director for the Maryknoll priests. He said that if God grants anyone a vocation to be a priest or a nun and if they don't do it, it's almost for certain they're going to hell. Then he tells us all about hell and how God let some people get a good look at it and how terrible it is.

He shouts and sometimes his voice gets real low, "You are sinful unless you follow the way of the Lord. Will you fail God, fail yourself, and fall into the fires of hell for all eternity?"

He screamed a lot about that fire and those brimstones and all and got everybody real scared. Then over on the girls' side of the church you hear soft crying.

The priest keeps pointing his finger at us and shouts, "Some of you sitting here, right here today will be cast into eternal damnation. Unless you follow the path chosen for you by God, you will almost most certainly be damned. You! Yes you! And you will burn in hell." Then "sob, sob." Christine Carney cries real loud. I guess she's real scared of going to hell. He points right at her then he says "You" and another "You" gets pointed at Earnest. Earnest ain't sobbing. He's turning around and smiling like he just got famous. But at least everybody knows Earnest actually made it to church this morning.

Dear John,

I asked Christine Carney, "How come you were you crying in church yesterday? You're real scared of hell, aren't you?"

But she says, "I'm not scared for myself but for all the poor souls of people like you and Earnest and Nicholas who are most certain to burn in hell if you do not seek forgiveness for your sins. I'm not worried for myself because I have seen and heard many signs that I'll be a nun and go to heaven."

I asked Christine Carney to tell me what kind of signs she got from God.

But she says, "They're too personal to talk about."

I guess I just got to keep looking for my own signs.

Dear John,

Well I figured maybe I'm not getting any really good signs because maybe my soul isn't pure enough. I just remembered this Friday is First Friday and on Thursday, that's tomorrow, the whole class is going to confession. I'm going to really confess everything, get a real clean soul and then maybe God will give me a really good sign.

Dear John,

The class all went to Confession this morning. It's embarrassing when a kid is in the confessional box for a long time because then you know the kid's a real big sinner. But Peter Ackerman was in there for about half an hour and Earnest for about half a minute. Every rule got exceptions.

Well, I really examined my conscience and had a great big list which I wrote down but that did not help all that much because you can't read in the dark confessional. But who wants a light? Then the priest can see who you are. Well, anyways, I forgot some of the sins. I have to go back next Saturday and get rid of the rest of my sins. God isn't going to give me a sign if I got some sins on my soul.

Dear John,

The nun told us about vocations today and she says there are two kinds of vocations. One is the religious vocation and the other is the married vocation. The highest vocation is the religion one and the lowest is the married one. People should get married only if they're weak and can't control their animal instincts.

I don't think I'm going to tell my dad what the nun said.

Dear John,

I asked Peter Ackerman, "How come you want to be a priest?"

He said, "I always wanted to be a priest. That's why I became an altar boy. I don't care that much about the money we make on weddings and funerals and going to Rye Beach. I just want to dedicate my life to God."

Dear John,

The nun gives us some practice tests. They are old tests from Brooklyn Tech and Bishop Loughlin. The girls get the same test as the boys for Bishop McDonald. The nun told us that girls can't go to Brooklyn Tech because that's for boys who want to be scientists but girls don't make good scientists.

Dear John,

I asked Peter Ackerman if he had any signs from God what told him he had a vocation to be a priest.

He says, "Sure lots. When I was praying one time, I felt a tap on my shoulder and I turned around and there was nobody there."

I told him "Me too. I had a tap on my shoulder too."

But then he says, "That's not a big sign. I've had big signs like lots of dreams about being a priest. God talks to us in dreams by showing us what He wants us to do."

Dear John,

Christine Carney's real mad at the nun for the first time. The reason is that Christine Carney always gets the best grades in everything, even science. Christine Carney told me, "I just happen to want to be a nun but if I wanted to be a scientist, I'd be a better scientist than any man."

Dear John,

Earnest overheard Christine Carney about the nun saying women don't make good scientists and all. Earnest says, "I am thinking finally there is hope for Christine Carney. Maybe she got a little spunk and won't always just try to be a goody two-shoes."

Dear John,

I was talking to Earnest about dreams.

Earnest says, "I get lots of dreams about stuff what God got nothing to do with."

Dear John,

I had a dream last night. It was about swimming through a tunnel and when I got out, there was a beautiful lady. I think it was the Blessed Mother. I think that's a sign.

Dear John,

I had another dream last night. I was an altar boy and then all of a sudden I'm the priest and I'm saying all the Latin that the priest says and then I'm saying the altar boy Latin too and then I turn around and I'm in church pews. I was all over the church at the same time. Then the old wooden church is on fire and I'm the fireman trying to put out the fire but it burns all the way down. I wake up and I am sweating. I keep thinking about my dream last night and then I remember that after I was a fireman I was a priest again and I look at the Church all burned to the ground and I said, "Ite, Missa est." That's what the priest says at the end of the Mass. It means "Go the Mass is ended."

Dear John,

Earnest does it again! He asks a question. Actually he asks more than one question. First he asks the nun how come you can't be a priest or a nun and also be married?

The nun shows us her left hand and says, "This is a wedding ring." Then she says that nuns are married. "We are married to God."

Then Earnest does it again. He says, "OK. I understand that because you can't be married to two people at the same time." But then he asks, "Are priests married to God?"

The nun answers, "No. God is a male and that would not work at all."

I can see the nun getting a little upset with Earnest's questions but then she gets really upset when Earnest asks, "If all the nuns are married to God, is God a polygamist?"

The nun is suddenly down at Earnest's desk and yelling, "You are blaspheming!" She is just about to wop Earnest on the head with her yardstick when the nun who's the principal opens the door.

After a short discussion the two nuns scowled at Earnest in a most nasty way. Earnest spent the rest of the day helping Mrs. Murphy, the school secretary, stuff envelopes.

Dear John,

Earnest told me, "I always heard that God works in strange ways. God's gotta be real strange to want to be married to this nun."

Then Earnest said, "I have a few more questions but I do not get to pose them to the nun. But when I am helping the school secretary, we get to talking about this and that and one thing and another which gives me an opening to ask her how come priests can not get married? Mrs. Murphy told me the truth. She said, 'I don't know.' The way I look at it, I think the nun would probably have the exact same answer if she told the truth."

Dear John,

I had another dream last night. I was a train going into a tunnel. There was a beautiful girl in the dream but it definitely was not the Blessed Mother. I think I had one of Earnest's dreams.

Dear John,

Earnest says "When it comes to women, God does not have very good taste."

Christine Carney heard Earnest and says, "I am shocked. God does not care about how women look. He only cares about their kindness, goodness, and virtues."

Earnest puts his hand to his chin and says, "Hmmm! Kindness, goodness and virtues? Most nuns got big problems in those areas too, especially that kindness situation."

Then Christine Carney says, "God works in strange ways."

Dear John,

Earnest is still talking about God marrying nuns. Earnest says, "Finally Christine Carney and yours truly got something we can agree about. God works in strange ways."

Then he adds, "I agree with Christine Carney about something else too. It is not so much about their bad looks which of course is a concern not to be ignored but it is more a matter of their meanness. I would not marry one of these nuns even if she walked with gorgeous gams and the rest of her was shaped like Betty Grable."

Dear John,

Earnest tells me about a dream he had. He says he was standing in the church and he can't find his way out. There are no doors. Then he's looking at the altar and the statue of the Blessed Mother winks at him.

Dear John,

I think me and Earnest got our dreams switched.

Dear John,

It is vocation week and we had a procession around the school singing hymns and two little kids in second grade were all dressed up. The boy was dressed like a priest and the girl like a nun. Then some nuns talked to the girls about being nuns while some priests talked to the boys. Father Lawler was here and he's taking some boys for a trip to the seminary in New Jersey. A seminary is the place where they make priests. Father Lawler rented a big bus and we can all go free so we can see what a seminary is like. It's a week from next Saturday. I hope I can go.

Dear John,

I asked Father Lawler if the seminary is free like Bishop Loughlin. He says it costs only $300 a year. I told my dad that the seminary costs $150 for half a year. It sounded better but my dad said, "That's a lot of money."

Dear John,

The new church is almost done and pretty soon they're going to tear down the pretty wooden one. That old one is about a hundred years old and I love it. But they got to tear it down so they can build a new rectory where the priests are going to live.

Dear John,

Earnest told me he thought it was pretty stupid to build a new rectory when the priests could have moved into the Victorian Mansion.

I sort of figured out what was really going on in that mansion and I think if the priests moved to that house, they wouldn't have enough holy water to make things right.

Dear John,

I ask my mom if I can go on the trip to the seminary and she smiles and says O.K. But then when we tell my dad, he says he does not like the idea. He does not want me to think about going to the seminary next year because I don't know enough about the world to give it up. He thinks I should go to Eastern District. He says, "That's where you will learn a lot about the world." Then he smiles and says very quietly, "Yes. That was the place I learned about . . ." But then his eyebrows go down and he is thinking, "Hmm. Bishop Loughlin might by O.K."

Dear John,

So far five boys from my class have signed up to go on the trip to the seminary and one of those boys is Earnest. Of course, Peter Ackerman is going. I hope I can go.

Dear John,

Christine Carney is still mad about what Earnest said about God having bad taste in women. She says, "God is merciful to boys like Earnest because he is ignorant. What Earnest said was not theologically correct."

Dear John,

I asked Earnest how come he's going on the trip to the seminary. He says he heard that the seminary got a swimming pool.

Dear John,

There was a story on the front page of the Daily Mirror about Eastern District High School. A teacher got beat up by some kids what were on dope.

Dear John,

My dad says I can go on the trip to the seminary Saturday. Maybe that's a sign.

Dear John,

As you can see I'm spelling better and I'm using grammar real well because we learned that in school. Well, we really learned it a long time ago but I did not ever bother with it before. But the best help I ever got in grammar was from Kathleen Kelly. After her last visit I never heard from her again.

But I figure, if maybe I'm going to be a priest, then I got to straighten up on everything, and that includes grammar.

Dear John,

I told Earnest that Christine Carney says he's not theologically correct.

Earnest says, "Correct is not the same as truth."

Dear John,

So sometimes Earnest shows a real smart streak.

Dear John,

Every Wednesday during lent I'm going to be an altar boy for the Stations of the Cross. I carry the big cross and lead the acolytes and the priest all around the church. That's pretty good because Peter Ackerman figured Father McNulty was going to pick him to do that but he picked me. Maybe that's a sign.

Dear John,

The main thing I forgot to tell the priest about in confession was all those bad thoughts I get about girls. I really got to stop talking to Earnest so much because he loves to talk about naked women and kissing and feeling them up and all. But I told Earnest that's a sin against the sixth commandment. But Earnest does not look worried.

Dear John,

I've been real worried about getting all the sins told in confession. So today I go and tell the priest some of the sins I forget to tell last week. It's kind of embarrassing telling him about the bad thoughts and stuff I talk about with Earnest. So I did not go into details. I just told him I committed adultery ten times. I don't think the priest heard what I said because he just told me to say three Hail Marys. I thought I'd at least have to say a few Our Fathers.

Dear John,

Tomorrow we go on the trip to the seminary. We got to get to St. John's High School by eight in the morning. Then the bus is going to take us to the seminary in Princeton, New Jersey. Earnest, Peter Ackerman and I are the only ones going from our school. The other kids didn't want to get up so early on a Saturday. Earnest usually does not like getting up at all on a Saturday morning but he bought a swimming suit at the St. Vincent DePaul Thrift Store and he wants to try it out.

Dear John,

The bus left right on time and we drove over the Williamsburg Bridge, through Lower Manhattan, into the Holland Tunnel and down US I to Princeton, New Jersey. The bus turned onto a winding road and through the trees we could see a castle-like building with towers and domes. Five guys all dressed in black greeted us like we had been friends for centuries.

Earnest asked, "Where's the swimming pool."

One guy said, "It's in the gym but first you'll want to see the chapel."

Peter Ackerman loved the chapel. Earnest didn't care all that much. I thought it was pretty but all the pews were turned side ways. That's so when they sing chants and hymns, God can hear them better. Father Lawler talks about how great it is to be a priest and one of the guys in a black suit talked about how great it was to be in the seminary. At the end Peter Ackerman asks questions about what you have to do to join and Earnest also asked a question, "Where's the swimming pool?"

Next we got a tour of the classrooms and the study hall and then we had lunch in a great big dining hall and two more guys in black talked about being in the seminary and then we got to play basketball, or handball, or baseball. They showed us this olympic size swimming pool with white tiles and three diving boards but they said we could not use the swimming pool today. After I played some basketball with some of the guys who do not wear black all the time, a priest who's the Prefect of Discipline talked to us about the seminary and how we should all consider that God may have given us a vocation. We should pray that we have a vocation because it's the most important thing in the whole world. I looked for Earnest but he wasn't there. Then it was time to go and there was Earnest waiting by the bus with his hair all wet. He said, "The swimming pool's great."

Dear John,

Father Lawler came to our school today and gave me and Peter Ackerman and Earnest applications to join the seminary. He says, "I was watching you boys during the trip to the seminary and I'm very impressed. I think you will be great priests." I figure he didn't watch Earnest all that close.

Dear John,

Peter Ackerman wasted no time in filling out his part of the application. He just has to get his mom to fill out some stuff and he figures he's in. I took mine home and put it in the top drawer of my dresser. I'm still waiting for a sign. I need a really big sign.

Dear John,

Father McNulty says I'm gong to be the crucifix bearer in the procession for the dedication of the new church in two weeks. I get to carry the big cross and lead the Bishop and the priests and the nuns and a lot of other really important people and the whole school. The procession starts in the old church. Then I lead them out and over to the new church.

Everybody has to sing hymns when they're walking. Maybe they want me to carry the cross so I don't sing.

Dear John,

I don't believe it! Earnest filled out his application, got his mom and dad to fill out their part and he sent it in.

Dear John,

I asked Earnest, "How come you made an application to join the seminary?"

He said, "The seminary is indeed a swell place and a neighborhood such as that would be more than a fair trade for the one within which we currently reside. I also like the place real well for another reason which is that it has got a great swimming pool and I figure it is either the seminary or Eastern District High and I do not wish to go to Eastern District. Besides maybe I will become nothing good if I don't become a priest."

I said, "What about signs. Did God give you any sign?"

Earnest says, "Yes indeed. I did receive a sign. It was this sign when I was at the seminary. It was on a door. It said, 'Swimming Pool'."

Dear John,

Peter Ackerman and Earnest sent in their applications. But I did not. I still don't know but I have to make the decision fast because the last day to apply is next week. Maybe I already got a sign but I missed it or maybe it was the tap on my shoulder or something else. Christine Carney already got accepted to join the convent high school. When she's not wearing her school uniform, she dresses all in black. She's getting in practice for being a nun.

Dear John,

Tomorrow's the dedication of the new church. We had to practice today. I have to lead the procession and all. The only problem is that I don't know my way around that new church as well as the old one. We got to start the procession at the old church and the Bishop takes the communion host out of the tabernacle and we all make a procession over to the new church. We practiced going in the back door to the sacristy and then down the side aisle and up the middle one. The priests spray holy water all over the place. Then all the priests and the Bishop are going to say Mass altogether. Next week they wreck the old church. I don't like that but you can't stop progress.

Dear John,

I asked Earnest what he thinks about the new church. He says it's O.K. to make a new church but he thinks they don't have to knock down the old church. He says they should keep both. The priests don't need a new rectory because there are lots of houses and even apartments what are empty and for sale around here.

Dear John,

I think Earnest is right. The priests should give up the rectory so they can save the old church. They should have moved into the Victorian Mansion but maybe that was a bad idea. Not enough Holy Water.

Dear John,

Things did not go all that well in the procession today. See there are two doors next to one another in the back of the new church. So I am leading the whole procession and

I open the door on the right side and I walk in. But the problem is that I was supposed to open the door on the left side. Too late! Before I can turn around and walk back the Bishop and priests already followed me in. So I just keep going because there are hundreds of kids and people behind the Bishop and the priests. Everybody is singing hymns and not looking where they are going and if I stop and back up, somebody might get crushed. It was kind of dark but I see this light switch and reach out and flip it on as we pass. There are stairs going down. So I go down. All the procession follows and the kids are singing and following me right down the stairs into the boiler room. The Bishop is busy tossing holy water all around the boiler room and getting everything wet and hissing. I keep right on walking and there is another stairs going up on the other side. So I walk up and open the door at the top of the stairs and we come out in the back of the church and then I walk down the middle aisle right up to the altar. The church is real crowded and everything went O.K. after that but Father McNulty was real mad at me and said, "You opened the wrong door and you almost ruined the whole ceremony." I said, "I'm real sorry I messed up so bad."

Dear John,

I feel really bad about messing up the whole ceremony and I keep thinking about it and last night I can not get to sleep and I stay awake almost the whole night. But then today everybody says the ceremony was beautiful and wonderful.

Earnest's mom said, "When we were in church, all of a sudden we could hear way in the distance these heavenly voices singing hymns but we couldn't see them and then they got louder and louder coming up from the boiler room. That was just about the most beautiful religious experience I ever had."

Earnest agrees and says, "The singing in the boiler room really did sound great."

Dear John,

Earnest's mom had another religious experience today. It's a baby girl.

Dear John,

Father McNulty told me that going through the basement was the best thing in the world because everybody's talking about the heavenly sound coming up from the floor and the pipes and everywhere. He said, "I'm sorry I got mad and yelled at you, Bobby. Maybe God was guiding you to choose that door so the music would be more beautiful. As a matter of fact, I'm going to have all choirs start singing in the boiler room from now on. The Bishop blessed the boiler room and he thought we planned it that way and he's going to insist on blessing the boiler rooms in all the new churches from now on. Yes, I'm sure God was guiding you because you made the right choice. You opened the right door after all."

Dear John,

That's the sign. God had me choose the right door even though it was the wrong door. I think God tells me to go the wrong way a lot because it winds up being the right way. That's got to be the sign.

Dear John,

I sent in my application to the seminary. My mom was real happy and even my dad helped fill out some of the dates of their wedding and my birthday and stuff.

Dear John,

I'm leading the Stations of the Cross for the first time in the new church. Same thing happened. After the stations were over I lead the priest and the other altar boys into a closet instead of the sacristy. Lucky it was a big closet. We all fit O.K. till I hit the wall with my nose. It was dark and I just thought it was the dark sacristy. When I told my mom about that, she said, "God made you choose the wrong door to humble you. Maybe you're getting too big for your own britches."

Dear John,

That Christine Carney thinks she's so great! Today we're playing slap ball during lunch and she walks right across the court between home plate and the pitcher's chalk box. Christine Carney walks right in front of me just as I am pitching a real good flooker to Patrick Garino. I yell, "Christine Carney, you stupid jerk get off the court."

Then Christine Carney stops and folds her arms in front of her and says, "Bobby Anderson, you must learn to be more courteous to a woman of the cloth. I have been accepted into the convent and you must respect my vocation."

Before I could think of something brilliant to say back, she unfolds her arms and very slowly walks away. I wish I could've thought of something real smart. But I got my plan. Same one I had last year. I saved the plan and everything I need.

Dear John,

Father Lawler's coming to meet my mom and dad tonight. He already went to see Earnest's and Peter Ackerman's parents. It's part of the application. He says he has to see what our home is like and ask our parents some personal questions. Earnest was real mad yesterday because Father Lawler was coming to his place and he had to spend two days cleaning. I had to vacuum and dust today but Father Lawler's a short guy. So I don't need to dust the tops of the cabinets.

Dear John,

Our meeting went very well. Father Lawler was very nice. He asked me why I wanted to be a priest and I said, "I think God wants me to become a priest. I prayed for some sign and got it, maybe a couple of them." I think he liked that answer.

After we talked a little, Father Lawler asked me to leave so he could talk about personal stuff with my mom and dad.

I asked my mom what they talked about and she said, "Father Lawler wanted to know what church we were married in, if we were devout Catholics, the date of our marriage, and when you were born."

Dear John,

I wonder what Earnest said when Father Lawler asked him why he wanted to be a priest.

Dear John,

Earnest got accepted. He's going to be a priest.

Christine Carney says, "God help the future Catholics!"

Dear John,

I asked Earnest what he told Father Lawler about why he wanted to be a priest. Earnest looked at me real hard, the most serious look I've ever seen, and said, "God works in strange ways. I work in strange ways. I think we'll work together real good."

Dear John,

Peter Ackerman's been absent from school for the last two days. That's kind of strange because he's never ever been absent before.

Dear John,

I got accepted. I'm going to the seminary and that's good because now I don't have to take those tests for any of the high schools. Peter Ackerman's still sick.

Dear John,

Earnest and I went to the movies to celebrate getting accepted to the seminary. Earnest figures we better get to see some movies now because in the seminary we'll get to see only movies like the one about Fatima and Donald Duck.

I always do the same stupid thing in the movies. My brain tells my legs it's the same as walking down the aisle in church. So before I go into the seat I genuflect. It's embarrassing, especially when I see Christine Carney sitting across the aisle laughing her dumb head off at me. I guess she's living it up one more time too.

Dear John,

I am sitting on the wooden steps of the old church and Father McNulty walks up a few steps and then he sits down next to me. He says, "Congratulations for being accepted into the seminary. God has given you the greatest of gifts."

I told Father McNulty, "I'm very sad that their tearing down the old church."

Father McNulty said, "Bobby, change is inevitable."

I asked Father McNulty, "But do they have to tear down something that's beautiful and warm and filled with so many memories?"

Father McNulty said, "Many things are changing in the world and everyone, even the Church is trying to keep up with the modern times. But those changes are only outward changes. Some things will never change. I imagine when you are an old priest, you'll say the Mass with the same ritual and the same Latin words long after I'm gone. The important things won't change because they help to keep us united and that's what the word catholic means. It means universal, all together united. I'll be looking down from heaven and I'll hear you say, 'Introibo ad altare Dei.'"

Dear John,

I almost forgot. Maybe that was a sign when I memorized all the priest's parts for the Mass. I sort of got a head start on becoming a priest a long time ago.

Dear John,

We started practicing for graduation yesterday and tomorrow we're having our class party. After eight years, it's gong to be hard saying goodbye to everybody, almost everybody.

Dear John,

Peter Ackerman hasn't been in school in about a week. So I asked the nun about him and if he's really sick all that bad.

The nun told me, "Peter's sickness is not of the body but of his soul."

Dear John,

The class party was O.K. If Kathleen Kelly still went to St. Mary's, maybe I would have danced but I did not dance. I was a wall flower. But maybe if Kathleen Kelly had not moved to New Jersey, maybe I would not be joining the seminary. The only ones who did not come to the party were Christine Carney and Peter Ackerman. Not that anybody missed Christine Carney. But we did miss Peter Ackerman. He's still sick. What did the nun mean?

Dear John,

Peter Ackerman got rejected. He can't be a priest. Patrick Garino told me Peter Ackerman got a letter saying he can't join. Peter Ackerman was absent from school for more than a week. I don't understand. Maybe they got Peter Ackerman's application mixed up with Earnest's.

Dear John,

Peter Ackerman came to school today and he looks real bad. I told him, "Peter Ackerman, I heard you got rejected. That ain't fair." He said, "It's the rule. People born out of wedlock cannot be priests. My mom and dad weren't married when I was conceived. My dad isn't even my real dad. I always thought God wanted me to be a priest but obviously he doesn't." Then he starts shaking and then crying and he runs off.

Dear John,

How come God did that? How did Peter Ackerman get conceived when his mom wasn't married? God makes us. Doesn't he check to see if our mom is married? How come Peter can't become a priest if God didn't check first? It's not Peter Ackerman's fault. Peter Ackerman always wanted to be a priest and he did all the right things to be a priest. Something's not right here.

Dear John,

I'm looking out by bedroom window today and I see Christine Carney walking down the street carrying some package. I know she's leaving for the convent right after graduation tomorrow. So I go to the kitchen and it's still wrapped in the wax paper in the back of the ice cube tray. It's my goodbye present to Christine Carney and I got the idea from Earnest. It's a little yellow snow ball which I have been saving ever since last winter. I've been saving it for a long time. Quick run down stairs. I almost bumped right into her and I say, "How come you weren't at the class party yesterday?"

Christine Carney said, "I have given up the world and its pleasures. Instead of going to the party, I stayed home and prayed for souls like yours. I just hope you and Earnest will do no great damage to Catholicism." She was smiling when she said that and I wasn't sure if she was teasing or being serious.

Well, in any case I just can't resist any longer. I take it from behind my back. Christine Carney's mouth's opens wide. It is just the perfect time . . . but I can't do it. Instead I just stand there and say, "I hope you do real good things as a nun, Christine Carney."

She says, "I'm actually sure you'll do great things as a priest, Bobby Anderson. God bless you." I say, "Good luck, Sister Christine." Then she smiles and puts out her hand to shake which surprises me. What even surprises me more is that I put out my hand to shake too. Only I forget the yellow snowball which is a little melted is still in my right hand. I pull back my hand just in time but Christine Carney thinks I'm teasing or something. She gets mad and starts walking away.

I drop the yellow snowball on the ground and I take my hand and rub it on my pants what gets little yellow streaks. Then I run after Christine Carney. I run in front of her and I said, "No, you don't understand. I pulled my hand away because it was dirty. Now it's clean."

Christine Carney smiled, a really big smile and we shake hands. But then something funny happens. Christine Carney put her arms around me and gives me the biggest kiss I ever got right on my lips. Then she smiles and turns around and walks away.

Dear John,

They're going to tear it down today. I'm writing this letter while I sit in the first pew of the old St. Mary's Church. It's not really a church anymore. It got unconsecrated when the Bishop consecrated the new one. The altar is empty, no candles, no sanctuary lamp, no tabernacle. The walls are bare, no stations of the cross, no statues, no banners. Nothing except all the things I remember about growing up. Some I don't even remember. Like I was baptized over there in that little room to the left of the entrance. But most of the things I do remember. I made my first communion at that altar rail and my first confession in that box against the right wall. An altar boy, weddings, funerals. June's funeral. The bull dozer's engine just started.

Dear John,

Now I'm outside sitting on the curb across the street from the old church. Not much left. The front wall's still standing. No it's not. It just came down thundering dust, now quiet rubble. It's over. It's like a part of my life that's over. Soon I'll be in the seminary, a new episode and more to come. But I need to go on from here without you. Goodbye John. Seminarians don't have imaginary friends. No need. We got Jesus and Mary and all the saints. Besides, I hate writing letters!

The End